Fair Competition: THE LAW AND ECONOMICS OF ANTITRUST POLICY

Fair Competition

THE LAW AND ECONOMICS OF ANTITRUST POLICY

JOEL B. DIRLAM *Connecticut College*

ALFRED E. KAHN *Cornell University*

GREENWOOD PRESS, PUBLISHERS
WESTPORT, CONNECTICUT

Reprinted by permission
of Cornell University Press

First Greenwood Reprinting 1970

SBN 8371-2971-0

PRINTED IN UNITED STATES OF AMERICA

TO *M. W. W.* AND *I. R. B.*

Preface

FOUR years ago, impressed by the mounting criticism by economists of current antitrust developments, we persuaded the Cornell Social Science Research Center to make us a grant for an exploratory study of vertical relationships between large and small business under the antitrust laws. We began by studying the economic implications of key court and commission decisions in the grocery and gasoline fields; but we came increasingly to realize the extent to which the antitrust laws embody broader social conceptions of equity and fair business dealing. We found that the decisions could not be fully understood or fairly appraised by economic standards alone. Hence we concluded that the appropriate question for economists to ask about antitrust policy is not whether this is the most efficient way of structuring or reorganizing the economy, but the inverted one: Does antitrust conflict seriously with the requirements of efficiency? In the current jargon, is fair competition "workable"? This is the question we try to answer in this book.

We focus our attention on the decisions of the last fifteen years that have given rise to the "new economic criticism"—the decisions illustrating divergent legal and economic conceptions of monopoly and competition. We treat only indirectly the traditional law of unfair competition, of misrepresentation, molestation, trade-mark infringement, and the like. We do not attempt to formulate a new law from scratch, but to analyze and evaluate the rationale of the law we now have. We are as aware as our readers are likely to be of the dangers of trying to extract from such a variety of statutes, decisions, and industries, or to force upon them, a consistent point of view. We have found the approach we suggest in the pages that follow a helpful one; we do not claim it is infallible.

A most welcome grant from Cornell's faculty Committee on Research Grants, together with the kind permission of the editors of the *American Journal of Economics and Sociology,* the *Harvard Law Review,* and the *Yale Law Journal* to draw freely from our articles, made it possible for us to complete the book.

From time to time over the last few years, we have profited enormously from the opportunity to discuss various aspects of our work with many people, among whom must be singled out Sarah Boone, Smith Wormley Davis, Robin Erle, Steven Gray, Peter Kaplan, Jonathan Swift, Stephen Rae, David Rossiter, and Samuel Simmons. We want to express our thanks also to Bruce Bryant, Priscilla Dirlam, Catharine Glassburn, Susan Jones, Joel S. Kahn, Rhoda Kahn, Sarah Michie, Michael Petty, and David Rosenthal, who have read parts of the manuscript and supplied us with invaluable suggestions with respect to content and style. John Merrill was extremely helpful in providing leads on the British monopoly problem; and Morris Adelman's provocative articles have been a continuous source of stimulation. We ought finally to acknowledge the forbearance of our wives, whose only defense during the difficult months just passed was to refer us from time to time to Simone de Beauvoir.

J. B. D.
A. E. K.

May 1954

Contents

PART I

The New Antitrust Policy and Its Critics

CHAPTER 1

The New Criticism of Antitrust

THE antitrust policy of the United States, so long enthroned above political conflict, supported by economists of all schools of thought (except the Marxian), and even judged worthy of export to assist in rehabilitating our fallen enemies, is now being called severely to account. From the business community come widespread grumblings, reminiscent to some extent of pre-N.R.A. days, though this time it is the general prosperity of the American economy rather than depression that has made it politically possible for businessmen to express their dissatisfactions openly. The fraternity of academic economists, too, is shattering into splinter groups, some supporting, some opposing what they conceive to be current antitrust doctrines. Scenting conflict, lawyers are joining—nay, leading—the fray, in the hope of formulating a brand-new set of statutes, administrative regulations, and judicial interpretations. It would be ironic if, as socialist Britain begins for the first time to build an antimonoply program, the free-enterprise United States should set out to emasculate this "economic Magna Carta" on the ground that it is inapplicable to modern market competition. The purpose of this book is to re-examine, as dispassionately as possible, the areas of antitrust policy that have been most responsible for, and are most vulnerable to, the current dissatisfaction.

Sources of the New Criticism

Like most social attitudes, the new criticism of antitrust is the product of a great number of converging historical and intellectual developments. And it is not itself a simple phenomenon: different people and groups criticize the law or its interpretation for different reasons and would amend it in different ways. But the attack on *economic* grounds is at once the most novel and the most threatening. The economists have provided the rationale for most of the other dissenters. When businessmen and lawyers call for amendments, asserting that the application of the laws in recent years has been too strict and that the zeal of the enforcement agencies has been not only excessive but misdirected, they do so in the name of "workable competition"—a concept supplied them by economists.

In short, the intellectual source of the contention that "our antitrust laws are crippling America" (the title of an article by David Lilienthal in *Collier's,* May 31, 1952) is in the current thinking of economists. This thinking has proceeded along two major lines: (*a*) developments in the theory of competition, and (*b*) factual analyses of concentration trends, market structures, and business behavior.

Before the publication in 1933 of Edward H. Chamberlin's *The Theory of Monopolistic Competition* and Joan Robinson's *The Economics of Imperfect Competition,* most economists confined their theoretical explanations of market behavior to two polar extremes: perfectly competitive markets on the one hand and pure monopolies on the other. The two books formalized a long-standing but theretofore unexpressed recognition that the two polar extremes are extremely rare: there are no perfect markets and no pure monopolies. Hence a central place was given in the new theory to hybrid markets—oligopolistic because they have few sellers, monopolistically competitive because each seller has some range of discretion in fixing his price.

For a time the new theories continued implicitly to accept pure competition as their norm or ideal [1] and to analyze the behavior of the hybrid markets in terms of the extent to which, under different conditions, they were likely to fall short of that ideal. But they gave rise to and strengthened a prevalent skepticism—understandable in the middle of the Great Depression—about the realism of relying on pure competition as a guide to

[1] But see note 5, below.

public policy. If monopoly elements are inevitably pervasive, is there any use in striving for pure competition? Disintegration of oligopolies or monopolies seemed to offer no solution in a world condemned by the ingenuity of advertising men and engineers to perpetual disproportion between the number of sellers of any given, standardized product and the number of customers. Economic policy had to adapt itself to the inevitability of big business, oligopoly, product differentiation, and other imperfect methods of competition.

Meanwhile the depression of the 1930's was weakening American devotion to the competitive ideal. True, many economists argued in the 1930's that price rigidity in monopolistic industries was in considerable measure responsible for the depth, length, and severity of the depression. Unemployment was widespread, so the theory ran, partly because monopolists had reacted to declining demand by reducing output instead of prices. So wants remained unsatisfied, and the resources that could satisfy them remained unemployed because at current, noncompetitive prices purchasing power was insufficient to put the unemployed to work.[2] Monopolistic output and investment restriction were to blame. However, the New Deal also introduced N.R.A., which, in quest of recovery, abandoned antitrust policy and adopted the businessman's ethical principle that the price cutter is a "chiseler." The failure of N.R.A. to produce recovery did not eradicate the skepticism it betrayed concerning the stability, efficiency, or feasibility of a competitive system. And in the later 1930's, under the influence of Keynes, many in the academic world as well began to question the theory that price cutting is an effective remedy for widespread deflation.[3] The proper cure, it was decided, is monetary and fiscal, not antitrust, policy.

The accomplishments of the American economy since 1940, for all its competitive imperfections, seemed to reinforce the lessons of the depression. The still monopoly-ridden capitalist

[2] See Gardner Means, *Industrial Prices and Their Relative Inflexibility*, 74th Cong., 1st Sess., Senate Doc. No. 13 (1935); Harold G. Moulton, *Income and Economic Progress* (Washington: Brookings, 1935).

[3] K. E. Boulding, "In Defense of Monopoly," 59 *Q. Jour. Econ.* 524 (1945).

economy of the United States showed new sources of dynamism —not merely in response to the heavy government spending of war years but through the widely (and erroneously) predicted postwar "depression" as well. Apparently purity of price competition was not so necessary to full employment and economic progress as had theretofore been believed.

In this atmosphere the idea gained favor that it was not only useless to try to make markets "purer"—it was also undesirable. By purely competitive standards the most important kind of competition is price competition; product differentiation through quality differentials and advertising introduces monopoly elements and is wasteful.[4] But now the author of the theory of monopolistic competition has pointed out that consumers may want product variation and change and may benefit from the assurance of quality provided by a familiar brand name.[5] Others have suggested that industries with an infinite number of infinitesimally small producers may be incapable of conducting expensive research programs or making the expensive investments necessary for technological change. Antitrust policy, it is said, cannot, as it is presently enforced, face up to these realities of a world of half-monopolies which may give consumers what they want more effectively than a never-never land of atomistic competition.[6]

Hence pure competition has given way to "workable competition" as the appropriate goal of public policy. In the process, old-fashioned competitive standards presumably enthroned by the antitrust laws have undergone a transvaluation. Price discrimination has come to be regarded not as a technique for exploiting selected buyers but as a necessary method of competitive

[4] G. W. Stocking and M. W. Watkins, *Monopoly and Free Enterprise*, Chap. 10.

[5] E. H. Chamberlin, "Product Heterogeneity and Public Policy," 40 *Amer. Econ. Rev., Papers and Proceedings* 85 (1950); however, see W. Adams, "Competition, Monopoly and Countervailing Power," 67 *Q. Jour. Econ.* 469, 470 n. 4 (1953).

[6] J. P. Miller, "Measures of Monopoly Power: Their Economic Significance," in National Bureau of Economic Research, *Conference on Business Concentration and Price Policy*, 1952, mimeo.

price cutting. Price agreement, or tacit collusion, is no longer monopoly, but a bulwark against the cutthroat competition that threatens all industries with heavy fixed costs. A few large buyers, forcing sellers to give them discriminatory concessions, are preferable to many because a big buyer can bargain more effectively with a big seller in the consumer's interest. A few large sellers are more desirable than a large number of small ones because only big producers can create new and better products for better living, as well as carry the burden of industrial mobilization for more effective killing.[7]

The association of technological progress with concentration of industry represents a partial reversal of the old-fashioned idea that competitive industries are more dynamic than monopolistic ones. Joseph A. Schumpeter had challenged the conventional assumptions on this point in his *Capitalism, Socialism and Democracy* by arguing that highly competitive industries have no margin of profit to finance innovations, and that perfect competition, resulting in immediate duplication of innovations by others, offers no supernormal profits to justify the inevitable risks. So John K. Galbraith, though despairing of the adequacy of price competition under oligopoly, concludes that an industry with a few large sellers is more likely to be progressive than any other: it has the funds and the prospect of high rewards for innovation. It is not despite but because of their structure that the oligopolistic chemical, electronics, automotive, and petroleum industries are so dynamic, while the atomistic agricultural, textile, and coal-mining industries are (without government assistance) chronically depressed and incapable of basic technological progress. This observation, and the corollary one of Schumpeter that modern innovation, continuously developing substitute processes and products, is extremely effective in eroding established monopoly positions, obviously casts doubt on a policy springing historically from a hostility to trusts. As Gal-

[7] See J. M. Clark, "Toward a Concept of Workable Competition," reprinted in American Economic Association, *Readings in the Social Control of Industry,* pp. 452–453; J. K. Galbraith, *American Capitalism,* Chaps. 7, 9, and 10.

braith sardonically observed, "The foreign visitor, brought to the United States by the Economic Cooperation Administration, visits the same firms as do attorneys of the Department of Justice in their search for monopoly." [8]

A number of studies by economists during the last twenty years have supplied factual support for the foregoing theoretical structure.

Some have demonstrated the ubiquity of monopolistic practices in American industry. Arthur R. Burns's *The Decline of Competition* showed how widespread were such impurities of competition as price leadership, market sharing, price inflexibility, and integration imposing serious competitive handicaps on small firms. The T.N.E.C. hearings and monographs and, more recently, Corwin Edwards' *Maintaining Competition* and G. W. Stocking and M. W. Watkins' *Monopoly and Free Enterprise* have supplied further documentation of these findings.

Others have suggested that perfect competition is a useless measuring rod against which to judge the economic performance of individual industries. Jesse Markham found competition highly effective in the oligopolistic rayon industry; [9] Donald Wallace had certain reservations about market control in the monopolistic aluminum industry, but only because he thought three or four producers would have made a better record than one; [10] W. R. MacLaurin concluded that progress and invention in radio, as in television, would have been impossible without the protection of the patent monopoly and the large resources of the few giant firms.[11]

Certain economists, investigating in great detail the familiar charge of the 1930's that concentrated industries generally pursued inflexible price policies during the depression, have demonstrated statistically that prices in manufacturing fluctuated closely with direct costs, and that there was no observable rela-

[8] *Ibid.*, p. 96.

[9] *Competition in the Rayon Industry* (Cambridge: Harvard U. Press, 1952).

[10] See pp. 152–154, below.

[11] *Invention and Innovation in the Radio Industry* (New York: Macmillan, 1949).

tionship between oligopolistic concentration and price inflexibility.[12]

Finally, we have the conclusions of others, based upon an admittedly scanty record, that there is little or no evidence of a trend toward increased concentration in the American economy since 1900.[13]

From these widely divergent studies it is possible to conclude that it is now less fashionable in economic circles to view with alarm the concentration of economic power. But the implications for antitrust policy are less clear. Depending upon one's point of view, one might conclude that the antitrust laws have been either ineffective or of great importance. If concentration has not increased, if prices in general tend to fluctuate with changes in direct cost, and if despite the widespread imperfections of the market the performance of many of our most concentrated industries has been at least better than it would have been under atomistic competition, one can argue either that there is no particular need for vigorous enforcement of the antitrust laws (since on the whole the economy has been behaving quite well) or else that the enforcement we have had has been very successful.

It has not been necessary for the "new critics" of antitrust to choose between these two possible interpretations of the historical evidence. Beginning in 1937, after more than twenty years of only perfunctory activity by the Department of Justice, antitrust enforcement was intensified, and produced some changes in the judicial interpretation of the laws. Therefore it is possible to believe—and who does not?—that the antitrust laws are our

[12] Alfred C. Neal, *Industrial Concentration and Price Flexibility* (Washington: American Council on Public Affairs, 1942); Richard Ruggles, "The Nature of Price Flexibility and the Determinants of Relative Price Changes in the Economy," in National Bureau of Economic Research, *Conference on Business Concentration and Price Policy*, 1952, mimeo; W. L. Thorp and W. F. Crowder, *The Structure of Industry* (T.N.E.C. Monograph No. 27; Washington: G.P.O., 1941), Pt. V.

[13] G. Warren Nutter, *The Extent of Enterprise Monopoly in the United States, 1899–1939* (Chicago: U. of Chicago Press, 1951); M. A. Adelman, "The Measurement of Industrial Concentration," 33 *Rev. of Econ. and Stat.* 269 (1951); A. D. H. Kaplan and A. E. Kahn, "Big Business in a Competitive Society," 47 *Fortune*, Feb. 1953, Sec. 2.

economic Magna Carta, helping to explain the superiority of the American economy, and at the same time to interpret the historical evidence as arguing that the antitrust developments of the last fifteen years have been unnecessary or harmful. It is not the traditional Sherman Act that needs changing; that would be unthinkable. It is only the excessively doctrinaire, legalistic, economically naïve interpretations recently originated by the enforcement agencies that have been unnecessary and require reconsideration in the light of new economic conceptions of workable competition.

While this argument is by no means entirely lacking in merit, it poses a dilemma for the new critics. Few economists or businessmen would disagree, at least for publication, with the widespread belief that the antitrust laws have helped keep the American economy—structurally monopolistic though it may be—competitive, by forcing businessmen to weigh their every action in the light of its proscriptions.[14] Yet most of the new critics also condemn just those revivifications of the antitrust laws that have, in contrast with the somnolence of the period 1917–1937, generated this caution on the part of business executives.

Nature of the New Criticism

In any event, there is no doubt that the articulate spokesmen of business, especially big business, have found it possible in recent years to speak out openly against the reinvigoration of antitrust enforcement. The following represents a fair sample of their complaints. (We should make it clear at the outset that if we thought these complaints entirely without foundation we would not consider it worth while to write a book appraising them.)

1. Because the statutes are unclear or have been interpreted unpredictably, no businessman, however conscientious, is immune from prosecution.
2. Consequently, cases are selected mainly on a political basis.
3. Enforcement (at least until January 1953) has been by

[14] E. S. Mason, in D. M. Keezer, "The Antitrust Laws: A Symposium," 39 *Amer. Econ. Rev.* 713 (1949); see also the remarks of Burns, *ibid.*, p. 695.

officials hostile to a free competitive system, and it has been carried out in a manner that makes vigorous competition more instead of less difficult for businessmen.

4. The antitrust laws have been interpreted in such a way as to protect smaller businesses from deserved competitive extinction; i.e., present interpretations confuse the preservation of competition with the preservation of competitors.

5. The government is attempting to substitute itself for the market in determining whether small or big business should do a particular job; the only appropriate judge is the consumer.

6. Businessmen should not be urged to compete, only to be turned against when they win out in the competitive struggle.

7. Big business is necessary for military mobilization, efficiency, and technological progress.

A statement on "Effective Competition" prepared by the Business Advisory Council of the Department of Commerce, and made public in 1952, offers a fair indication of the specific instances in which a large portion of the business community thinks the antitrust laws have gone astray. In the name of effective competition the Council apparently would have (*a*) permitted the large oil companies to get together in the 1930's and buy up independently refined gasoline in order to stabilize (raise) prices; (*b*) found nothing objectionable in the practices that led the courts to condemn A & P (including the exaction of discriminatory discounts and predatory local price cutting); (*c*) refrained from applying the antitrust laws to newspaper monopolies or "medium-sized theatre chains," because cases of this sort illustrate a recent tendency "to define an area or product-line or market fitting the alleged culprit in the case"; (*d*) permitted the rigid steel conduit or other industries to follow a basing-point system because there was "little positive evidence of conspiracy"; (*e*) reversed judicial interpretations of the Robinson-Patman Act said to prohibit "price reductions . . . if they may possibly injure competitors," although the act actually condemns only selective or discriminatory price reductions. The report also sees no possible conflict between the patent system and "effective competition," because "no patent monopoly can have any real value to its owners or to licensees unless it improves values."[15]

We endeavor to trace in detail, in Chapters 3 and 4, the path which interpretations of the antitrust laws have taken in recent years, in order to appraise the tendencies that have given rise to this sort of complaint. Nevertheless both the tendencies and the complaints deserve a brief summary at this point.

During the period 1939–1953, courts and commissions do seem to have approached condemning, per se, business size, integration, monopoly power, and mere fewness of sellers. They have sometimes reached such decisions with little more evidence of collusion or unreasonable exclusion of competitors (the traditional proofs of illegality) than the commission of acts by which size or market power were acquired. They have, similarly, condemned such business practices and procedures as tie-ins, exclusive dealing, sales under full requirements contracts, and price discrimination, when they have had the effect—perhaps only one among many and perhaps incidentally—of disadvantaging individual competitors, without regard to whether they have weakened the vitality of competition in the market as a whole.

There has been, therefore, some dilution of the traditional "rule of reason," which permitted the courts previously to consider economic justifications for allegedly restrictive, collusive, or exclusive practices. The economist critics of these developments point out that such market impurities as are mirrored in static market data like business size, market shares, and the possession of strategic advantages over competitors, or in business practices and arrangements that impose some handicap on competitors are not unequivocal evidences of the effectiveness or ineffectiveness of competition. They may be the outcome of success in the competitive struggle, of superior enterprise or efficiency. To condemn the outcome may be therefore to damp competitive initiative. They may be indispensable instruments or methods of competition in modern markets, mutually acceptable arrangements between seller and buyer, supplier and distributor, merger and mergee, which permit them on balance to vie more effectively for the custom of buyers. Neither the amount of commerce

[15] The citations for these five conclusions are to the following pages of the *Report:* (1) 6; (2) 6; (3) 13, 14; (4) 7; (5) 1, 7.

directly involved nor the presence of mere power to exclude nor loss of business by individual competitors is an adequate criterion of the economic effects of moves toward increased size or integration, or of these business practices. Therefore, we are told, an economically intelligent policy must investigate the net effects of business structures and actions on over-all economic performance, measured in terms either of concrete economic results or of the continuing vitality of competitive forces in the market as a whole. These are the tests of whether competition is workable, though impure; and these are the tests that should henceforth guide antitrust. What is required is to rehabilitate the rule of reason, which in a rough sort of way used to keep the antitrust laws compatible with workable competition.

Here we see the culmination of the developments in economic thought summarized earlier. It is no longer compatible with the teachings of economics to adopt doctrinaire positions on antitrust policy—whether toward business size, fewness of sellers, "trusts," price-fixing conspiracies, or any other business practice. The crucial test of virtue is industry performance. Does it give the people "what they want"? Is the industry working sufficiently well to justify a hands-off policy on the part of the government?

One cannot dispose of these new economic norms of workable or effective rather than pure or perfect competition merely by pointing out that they are vague, shifting, or pragmatic, or not much of a standard at all, unless one can point to some "workable" alternative. An economist appraising the structure or performance of a market or industry cannot confine his efforts to demonstrating the ways in which either falls short of the purely competitive standard. The proponents of workable competition have made the case convincingly that purity is both unattainable and undesirable. The preferable ideal is one of balance: sellers sufficiently few for efficiency and progress, yet numerous enough to give the buyer real alternatives and to prevent monopolistic exploitation and restrictionism; buyers big enough to offset the power of sellers yet not so powerful as to exploit them or the public; control over supplies and markets, whether by contractual arrangements or financial relationships, to permit desirable long-term investments and the risking of savings, yet not such dominance as excessively to restrict the competitive opportunities of new entrants; sufficient limitation of rivalry between competitors to avoid cutthroat competition, yet not so much as to produce excessive monopoly power.

Are the antitrust laws—limited by the nineteenth-century ideal from which they sprang and reinvigorated by recent judicial interpretations—incapable of producing the kind of a balance necessary for workable competition under conditions of modern technology? This is the question we will try to answer.

Though our main purpose is to assess the new criticism of antitrust primarily in its own terms, i.e., by investigating the economic consequences of the "new Sherman Act," we shall want also to ask whether this balancing procedure can ever be prescribed by economic analysis alone. Noneconomic criteria always creep into economists' qualified verdicts about the workability of particular competitive situations. Can one on purely economic grounds draw the line between power enough and power too much, or between its reasonable and excessive exercise? Or can one decide whether or not an industry should be permitted to run along accustomed lines on the basis of whether it is giving consumers what they want, when "what consumers want" is to a considerable extent a function of what they have been getting? The only alternatives customers know are those that have been presented to them by the same accustomed patterns of business structure and behavior. Here public policy may defy the economists. The latter have shown a tendency in recent years to worry only about the power that is a power to increase prices; but there are other forms of economic power about which the community may legitimately be concerned. Economists have also shown a strong tendency to define welfare in terms of efficiency in doing accustomed things in an accustomed way, to define competition in terms of the forms it takes today, and to insist that those are the only possible goals, practices, and forms even though the community may find some of them socially unacceptable. The history of every law promulgated to eliminate a social evil is marked by complaints before the fact by interested parties that this or that provision would be impossible to live with, that it defied "economic principles," that the current way of doing things was the only possible way, and with evidence after the fact that, once they were forced to do so, the complainants found it possible to live very happily indeed under the new dispensation.

The Rationale and Purposes of Antitrust in a Democracy

The antitrust laws were not conceived, either in 1890 or 1914, as statutes for general economic planning. They were intended only to prevent the unfair exertion of bargaining power and to strike at gigantic monopolistic consolidations.[16] Both Senator Hoar, who wrote the bill that was finally passed, and Senator Sherman stated that they had no objection to combinations that were lawfully achieved, that were not formed for the purpose of eliminating competition, and that did not engage in unfair methods of competition. Thus, these sponsors of the Sherman Act were not hostile to mere size or market power. Likewise the Clayton and Federal Trade Commission Acts were not designed to prevent bigness from triumphing, if it did so "in the field of intelligence and economy." [17]

Public policy toward monopoly does not stop at this point. "The public will not tolerate the mere fact of being dependent upon the good will of a private monopolist to use his power humanely." [18] Where competition has disappeared beyond recall, or is an impractical or inadequate method of protecting the public, the alternative is direct intervention by a regulatory commission or public ownership. The point at which the public decides that a seller is a monopolist, or a monopolist about whose humanity it need be concerned, cannot be drawn with a hard and fast line: note the continuous historical changes in the definition of "public utilities" or of "industries affected with a public interest." [19]

16 Compare Miller, *Unfair Competition*, pp. 23–26, and Watkins, *Public Regulation of Competitive Practices*, pp. 35–38, 43.

17 Woodrow Wilson, *The New Freedom* (New York: Doubleday, Page & Co., 1921), p. 165.

18 Clark, *Social Control of Business*, p. 126.

19 See Irston R. Barnes, *The Economics of Public Utility Regulation* (New York: Crofts, 1942), Chap. 1.

Governmental regulation of bargains between businesses, or between sellers and buyers, may be thought of as having two broad purposes in a free enterprise society.

1. *Controls are supposed to ensure that the bargaining process (and, only if necessary, the outcome of the process as well) conforms to the community's sense of equity, or fairness.* When the government set up a commission to fix reasonable railroad rates, required that corporations provide certain information to purchasers of their securities, and sponsored collective bargaining under the Wagner Act, it was trying to put the parties to various types of transactions on an equal footing.[20] The first of these examples represented a replacement of the bargaining process, in order to achieve the same end. The second and the third, like the antitrust laws, sought to ensure fairness by setting up circumstances of substantial equality of power, under which free bargaining might be permitted to continue as the heart of the economic process. And although the antitrust laws do not attack inequalities of power as such, the second section of the Sherman Act clearly mirrors the community's distrust of excessive power, purposefully sought or unfairly achieved.

2. *Controls are also supposed to preserve the competitive system of checks and balances and assist its functioning.* As the sponsors of the Sherman Act realized, the purpose of regulating business transactions is to preserve a system in which gain is sought and obtained by efficiency in bargaining with customers, and to discourage the quest or achievement of market advantage by methods that are unfair or collusive. The purpose, in short, is at once to preserve the competitive process and to channel it along socially productive lines. There is no way of proving that a competitive system is actually more "efficient," whatever that means, than a noncompetitive one. In many ways competition, particularly such imperfect competition as alone is attainable in an imperfect world, involves serious wastes. A perfectly planned monopoly *could* conceivably be more efficient, by certain standards.[21] Yet the general assumption of the drafters of the Sherman

[20] See John R. Commons, *Institutional Economics* (New York: Macmillan 1934), pp. 343–345.

[21] E. A. G. Robinson, *Monopoly* (London: Nisbet, 1941), Chap. 6.

Act was that, if unfair tactics and excessive merging were prevented, incentives and punishments enforced by free consumer choice would so order industry as to benefit the community. This is still the essential premise of a free enterprise economy: that in the long run such a system, operating through competitive markets, provides the most effective means of promoting economic progress, economic justice, and the general welfare.

Clearly we are not devoted to a competitive system only for "economic" reasons. It is also associated with such social and political ideals as the diffusion of private power and maximum opportunities for individual self-expression. If the economy will run itself, governmental interference in our daily life is held to a minimum.

This last purpose of preserving competition must also condition the kind of policy adopted to preserve it. As J. M. Clark has suggested, one principle of government intervention in economic life is that it exercise an "economy of coercion." It was precisely the appeal of antitrust intervention that by preserving the competitive regulator it would in the end minimize coercion. It represented, paradoxically, a departure from laissez faire in the ultimate interests of laissez faire. In this light, one must give heed to widespread recent criticisms of antitrust that no businessman today really knows what the law says, that everyone, no matter how scrupulous his efforts to live within the law, stands in danger at one time or another of being indicted or subjected to a civil suit for violating it.[22] It is clearly important, in evaluating the new Sherman Act, to ask to what extent the above-mentioned complaint is valid and, if it has substantial validity, to seek alternative standards for antitrust that might do a better job of economizing coercion.

22 M. P. Madison, "Proposed Amendments of the Federal Antitrust Law and Its Relation to 'Big Business,'" *Antitrust Law Symposium 1952*, pp. 106–121 (these annual volumes are hereafter referred to as, e.g., *1952 Symposium*); T. E. Sunderland, "Changing Legal Concepts," 24 *Jour. of Business* 235 (1951).

The Problem of Conflicting Goals and the Role of the Economist

There are indissoluble links between these two fundamental purposes of the antitrust laws. Fair competition is supposed to promote efficiency, and it is hoped that rules of fairness will ensure the preservation of competition itself; free competition is supposed to promote economic justice. Nevertheless the ideal of fairness embodies values other than those usually conceived by economists in defining maximization of economic welfare, and there may even be conflicts between the two. The initial impact of unfair competitive practices is on the businessman in his role as a seller; although it is usually assumed the consuming public will in the end benefit by prohibiting such practices, the first purpose is to protect competitors. Society may be prepared, as in the case of the "fair trade" laws, to define as unfair competition practices that might serve the public without destroying competition itself.

The economist cannot say to society that in all such cases of conflict the interest of the disadvantaged competitor must be sacrificed to that of the consumer. One cannot simply equate the "public interest" in a democracy with the "consumer interest," defining the latter as the interest of all citizens "in getting more and better goods for consumption at ever lower prices." [23] Realistically considered, "optimum" output, or "welfare" economics or other similar concepts, apply to only one of many types of social activities, each of which has a different scale of values. It is not true, even though Adam Smith said it and even though his saying it was salutary at a time when public policy was excessively indifferent to the principle, that "consumption is the sole end and purpose of all production." [24] We all have interests as producers (or as citizens of an urbanized civilization) as well as interests as consumers. Conflicts—particularly between the values and interests of producers and consumers, or between this group of producers and that, or between "economic welfare" and other values—are the order of the day. They are resolved

[23] V. Mund, *Government and Business,* p. 63.

[24] *Wealth of Nations* (Modern Library Ed.), Bk. IV, Chap. 8, p. 625.

pretty much on the assumption that neither one side nor the other invariably takes precedence.

The resolution of these conflicts of interest and values is a political, not an economic, function. What then are we to make of the widespread criticism of antitrust laws today that they have been employed for "political" purposes, and that cases are selected on the basis of political considerations? A statement to this effect by Justice Jackson, then Attorney General, has become part of the folklore of current antitrust commentary. It is an interesting semantic development that the word "political" should now, among some economists (formerly known as "political economists"), pass without question as a term of opprobrium. The word may deserve its derogatory connotation in some instances—if, for example, the administration in power selects companies to prosecute on the basis of their campaign contributions. But this is seldom the contention. The implication is usually that Congressional pressures and prospective electoral considerations rather than economic criteria determine the selection of cases; that big business is likely to suffer because it controls fewer votes than the groups who applaud attacks on it.[25] This too may be an unfortunate method of selecting cases. But the process of selection cannot and should not be an exclusively "economic" one. The question must always be (over and above that of "Can we win the case?"): What values, what interests are served by bringing this rather than that suit? In every criminal case the prosecuting attorney must make the same choice, bearing in mind also, it is to be hoped, the supreme value of equality of all citizens before the laws. If the local representatives of even a very efficient big business have unfairly injured a small competitor, or applied what society judges to be an unfair amount of coercion to an independent businessman, it may be an entirely reasonable *political* decision to bring the company before the bar, regardless of whether the single action fits into a general program for improving the economic performance of American industry. The separation of the reasonable and fair from the un-

[25] Madison, in *1952 Symposium,* p. 108, esp. n. 8; Adelman, "The Great A & P Muddle," 40 *Fortune* 122, 123 (Dec. 1949); see also Donald Dewey, "Antitrust Policy and the Big Buyer," 17 *Jour. of Marketing* 283 (1953).

reasonable and unfair is inevitably a political process. But this fact does not in itself make the distinction arbitrary.

Moreover, as we have already suggested, one is entitled to particularly grave doubts whether the techniques of welfare economics—that take as the basic datum "consumer interests and desires" as presently manifested by free choice in the market and ask only how society can best be organized to meet *these* desires at lowest cost—have a strong case for applicability to public policy decisions. In our society the individual's consumption pattern and the businessman's costs are surely not determined by truly untrammeled choices or truly free bargaining. Instead it is the business culture which imposes more or less invariable standards of the "good life" on consumers and fixes interest rates, wages, and other costs of doing business.[26] And constantly disrupting the consumer's tranquillity are the advertising agencies. It is not true, as the *New Yorker* says, that there has always been an ad-man, or, at least, as many as plague us today. He is getting more and more expert in altering consumption patterns, using each nugget of information that social psychologists turn up for his own purposes,[27] to give us dry "beer," shirts worn by one-eyed men, tonic sold by bearded distributors, color television, and 200 horsepower cars for which our cities have no room. A large portion of our "highest per capita income in the world" consists in expenditures that are necessary to offset the horrible consequences of our unplanned, ugly, dirty, crime-ridden cities, and to keep up with the ubiquitous ad-man. It is therefore difficult to take seriously as the ultimate criterion of policy either the consumer interest, as manifested by the choices consumers actually make, or the preservation of the "dynamic tendencies" that determine what those choices will be as well as satisfy them.[28]

At the same time, if a democracy is to make an intelligent

[26] See the elaboration of this point in C. E. Ayres, *The Industrial Economy* (Boston: Houghton Mifflin, 1952), Chaps. 13 and 14.

[27] See any issue of the *Jour. of Marketing*.

[28] On much of the foregoing, see the eloquent statement of Clark, *Guideposts in Time of Change* (New York: Harper, 1949), Chap. 3; also Ben W. Lewis, "It's Political (Repeat Political) Economy," 9 *Antioch Review* 369 (1949).

choice between goals, it must be able to balance sacrifices against achievements. The real difficulty is to measure the costs, for example, the economic costs, if any, of requiring "fair dealing" for competitors. Often, we shall see, the critics of recent antitrust developments have seen conflicts where none existed or have magnified beyond all reason the efficiency costs of this or that decision. Economics is not an exact science; in many ways it is not a science at all. Yet to hear some economists predicting dire consequences of antitrust decisions whose purpose was to assure competition solely on the basis of relative efficiency, with fair and equal access to supplies and markets, one would think that the tools of economic analysis were keen indeed. It is not an unfair question to ask such economists, "If you are so sure you can predict the consequences of antitrust decisions, why can you not predict the course of the stock market?"

Most of the cases brought up under the antitrust laws present the Federal Trade Commission or the courts with the problem of reconciling interests of consumers with those of producers, or of conflicting groups of producers, under circumstances where it would be absurd to say that one interest clearly and absolutely outweighs the other. Decisions must always be tentative. We accept this procedure without question when there is collective bargaining over wages or contract arbitration. No one supposes that the decision reached is based upon absolute, invariable economic standards of efficiency or of the public interest which take precedence over the interests of the parties concerned. We demand no simple economic rationale for the laws prohibiting unfair labor practices. Although we quarrel about their precise definition, few of us doubt the need for such rules. So it is with competition between businesses. Almost every important case under the new Sherman Act, as we shall see, involves precisely this issue of fair treatment for suppliers, competitors, and customers, immediate or ultimate. All the economist can do is to indicate where, if at all, a decision in the interest of equity involves a sacrifice of the interests of others. And he has an obligation, in so doing, to avoid overstating the ability of economics to predict the direction, let alone to measure the dimensions, of these consequences.

Areas of Conflict

In the chapters that follow we appraise the feasibility of adopting the economic standards for antitrust proposed by the new critics. In Chapter 2 we discuss these standards and contrast them with the traditional legal criteria of monopoly and unreasonable restraint. In Chapters 3 and 4 we trace the path of the law in the last decade, to see to what extent it has departed from the traditional legal criteria and weakened the traditional rule of reason. In the process we consider, at least incidentally, the appropriateness of antitrust policy as presently interpreted and in comparison with possible alternative formulations, in the light of the broader, noneconomic goals briefly discussed above.

In Part II we attempt an economic evaluation of recent antitrust cases in each of the areas where the current criticism argues that the law has gone astray. The purpose will be to see whether and wherein the new Sherman Act does indeed conflict with the requirements of efficient, workable competition. In this last task we shall attempt to weigh the purely economic evidence, insofar as it can be surmised from, and the rough tools of economic analysis applied to, the half-revealed facts of business life. At the same time we shall consider to what extent the pattern of enforcement revealed in these cases is perhaps also, or alternatively, justifiable as a means of achieving the other purpose of antitrust —justice or equity—and, if so, to what extent the community may have to pay in reduced efficiency for the decisions reached. The simple question for economic analysis here is whether fair competition is unworkable.

Recent antitrust suits in the following areas have engendered the most controversy. Chapters 5 to 8 consider each separately.

1. *Integration.* A firm is integrated when it operates in more than one market, performs more than one function in a process of production and distribution, or produces a variety of products. It may integrate by merger, acquiring another company, or by internal expansion, constructing the new facilities itself. The phenomenon of integration raises the possibility that nonintegrated competitors will be shut out of markets, or unable to acquire necessary supplies of raw materials, or subjected to a

variety of "squeezes" unrelated to their relative efficiency in serving the public. At the same time, integration may also have strong economic justification and may make competition more effective. To take the most obvious kind of example, a petroleum refinery that operates both a simple distillation and a thermal cracking unit or a steel mill that operates side by side a blast furnace and a bessemer converter can make use of certain by-products, like gases or heat, which would be wasted if the steps were performed disconnectedly. The possible improvements in efficiency are not confined to such engineering savings from integrated productive operations. A farm machinery manufacturer who can give his salesmen a full product line to carry may make fuller use of the gasoline and time they use in distributing his products than if he had only one product to sell. And the economic advantages are not limited to efficiency: by integration a firm may uncover new supplies of raw materials, offer customers new products or alternative sources of old ones, and reduce costs and prices through by-passing or supplanting a monopolist.

The general problem of public policy with respect to integration can be simply stated, but it is not easy to resolve. It is necessary to decide, on the basis of motives, actions, or consequences, whether particular acts of integration or of an integrated firm are on balance socially and economically acceptable. And what if the motives and consequences were mixed? The questions for us to investigate then are: By what criteria may an antitrust policy distinguish between the socially acceptable and inacceptable? How have recent antitrust decisions drawn the line? And have the results been economically unfortunate?

2. *Exclusive dealing, full requirements contracts, and tie-ins.* Like integration, these practices may represent unreasonable methods of shutting competitors out of markets and may therefore weaken the force of competition. On the other hand, it would be economically undesirable to forbid them outright. Like integration, they may permit reduced costs or improved service, without serious impairment of the similar efforts of rivals. A full requirements contract may be best adapted to the needs of the buyer, who wants to be assured of supplies for a production season, as well as of the seller, who may require such an assurance to

justify incurring a heavy production or distribution expense. The reasonableness of a particular use of one or another of these exclusive arrangements may depend on the motives or the consequences, actual or prospective. In any case the decision can be made only after an examination of the relevant facts in each case. So here again, in our appraisal of the new Sherman Act, we shall see how the courts have reached their decisions in each of the leading cases, in order to decide whether the rule of reason has been ignored, whether the public has been exposed to possible injury, and whether better alternative standards might be applied in the future.

3. *Price discrimination.* A seller may, by price discrimination, ruthlessly exploit his customers or drive competitors out of business. Yet like other competitive practices, discrimination cannot be objectionable per se. Public utilities take advantage of differences in the elasticity of demand of different classes of customers to charge different rates, depending on what each traffic will bear, and in so doing achieve higher output and lower cost, from which all buyers benefit. Sellers in unregulated markets may use discriminatory prices for the same purpose. The offer of selective price cuts, perhaps under the pressure of a valued customer, perhaps in order to meet the price of a competitor, is a necessary part of the competitive process.

There are really two primary problems of policy with respect to this practice. The first is to decide whether a particular pricing policy may be fairly characterized as discriminatory. To charge different unit prices for different quantities purchased, or at different times, to offer different discounts to customers performing different functions, to charge delivered prices that result in higher mill nets on sales to those near the plant of the seller may or may not constitute price discrimination, and may or may not be economically undesirable. The second and more important problem is to determine whether in each particular case the practice (whether or not correctly labeled as discriminatory) contributes to more intensive competition or in some way unfairly limits access to the market by competitors of the seller or by his less-favored customers. The price discrimination section of the antitrust laws has probably been its most controversial one in recent years, and cases under it have certainly evoked the most widespread criticism on economic grounds. Chapters 7 and 8 will attempt to test these arguments and the decisions which have evoked them.

The foregoing topics do not exhaust the controversial developments generally referred to as constituting the "new Sherman Act." The major omission (since most of the cases involving sheer business size are also integration cases) is the group of cases of alleged price-fixing and market-sharing "conspiracies" where there was either little or no direct evidence of conspiratorial agreement among competitors (the decisions turning on "presumptive" or "implied" conspiracy, or mere "conscious parallelism of action"), or where the condemned agreements may have had other, more defensible purposes (e.g., patent pooling, the provision of market information through trade associations, or joint development and exploitation of foreign markets or sources of raw materials), or where the so-called "conspirators" were in fact affiliated companies or the officers thereof, really constituting a single transacting unit. Although we consider these developments in somewhat less detail, all underlie and are discussed in our general analyses in Chapters 2 and 9. Since most of these cases involved also issues of business size, market dominance, integration, or some of the abovementioned competitive practices, they appear also in the intervening chapters.

CHAPTER 2

Legal and Economic Standards for Antitrust Policy

ONE of the most ironic aspects of the widespread criticism of the antitrust laws today is that before the era of the new Sherman Act academic economists, almost to a man, criticized the antitrust authorities for their inactivity and the laws themselves (as interpreted by the courts) for their impotence. The call of the "new critics" for restoration of the rule of reason is matched only by the complaints of the "old critics" that the rule of reason had been so interpreted as to hamstring antitrust enforcement in dealing with the gentlemanly monopolistic techniques of the 1920's.[1]

The primary purpose of the present chapter is to weigh the traditional legal standards of monopoly and monopolizing against proposed alternative, "economic" standards, in order to see whether it is indeed time for a basic reorientation of antitrust.

In general, we affirm and defend both the traditional theory of the antitrust laws and recent developments in their interpretation. The defense is not unqualified; it could hardly be so, in

[1] See, among others, Eliot Jones, *The Trust Problem in the United States* (New York: Macmillan, 1921), pp. 492–498; Myron W. Watkins, *Industrial Combinations and Public Policy* (Boston: Houghton Mifflin, 1927), pp. 253–273, 289–291; Dexter M. Keezer and Stacy May, *The Public Control of Business* (New York: Harper, 1930), pp. 49–57, 95–96, 233–234; and Watkins, "Business and the Law," reprinted in American Economic Association, *Readings in the Social Control of Industry*, pp. 48–75.

view of current uncertainties and substantial contradictions between this decision and that, this law and that. Our argument here assumes what we hope to prove in Chapters 3 and 4—that the law has not changed as much as some commentators have implied, and that it is therefore possible to support at one and the same time the traditional approach to antitrust and its current revivification while rejecting proposed economic alternatives. The argument suggests that a recognition of the purposes and requirements of a rule of law and of the serious limitations of economic criteria of monopoly counsels greater moderation than has distinguished much recent commentary.

In so arguing, we shall find ourselves in some respects upholding the traditional theory of antitrust against the enthusiastic supporters as well as the critics of what both conceive to be a new Sherman Act. Both have in common not merely a misleading conception of how far the law has changed,[2] but also a belief that objective economic analysis supports their radically divergent arguments. Their conflicting economic views help to underline our own opposing contention that economics does not offer clear-cut objective criteria for antitrust superior to those which have long prevailed.

Monopoly at Law and Its Rationale

In a society grounded in individualism, the function of government consists very largely of setting boundaries to individual action. For the free enterprise area of the economy, the law merely fixes the rules of the game. So the antitrust laws involve the government in no entrepreneurial activity proper and require no detailed review of either basic investment commitments or run-of-the-mill business decisions. Instead and appropriately, they proscribe specific *actions* deemed socially undesirable: contracting, combining, or conspiring to rig the market, as well as monopolizing, discriminating, tying-in, and competing unfairly, whether in concert or independently. These prohibitions may be

[2] Compare remarks of Edwin G. Nourse and A. D. H. Kaplan in the panel discussion on "The Economics and Legality of Bigness," *Current Business Studies* (Trade and Industry Law Institute), Feb. 1950, pp. 22, 50, with Walter Adams, "Is Bigness a Crime?" 27 *Land Economics* 287–289 (1951).

summarized as embracing the substantial elimination of competition either by agreement or by unfair (predatory) rivalry, in short, by collusion or exclusion. Of these offenses, monopolizing is the most equivocal. It might be taken to forbid mere possession of monopoly power, and hence to outlaw a market situation rather than a course of conduct. In fact, it has been clear, until recently at least, that monopolizing meant the acts incident to attempts to acquire or maintain substantial monopoly power.[3]

The economic rationale of the law rests on two assumptions. The first is that the will to "get ahead," to outdo others, in short, to compete, is so strong and so widespread that it needs only to be channelized by negative prohibitions. The second is that cost functions and optimum business size in most industries are such that out of fair rivalry the numbers of sellers (and buyers) emerging will not be so small as to weaken seriously the force of competition in the market. These assumptions have often been questioned [4] but seldom refuted on the basis of concrete examinations of the structural pattern and performance of specific industries. It follows that the law need only prevent the deliberate impairment, misdirection, or suppression of competition to protect both the public interest and the legitimate interests of business competitors.

The common law rules dealing with restraints of trade and unfair competitive practices were concerned less with protecting the consumer than with protecting businessmen's freedom to compete. The antitrust laws sought both ends, finding no incompatibility between them. The recent criticisms of antitrust argue, essentially, that the enforcement agencies have confused the two and, in consequence, have weakened the force of competition. Unfortunately, the distinction between preserving competition and preserving competitors (particularly since the former may obviously be interpreted to embrace the protection of business-

[3] See Mason, "Monopoly in Law and Economics," reprinted in American Economic Association, p. 41 n.; also Watkins, "The Sherman Act and Enforcement—Discussion," 38 *Amer. Econ. Rev., Papers and Proceedings* 206 (1948).

[4] See, e.g., Galbraith, *American Capitalism,* Chap. 4; Levitt, "The Dilemma of Antitrust Aims: Comment," 42 *Amer. Econ. Rev.* 893 (1952).

men from competitive handicaps unrelated to relative efficiency) is by no means so clear or so easily made as is implied alike by the rationale of antitrust and by the contentions of those economists who have been criticizing antitrust enforcement agencies (including the courts) for failing to make it.

The Market Structure Test of Monopoly

Economists have developed two fairly distinct tests of monopoly. One test looks to market structure for evidences of those characteristics from which, according to the theory of the firm, undesirable results must follow. The other criterion applies the maxim "By their fruits ye shall know them." It may begin by identifying structural impurities, but its primary emphasis is on the economic record, i.e., market performance. Only if the results are "bad" is the monopoly power deemed excessive. The two tests are not mutually exclusive; it is seldom suggested that either be applied without consideration of the other; and both assume that a radically imperfect market structure will sooner or later produce a defective performance. However it is clearly one thing to judge the market situation itself (on the ground that "an industry which does not have a competitive structure will not have competitive behavior,") [5] and quite another to evaluate the results, judging the structure mainly in terms of those findings.

Of these two concepts, it was the former which alone underlay Mason's contrast of "monopoly in law and economics." Following Chamberlin, he observed that to the economist monopoly describes a market situation in which an individual seller has the power to influence price. Such exploitative monopoly power may appear without collusion or exclusion, that is to say, it may arise in the absence of the traditional legal evidences of unreasonable restraint of trade or monopoly. Conversely, illegal actions may fail to create the exploitative power which alone signifies monopoly to the economist. Although Mason judiciously made no such recommendation, one possible implication of the contrast he drew was that the "antiquated and inadequate" law should be

[5] George J. Stigler, "The Case against Big Business," 45 *Fortune,* May 1952, p 167.

altered to conform to the theory of imperfect competition.[6] Galbraith has shown no hesitation in drawing this conclusion. He declares forthrightly that the laws are inevitably defective because they cannot reach oligopolists except if they misbehave; that, because of oligopoly, "competition . . . has, in fact, been superseded." [7]

Other economists have explicitly drawn the implication that antitrust policy ought to be directed not only against single sellers, but also against oligopoly (or other kinds of monopoly markets) per se. The National Resources Committee, and some members and witnesses of the T.N.E.C. and Celler Committee had a most respectable support in oligopoly theory for their concern with concentration ratios (measuring the percentage of output or sales in individual industries accounted for by a given number of the largest firms) and their assumption that mere fewness of sellers is an evil in itself.[8] Arthur R. Burns's monumental proof of the "decline of competition," which is really a thorough demonstration of the absence of pure competition, concludes that direct public regulation is required to do the job that competition no longer does. On the other hand, Eugene V. Rostow, finding similar tendencies in industrial structure and market behavior, argues that the laws should attack monopoly power per se and applauds such tendencies in the "new Sherman Act." [9] Morris Adelman has stated that "until and unless we decide that the real problem is market control and how much and what kind

[6] Mason, in American Economic Association, pp. 37–43.

[7] *American Capitalism,* p. 119; see also Chap. 5 and his "Monopoly and the Concentration of Economic Power," in Ellis (ed.), *A Survey of Contemporary Economics,* pp. 102, 118–119, 127.

[8] See, e.g., National Resources Committee, *The Structure of the American Economy,* Pt. I (Washington, G.P.O., 1939), pp. 102, 110–116 and Chap. 8; House Committee on the Judiciary, Subcommittee on Study of Monopoly Power, *Study of Monopoly Power* (hereafter, Celler Committee), Hearings, 81st Cong.. 2d Sess., Serial No. 14, Pt. 1, pp. 91 (Tom Clark), 102–103 (Cong. Celler and Sen. O'Mahoney), 110 (John D. Clark), 206–207 (John Blair), 338 (Walter Adams), 366 (Herbert Bergson).

[9] "The New Sherman Act: A Positive Instrument of Progress," 14 *U. of Chicago Law Rev.* 567 (1947); "Monopoly under the Sherman Act—Power or Purpose," 43 *Ill. Law Rev.* 745 (1949). See also Adams, in 27 *Land Economics* 287 (1951).

we ought to permit, the situation will remain confused." [10] And Ward S. Bowman, Jr., has therefore proposed that a presumption of illegal monopoly power attach to all multiplant firms accounting for more than 10 or 15 per cent of their respective industries' sales.[11] Implicitly or explicitly, and despite substantial differences between them, all the foregoing writers have adopted the first concept of monopoly distinguished above, and some of them have stressed the necessity for a broad-scale structural transformation of markets.

It is ironic that many economists, trained in the Chamberlinian tradition, now chide the Department of Justice and the courts for learning their lessons too well. But the courts have not followed the lead of the theory of monopolistic competition as far as some critics (or friends) of recent decisions would have us believe, and they have been wise not to do so. Our view is that if they will only resist some of the policy implications of the new economic criticism as well, the antitrust laws will continue to play an effective role in preserving workable competition.

The concept of workable competition strongly suggests the expediency of the traditional approach to antitrust, in preference to applying a market structure test. If monopoly elements inevitably pervade the economy, and are in some measure essential to a good performance, it would clearly be quixotic to attack monopoly as such. If the courts were really prepared now to outlaw "the power to raise prices," as some enthusiastically read the recent *American Tobacco* decision,[12] few industries would be exempt. The economy would have to be "purified" right out of the twentieth (and every other) century. Yet there exists no generally accepted economic yardstick *appropriate for incorporation into law* with which objectively to measure monopoly power or to determine what degree is compatible with workable competition.

The heart of the problem of policy would be to determine *how much* power to raise prices, enjoyed for *how long,* is objection-

[10] "Effective Competition and the Antitrust Laws," 61 *Harv. Law Rev.* 1317 (1948).

[11] "Toward Less Monopoly," in 101 *U. of Penn. Law Rev.* 589 (1953).

[12] See p. 71, below.

able. Most proponents of this test would probably regard the cigarette industry as one exemplifying excessive market power. Yet even here the evidence is not unequivocal. Great stress has been laid on the flagrant price increases of 1931. Yet the consequence was an increase of the market share of the ten-cent brands, within a period of seventeen months, from 0.28 to 22.78 per cent, and a precipitate price retreat by the Big 3.[13] By what acceptable law could the market structure in cigarettes have been subjected to direct attack?

The scrutiny of the law might, instead, be directed at the sources of monopoly power (product differentiation and difficulties of entry by new firms), rather than toward the power itself. But these causal factors, similarly, either are not measurable or are not, taken individually, unequivocal in their implications concerning the workability of competition. Whether their influence is, on balance, beneficent or harmful depends on a host of conditioning circumstances that defy incorporation into legal prohibitions. Every market structure is in large measure *sui generis.*

Product differentiation, for example, is often a means of competition that serves the public by providing minimum assurances of quality and by catering to a real consumer desire for product improvement or variation.[14] Difficulty of entry, when not deliberately devised or imposed, and the special obstacles posed by massed patents scarcely provide a sufficient basis for antitrust action against firms whose monopoly power they may enhance.

[13] *American Tobacco Co.* v. *U.S.,* 328 U.S. 781, 805–806 (1946).

[14] Compare Chamberlin himself, in 40 *Amer. Econ. Rev., Papers and Proceedings* 86 (1950), with Mund, *Government and Business,* pp. 122–123. At the same time, Chamberlin's contention that it is impossible to condemn (all? or even specific instances of?) product differentiation in terms of welfare considerations because people want variety ignores the fact that the "variety" consumers "want" is not a pre-existing datum but is deliberately cultivated by the kinds of limited competition which some businesses have chosen to adopt. If "welfare economics" cannot evaluate such a situation, it is fraudulently named. See, on this general subject, Arthur P. Becker, "Psychological Production and Conservation," 43 *Q. Jour. Econ.* 577 (1949), and our discussion in Chap. 1, above. On some other pitfalls of a market structure test, see G. E. Hale, "Size and Shape: The Individual Enterprise as a Monopoly," 1950 *U. of Ill. Law Forum,* Winter, 525–528.

Similarly, there are serious dangers in setting upper limits to business size or market shares, *ex ante*. They include the difficulty of defining products and markets in a way that will be generally acceptable and will stay put (what about the substitutability of one product for another?); the unmeasurable economies of scale, including the economies of experience, technical skill, and research; the possible damping effect on business enterprise of such upper limits; the possible compatibility of oligopoly and forthright rivalry (particularly in innovation); and finally the tendencies of giant business units constantly to change their product "mixes" and thereby to intensify interproduct and interindustry competition.

Rarely does the cause of effective competition demand an attack on an industry merely because of the fewness of the firms that make it up. A broad sampling of opinion among economists, of a wide variety of general attitudes toward big business and the antitrust laws, discloses a surprising concurrence in the view that pure, noncollusive oligopoly is not the problem that has been popularly depicted. Mason, Clark, Schumpeter, and Chamberlin have pointed out that fewness of sellers and product differentiation need not be incompatible with effective rivalry in the public interest, just as great numbers of sellers do not assure a satisfactory performance. Galbraith makes no effort to reconcile his statements about the ineffectiveness of competition under oligopoly with his equal stress on the indeterminacy of the economic results in such markets and his extolling of oligopoly as the market structure best suited to produce innovation. His theory of countervailing power only partially resolves this contradiction.[15] Stocking and Watkins on the one hand and Kaplan on the other have exposed the infrequency of the conjuncture of the numerous and varied circumstances required for a purely oligopolistic market to yield a monopoly outcome without collusion.[16] William Fellner has concluded that a combination of the tradi-

[15] Cf. statements cited in note 7 above with those in his *American Capitalism,* Chap. 7, and his chapter in Ellis, pp. 102, 119–120, 127–128.

[16] Stocking and Watkins, *Monopoly and Free Enterprise,* Chaps. 4 and 5; Kaplan, *Big Enterprise in our Competitive System,* Chap. 3. See also J. Fred Weston, *The Role of Mergers in the Growth of Large Firms,* Chap. 6 and App. A.

tional antitrust policies and ancillary government actions directed at reducing barriers to entry might suffice to produce workable competition.[17] Markham's argument that price leadership alone (in the absence of collusion, coercion, or exclusion) is not a serious problem supports this view.[18] Carl Kaysen suggests that a relatively slight extension of the antitrust concept of collusion to cover such a rigid price leadership as fairly clearly signifies an "agreement to agree" would suffice,[19] and Milton Handler has put forth similar reasonable criteria for identifying presumptive conspiracies. Such an extension of antitrust does represent a change in degree; the prohibition of collusion shades into a positive order to act like competitors. But the test is still market behavior, not structure or results; and it is a test (as Handler points out) in keeping with the traditional doctrine of conspiracy, although with this important change: that the evidence of illegal "action" may be found primarily in a failure to compete, mirroring a presumed common understanding, rather than in direct conspiratorial activities.[20] All these opinions suggest that the antitrust laws need not and should not condemn oligopoly as such.

The market structure concept of monopoly still has an important role to play in antitrust policy. It must supply evidence of market power that defendants have allegedly "abused" or obtained illegally. It must supply guidance for legal remedies when a business has habitually indulged in illegal practices by suggesting (for removal) the market elements that fostered illicit conduct. And the avoidance or offsetting of industrial concentration may very well assume a central position in guiding other

[17] "Collusion and Its Limits under Oligopoly," 40 *Amer. Econ. Rev., Papers and Proceedings* 60–62 (1950).

[18] "The Nature and Significance of Price Leadership," 41 *Amer. Econ. Rev.* 891 (1951). A. R. Oxenfeldt's criticism does not destroy Markham's thesis that price leadership may be compatible with effective competition. 42 *Amer. Econ. Rev.* 380 (1952).

[19] "Collusion under the Sherman Act," 65 *Q. Jour. Econ.* 263 (1951).

[20] "Anti-Trust—New Frontiers and New Perplexities," 6 *The Record* 62–68 (1951). The foregoing summaries are of course sketchy. There are others, like Burns, Kreps, and Lewis, who would disagree with much of this. See their contributions to Keezer, in 39 *Amer. Econ. Rev.* 689–724 (1949).

government policies bearing on business performance. There is a need for government measures ancillary to antitrust, to curb and counteract the forces that help generate monopoly power: revising the tax laws (for example, what sensible justification can be advanced for permitting unlimited deductions of advertising expenditures in computing taxable income under the corporation income tax levy?), organizing technical research and assisting private, co-operative research organizations, providing credit facilities for new ventures, defining quality standards and enforcing grade labeling, underwriting full employment, ensuring sustained, adequate supplies and fair distribution of scarce raw materials, assisting private parties to resolve patent infringement controversies, and so on. Such measures are, of course, not at all incompatible with the traditional focus of antitrust. On the contrary, they would merely further implement the traditional conception of unfair competition by attacking positively what the law already attacks negatively—competitive disadvantages not attributable to inefficiency.

The Market Performance Test

Should antitrust scrutiny be focused mainly on market performance? In 1949 Mason suggested this test as one possible way of deciding, at law, whether an industry is workably competitive.[21] More recently, Clare E. Griffin has provided a judicious expression and elaboration of this thesis.[22] Both concepts (market performance and workable competition) are essentially pragmatic. How intense a rivalry, how many sellers, how standardized a product, how easy entry, how much independence of action among sellers are required for workability? Enough, it is averred, to give the consumer a real range of choice, to ensure efficiency, to hold profits to reasonable levels, to yield technological progress and a passing on of its gains in lower (though not necessarily cyclically flexible) prices, while avoiding cutthroat competition. The law, these economists imply or openly suggest, should evaluate the economic results in the light of the available alter-

[21] "The Current Status of the Monopoly Problem in the United States," 62 *Harv. Law Rev.* 1266–1271, 1280–1285 (1949).

[22] *An Economic Approach to Antitrust Problems.*

native market structures and attack the structure only when the foregoing tests warrant it.[23]

It is perhaps an exaggeration to imply that adherents of the workable competition test propose to judge market structures exclusively in terms of performance. Most of them appear to believe that it is possible to formulate certain minimum structural requirements (notably the familiar one that the buyer have a sufficient number of real alternatives among which to choose) less rigid than pure competition, which will assure the most effective performance attainable. S. C. Oppenheim, cochairman of the Attorney General's National Committee to Study the Antitrust Laws, would have each decision turn on an economic appraisal of the interaction of "structure, behavior and accomplishments" of the defendant industries.[24] But an increasing number are finding an effective performance compatible with such impure conditions as to cast doubt on any attempt to formulate a structural norm.[25]

Of course, the courts have always scrutinized the behavior or performance of defendants in antitrust cases. They have examined data on prices and profits, where relevant in appraising charges of restraint or monopolizing. But they were looking for evidence bearing on the propriety of the firm's conduct in terms of the traditional legal offenses; they were not basing their decisions substantively on the economic record. No doubt the courts were impressed in the old *Standard Oil* and *American Tobacco* cases [26] by a record of exorbitant prices and profits. But the crucial determinant of the majority opinions was the record of mammoth mergers and flagrantly coercive and exclusive tactics. There is little evidence that recent decisions (as distinguished from the decrees) have been seriously influenced by *economic* evaluations of business performance. The Supreme Court

[23] Markham, "An Alternative Approach to the Concept of Workable Competition," 40 *Amer. Econ. Rev.* 361 (1950).

[24] "Federal Antitrust Legislation," 50 *Mich. Law Rev.* 1190 (1952).

[25] Griffin, pp. 59–61; R. B. Heflebower, "Economics of Size," 24 *Jour. of Business* 265–268 (1951).

[26] *Standard Oil Co. of N.J.* v. *U.S.,* 221 U.S. 1 (1911); *U.S.* v. *American Tobacco Co.,* 221 U.S. 106 (1911).

stressed the price gouging by the Big 3 cigarette companies in 1931 not in passing judgment on their economic performance, but because, it held, "the . . . record of price changes is circumstantial evidence of the existence of a conspiracy. . . ." Similarly, as it was careful to point out, the heavy advertising expenditures of the Big 3 were "not here criticized as a business expense . . . ," [27] but as an instrument of exclusion. In the *Alcoa* case Judge Hand waived any consideration of the company's economic accomplishments as "irrelevant." [28] To United Shoe Machinery's contention that its monopoly was required in the interest of efficiency and fundamental research, Judge Wyzanski gave "the shortest answer[:] . . . that the law does not allow an enterprise that maintains control of a market through practices not economically inevitable, to justify that control because of its supposed social advantage." [29]

When courts and administrative commissions are devising remedies for past antitrust violations, they must of course compare market performance under the condemned and the projected alternative market structures. But as the basic, self-sufficient guide to public policy, economic performance is as much open to question as is the test of market structure.

Mason's proposal is mainly that antitrust authorities make greater use of this criterion in selecting cases. Griffin, similarly, suggests its application mainly in selecting cases, framing decrees, and considering legislation. Hence the area of disagreement between proponents of the performance and of the traditional tests may easily be exaggerated.

However, a substantial conflict remains. As to the choice of cases, for example, one aim of the antitrust laws is to raise the plane of competition. For this reason there are grounds for prohibiting certain *actions* without exception, in all circumstances, entirely apart from considerations of economic engineering.

More important, if performance is to be relevant in the selection of cases, the justifiability of each selection by the enforcement agencies must be open to judicial scrutiny on the same

[27] *American Tobacco* v. *U.S.*, 328 U.S. 781, 804, 797 (1946).

[28] *U.S.* v. *Aluminum Co. of America,* 148 F.2d 416, 427 (1945).

[29] *U.S.* v. *United Shoe Machinery Corp.*, 110 F.Supp. 295, 345 (1953).

grounds. Hence the assessment of economic results would become an inevitable, and perhaps the determining, consideration in the process of adjudication as well.[30] And when we turn to the discussion of specific cases, we find among most proponents of this test a persistent undertone of criticism—that very "new criticism" with which the present essay is concerned—of recent prosecutions and decisions for attacking certain restraints of trade without regard to mitigating evidence of "good" economic results. The asymmetry of their argument is indicated by Griffin's reassurance that a *poor* performance should not be ground for legal action in the absence of a restraint of trade. Performance is thus to serve primarily as ground for exoneration, presumably of such recent defendants as Alcoa, National Lead, A & P, the Cement Institute, Standard of California, and Standard of Indiana. An effective antitrust policy should probably lean the other way, if at all, refusing to condone essentially anticompetitive activities merely because the industry's economic performance is "good," yet (following Handler) finding in noncompetitive market behavior at least a presumption of illegal conspiracy.

Market performance is not necessarily a sign of competition or monopoly at all.[31] It is a "way of looking at competition," in Mason's words, only in the sense that it looks for the results which idealized competition is supposed by static theory to achieve. And if the results are "good," the market which produced them becomes, *ipso facto,* "workably competitive."

Such an approach has an obvious attraction. Ignoring the irrelevant forms, dismissing the complexities of traditional legal inquiries, it judges situations in terms of what really counts, their results. It accords with the plausible aphorism that there can be too much competition as well as too little. It recognizes the commonplace axiom that competition is, after all, not an end in itself. We may agree with the aphorism while maintaining that it has very little to do with the practical possibilities and actual pur-

[30] See Griffin, pp. 90–92.

[31] See Edwards, "Public Policy and Business Size," 24 *Jour. of Business* 285 (1951); Lewis, in Keezer, 39 *Amer. Econ. Rev.* 706–707 (1949); and Adams, "The 'Rule of Reason': Workable Competition or Workable Monopoly?" 63 *Yale Law Jour.* 349 (1954).

poses of antitrust; the cure for "too much competition" is not to permit self-regulation of industry but to attack separately the circumstances that make it "too much"—consumer ignorance, the business cycle, the immobility of labor. As for the axiom, while the general American bias in favor of competition is indeed rationalized largely by an expectation that in the long run it will produce the best economic results, it is also true that fair competition is, indeed, an "end in itself." For, as we have argued in Chapter 1, it is indissolubly linked with the values of free enterprise, equality of economic opportunity, the channeling of the profit motive into socially constructive channels, distributive justice, and the diffusion of economic power.

To put the matter bluntly, the market performance test looks at the wrong end of the process. The essential task of public policy in a free enterprise system is to preserve the framework of a fair field and no favors, letting the results take care of themselves. Obviously, if the results go too far astray, Congress may have to re-examine and reconstitute the institutional framework, either in particular phases or in its entirety. Obviously, too, where it appears that some antitrust proscription is responsible for the poor performance, that proscription should be revised. But the arresting aspect of much of the current criticism of antitrust is its failure to produce concrete economic evidence that the kinds of market structure and behavior consistent with the antitrust laws actually fall short in their performance in ways which only a relaxation of those statutes will remedy. It will, of course, be our purpose in later chapters to document this contention.

Most advocates of a workable competition test for antitrust would deny the charge that they would look only to the results. They claim to trust competition to produce an acceptable market performance. For example, the Business Advisory Council of the Department of Commerce, after making clear its antipathy to an interpretation of the antitrust laws that would make size an offense, states, "The government, instead of attempting the impossible task of deciding where Bigness is more or less efficient, should rely upon the powerful action of Effective Competition. . . ."[32] One interpretation of this statement might be that

[32] *Effective Competition,* p. 16. Cf. note 49, below.

the determination of whether there has been an antitrust violation should omit consideration of the end results or of the efficiency of the defendants. However, the Council immediately proceeds to list some eleven separate tests which the courts and administrative agencies are to apply before they can conclude that a specific practice should be forbidden—in line with their earlier statement of principles that "every effort should be made to determine the effect of the particular practice on public welfare." [33] The list is a grab bag almost all of whose contents (including "*efficiency*") have this one characteristic in common: they are tests of market performance or results.

The insistence of economists on economic tests might be understandable had they in fact developed objective standards capable of commanding general acceptance. Certainly the second deficiency of the market performance test as a substantive basis for antitrust is its vagueness and uncertainty. The grounds on which the courts have for over fifty years refused to evaluate the reasonableness of prices collusively fixed still command respect today.[34] For example, in the *National Lead* case, the court held that a series of international cartel agreements, dividing up the world titanium market, were in violation of the antitrust laws. Surely Judge Rifkind's logic in refusing to consider a defense based on the industry's accomplishments was sound; even the facts of rapid expansion of titanium output and reduction in its price could not, except by an untenable *post hoc, propter hoc* argument, justify on economic grounds a total cartelization of world trade.[35] No basis has been shown, or could be found, for the contention that restrictive covenants (in contrast with non-restrictive cross licensing) were essential to this progress.

These refusals to judge performance in the presence of illegal restraints are particularly apposite because the test of workable competition has been suggested more often in defense or exculpa-

[33] *Ibid.*, p. 3.

[34] See *U.S.* v. *Trans-Missouri Freight Assn.*, 166 U.S. 290, 331–332 (1897); *U.S.* v. *Addyston Pipe and Steel Co.* 85 Fed. 271, 283–284 (1898); *U.S.* v. *Trenton Potteries Co.*, 273 U.S. 392, 397–398 (1927). See in precisely the same vein the opinions of Judges Hand and Wyzanski, notes 28 and 29, above.

[35] *U.S.* v. *National Lead Co.*, 63 F.Supp. 513, 525 (1945).

tion of antitrust violations than as an independent basis for attacking companies or industries. If "efficiency," "progressiveness," and "usefulness for national defense" are to acquit a company or industry, the government should presumably condone most instances of cartelization or monopolizing in the fields of electronics, chemicals, petroleum, and chain store distribution, regardless of whether the specific restraints had anything to do with good over-all performance. So Griffin criticizes the *A & P* cases because they were obviously not "inspired by an attempt to root out inefficiency and sluggishness . . ." and states that the company's real sin was that it was "too efficient." [36] The antitrust laws do not and could not make inefficiency and sluggishness offenses in themselves. The laws may legitimately be criticized only if in attacking what they *are* supposed to attack they at the same time discourage vigorous and economically beneficent competitive efforts. Such an indictment of the *A & P* case has yet to be made.[37]

Or is the determination to be left to the courts or administrative commissions whether, in the absence of the restraints, progress might or might not have been even more rapid, prices and profits even more reasonable? This would certainly prove a most elusive test. The burden surely rests on the critics of the antitrust laws to demonstrate that such a reform is necessary, that *those actions which the law prohibits* are indeed requisite to a good performance. This is something that for the most part they have failed to do.

It is not sufficient to demonstrate, as Mason does, that a doctrinaire market structure test conflicts with the requirements of acceptable performance.[38] He points out that (*a*) the economies of scale may dictate too few sellers for pure competition; (*b*) sellers may be sufficiently numerous for pure competition, yet remain inefficient or unprogressive; (*c*) certain kinds of collusion (e.g., regulation of marketing practices on the Chicago Board of Trade) may make competition more perfect; (*d*) a certain amount of market control may be necessary to promote innovation.

[36] Page 68. [37] See pp. 166–169, 211–216, and 234–241, below.
[38] In 62 *Harv. Law Rev.* 1269–1271 (1949).

The traditional *legal* criteria of monopoly do not come out on the wrong sides of these dilemmas. (*a*) Even the new Sherman Act does not condemn sellers merely because they are large or few. The law in action, therefore, is entirely in keeping with J. M. Clark's suggestion that firms not be attacked merely for increasing their market shares by winning customers in fair competition, but be subjected to scrutiny where they have grown by merger or by pressing bargaining advantages unrelated to efficiency.[39] (*b*) In excessively atomized industries efficient new firms may enter or existing ones integrate. This is the only possible general prescription for improving industrial performance short of public regulation or operation (and apart from ancillary governmental promotional activities, which are entirely consistent with antitrust). (*c*) The courts have explicitly exonerated beneficent trade association activities like those of the Chicago Board of Trade.[40] (*d*) As for the requirements of innovation, economists have yet to demonstrate that such collusion and monopolizing as the laws condemn have on balance contributed to progress, rather than to restriction and retardation, with the end of preserving existing equity values against competitive depletion or displacement. Significantly, when Griffin, in his critique of the antitrust laws, comes to discuss the prerequisites of innovation, he shifts to a demonstration of the inadequacy of perfect competition.[41] What this argument has to do with antitrust is nowhere demonstrated.

Alternatives in a Free Enterprise Economy

Only two general methods of regulating private business appear practicable. One is to establish fairly definite standards in statutory law, leaving businessmen free within those limits to pursue their own interest. So far as the writers can see, such standards can only be standards of conduct. In this case, legal uncertainties will arise only at the boundaries, though these boundaries between permissible and illegal actions may admittedly be vexatiously elusive. It is difficult to envisage equally clear criteria

[39] "The Orientation of Antitrust Policy," 40 *Amer. Econ. Rev., Papers and Proceedings* 96–97 (1950).

[40] *Board of Trade of City of Chicago* v. *U.S.*, 246 U.S. 231 (1918).

[41] Pages 69–73.

of acceptable and unacceptable economic performance. Poor results may issue through no conscious actions or fault of the businessmen concerned. A progressive and efficient company may yet violate the law in ways which contribute little or not at all to its good performance, or which may have kept the record of its industry from being even better.

The only effective alternative to using a firm's conduct as a standard is to formulate only the most general criteria into law, leaving to an administrative commission broad and pervasive powers of investigation, reorganization, and regulation, industry by industry. Such a commission would have to decide, in each case, whether particular market structures are excessively monopolistic. This decision would have to be based, in turn, primarily on a finding that prices, profits, salaries, or wages had been too high or too low, capacity too great or too little, progress in reducing costs, improving quality, introducing new products too rapid or too slow; and the regulatory agency would have to be empowered, on the basis of such decisions, to fashion appropriate alterations in business structure. Here, as a sample, is the relevant (but not exclusive) list of tests suggested by the Secretary of Commerce Business Advisory Committee for application by the courts (!) in antitrust suits:

Alternatives available to customers or sellers
Volume of production or services
Quality of the services or goods
Number of people benefited
Incentives to entrepreneurs
Efficiency and economy in manufacturing or distribution
The tendency to progress in technical development
Prices to customers and suppliers
Conditions favorable to the public interest in maintaining American investments abroad and in defending the country from aggression
The tendency to conserve the country's natural resources
Benefits to the public interest assuming the relief requested by the government in the proceedings.[42]

And these are proposed as part of a program to relieve businessmen of the uncertainties now said to emanate from the antitrust laws! Or perhaps the theory is that since any antitrust defendant

[42] *Effective Competition*, p. 17.

should be able to qualify for one or another of these defenses, uncertainty will disappear because conviction is impossible.

It is questionable whether any group, judicial or administrative, is competent to make such decisions; whether such delegation of responsibility would be politically acceptable; and whether such a change would make for greater clarity and dependability of businessmen's expectations than the antitrust laws as they now stand.

If the law is sound in condemning actions rather than market power or inadequate performance, the problem remains of appropriately defining the actions that it should prohibit. The most vexatious problems arise in applying the traditional legal proscriptions to big, integrated business units. Almost all the most controversial cases under the new Sherman (and Clayton) Act have involved problems of large size, integration, or associated competitive practices. Here we encounter the familiar dilemma of the "double standard," that is, the ambivalence of the law in dealing with restrictive agreements between separate firms on the one hand and proprietary concentrations of market power on the other. If the economic tests be rejected, the double standard is inevitable. The only circumstances in which antitrust proceedings against big business units (or their organizers) are warranted are when the units overstep the rules of a free enterprise system: rules prohibiting monopolizing, either by collusion or by exclusion (which is, by definition, unreasonable).[43] This is our thesis.

The Rule of Reason

The basic antitrust dilemma in this area, which makes it impossible for public policy ever to adopt simple, objective, mechanically applicable and universally acceptable criteria, arises from the fact that business size and integration almost inevitably confer certain unfair competitive advantages, unrelated to efficiency, and give rise to corresponding possibilities of the extension of monopoly.[44] The development of some kind of a rule of

[43] In our view, exclusive tactics, properly defined, are themselves unreasonable acts. See pp. 96–98 and 117–119, below.

[44] See our fuller discussion of this subject in Chap. 5, below.

reason in antitrust jurisprudence has therefore been inevitable. The rule of reason has taken two forms.

First, the courts generally took the position, at least between 1911 and the *Alcoa* decision in 1945, that large firms, whatever their control of the market, were to be judged primarily by one criterion: did the circumstances of their formation and the characteristic pattern of their market behavior evince an intent to monopolize? This was the test of unreasonable restraint and illegal monopolizing, and it was a test of conduct. It would be an exaggeration to imply that the courts devoted no attention to market structure. In the *U.S. Steel* and *Harvester* cases, the majority professed to find little evidence of monopoly power, even though convincing evidence was available to show that the mere existence of those giants exerted a substantial deterrent effect on price competition. But the decisive influence in the *Steel* decision was, surely, the lack of evidence of coercive, predatory, or exclusive tactics; hence no intent to monopolize was imputed. (The *Harvester* case is less clear on this score because the specific issue for adjudication was whether an earlier consent decree had established competitive conditions in the industry.) And even in the *Standard Oil, American Tobacco,* and *Reading* cases, the undeniable monopoly power enjoyed by these companies appears not to have been the decisive factor. It obviously could not have been decisive in the vacuous *United Shoe* decision of 1918.[45]

Second, the prohibitions of the Clayton Act were qualified by the cost-saving and good faith defenses (Sec. 2) and by the necessity for demonstrating a tendency substantially to impair competition (Secs. 2, 3, and 7). The discussion which follows makes no attempt systematically to differentiate Sherman and Clayton Act proceedings. Technically the same rule of reason cannot apply to both. The determination of whether a firm is in fact engaging in the vaguely defined practices condemned by the Sherman Act often necessitates an inquiry into intent, as we shall argue. On the other hand, the Clayton Act prohibits specified practices; hence its rule of reason must hinge not on intent but on substantiality of effect. However, the distinction is not worth

[45] See Stocking and Watkins, *Monopoly and Free Enterprise*, pp. 271–278.

drawing too sharply. The Sherman and Clayton Acts are inevitably intertwined, since the practices listed by the latter may themselves constitute methods of violating the former. Sherman Act monopolizing cases have usually considered the effect of the firm's actions on competition in the market. And intent is often an inevitable consideration in Clayton Act cases, notably in appraising the good faith defense of price discrimination under Section 2. Finally, there has been some tendency progressively to exempt antitrust authorities from the burden of demonstrating "specific" intent even in Sherman Act monopoly cases. This dilution of the rule of reason, which has tended further to obliterate the boundaries between the two statutes, has been accompanied by and associated with a corresponding weakening of the qualifications of the Clayton Act. So, again, the two developments may most satisfactorily be considered together.

The economic criticism of antitrust springs largely from a dissatisfaction with such an allegedly subjective criterion as intent. It is often extremely difficult to apply; the evidence is often equivocal. More important, the new critics would probably agree not only among themselves but also with advocates of rigorous market structure tests that intent is an irrelevant consideration in economic rule making. The antitrust laws should be framed in terms of objective standards rather than moral judgments, in terms of consequences rather than intentions. The relevant test, whether of integration or of competitive tactics, they would hold, is the persistence or (imminent?) suppression of competition as an effective force in the market. And the measure of the competitiveness of markets (here the new critics part with the old) is economic performance. The following quotation from Adelman illustrates this point of view:

> What we need . . . is a painstaking examination of the economic facts of the individual case. Whether the competition offered by the firm in question was but an attempt to destroy competitors for the sake of a longer-run objective of monopoly depends less on intent than on the structure of the market, and the strength of actual and potential competition. And since every market contains elements of monopoly, the "undue" or "unreasonable" nature must be deter-

mined by their influence in restricting output, raising prices, stifling progress and innovation, and the like.[46]

Unhappily, the "objective" standard, the vitality of market competition, is disturbingly elusive. Among economists urging its adoption are those who feel that the rule of reason of 1911 represented a departure from that test and those who feel it embodied just such a test; those who feel it was precisely by such a standard that U.S. Steel was exonerated in 1920 and 1948 and those who felt, with the Supreme Court minorities, that application of an objective economic standard would have compelled a decree of dissolution.[47] The same range of opinion, using the same test, may be documented with respect to a number of other cases. How one decides whether competition was appreciably constricted by the activities of A & P, Standard of California, Yellow Cab, the movie companies, New Orleans Times-Picayune, or J. I. Case, or by the financial link between du Pont and General Motors—all of these the objects of antitrust suits—depends on how one measures competition and defines the relevant market areas. Within certain markets, in certain meaningful respects, competition was unquestionably restricted by each. It would be interesting to take a poll among economists, asking them to choose, for example, between the appraisals by Supreme Court Justices Frankfurter and Jackson of the economic impact of ex-

[46] "Integration and Antitrust Policy," 63 *Harv. Law Rev.* 49–50 (1949). Yet at another time Adelman explicitly, and in our judgment correctly, disavows any suggestion that antitrust policy turn on the government's determination of whether economic results are "good" or "bad." "Business Size and Public Policy," 24 *Jour. of Business* 273 (1951). For a criticism of the stress on intent, see also Sigmund Timberg, "The Case for Civil Antitrust Enforcement," 14 *Ohio State Law Jour.* 317–323 (1953).

[47] Cf., on the one hand, references in note 1, above, and Stocking and Watkins, *Monopoly and Free Enterprise*, pp. 304–310; and, on the other hand, Kaplan, *Big Enterprise*, Chap. 2; Kenneth S. Carlston, "Antitrust Policy: A Problem in Statecraft," 60 *Yale Law J.* 1073, 1076–1080 (1951); and the majority opinions in *U.S.* v. *U.S. Steel Corp.*, 251 U.S. 417 (1920) and *U.S.* v. *Columbia Steel Co.*, 334 U.S. 495 (1948). See also Oppenheim's citation of, among others, these two opinions as "refuting" Justice Frankfurter's contention in *Standard of California* that the courts are ill equipped to make such economic appraisals. 50 *Mich. Law Rev.* 1161 (1952).

clusive dealing contracts in the West Coast gasoline market; the first is from the majority opinion, the second from a dissent:

> It would not be farfetched to infer that their effect has been to enable the established suppliers individually to maintain their own standing and at the same time collectively . . . to prevent a late arrival from wresting away more than an insignificant portion of the market.
>
> I am not convinced that the requirements contract as here used is a device for suppressing competition instead of a device for waging competition. . . . The retail stations . . . are the instrumentalities through which competition for this ultimate market is waged.[48]

The fact is that economics offers no objective measure of the vitality of competition, in all its aspects, or any way of balancing its possible attenuation in certain respects or in certain markets —where the advantages, tactics, or consequences of market power may have taken the toll of existing firms, discouraged the entry of others, or softened the price rivalry among those that remain —against its intensification, by the same firms and similar market practices, in other markets or in other respects. Economic analysis cannot provide conclusive tests of the efficiency or inefficiency of integration; [49] the determination must be left to the market, not to the government.

Nor does the "objective" standard proposed by the economist-critics of antitrust, viz., market performance (however it may be measured), meet the argument that gave rise to the Clayton and Federal Trade Commission Acts: that it may be desirable to forbid certain unfair actions before they have had an opportunity to do appreciable damage. Of course, Congress did not prohibit the enumerated practices outright; as we have already pointed out, it would have been a mistake to do so. On the other hand, it would be a mistake also to judge their legality only on the basis

[48] *Standard Oil Co. of Cal.* v. *U.S.*, 337 U.S. 293, 309, 323 (1949). To take another example, Kaplan describes the keen competition in the manufacture of cans (*Big Enterprise,* Chap. 6); Stocking and Watkins demonstrate its inadequacy (*Monopoly and Free Enterprise,* pp. 167–182). And both are right!

[49] Cf. "Economic policy should be based on actual facts about the relative efficiency of integrated and non-integrated firms." Adelman, "The A & P Case," 63 *Q. Jour. Econ.* 246 (1949).

of an exhaustive estimate of the economic performance of the industries concerned. To require convincing proof of even a "reasonable possibility" of over-all deleterious consequences, involving a tenuous comparison of unpredictables, weakens the prohibition of practices that experience and logic demonstrate tend to have certain anticompetitive effects (whatever their influence on the market as a whole).[50]

Finally, the objective economic standard fails to satisfy the need for rules of fair business dealing, entirely apart from any observable impact of unfair (or inherently exclusionary) tactics on market structure or performance. To paraphrase the poet, execrably: no firm is an island; the unfair elimination of any one business in some way diminishes every other; no one can say in what imponderable ways it weakens the vitality of all. And even if the only injury were to the few individuals subjected to unfair competitive pressures, it does not follow at all "obviously," as Oppenheim would have it, that laws seeking to regulate "the plane of competition between individual competitors" should be brought into conformity with the general antitrust statutes "aimed at preventing restraint of trade and monopoly." [51]

We return thus to the traditional conception. The function of antitrust can only be to see to it that no one attempts to stifle or pervert the process of competition by collusion, by unreasonable financial agglomeration, or by exclusion. Illegality must inhere in the act, not in the result.

The Strategic Role of Intent in the Rule of Reason

The test of intent is only a means of defining the act. In the words of Chief Justice White, in the *Standard Oil* decision, the antitrust laws condemn

> all *contracts* or *acts* . . . unreasonably restrictive of competitive conditions, *either* from the nature . . . of the contract or act *or* where the surrounding circumstances were such as . . . to give rise to the inference or presumption that they had been entered into

[50] *Cf.* W. B. Lockhart and H. R. Sacks, "The Relevance of Economic Factors in Determining Whether Exclusive Arrangements Violate Section 3 of the Clayton Act," 65 *Harv. Law Rev.* 933–940 (1952).

[51] 50 *Mich. Law Rev.* 120 (1952).

or done with the intent to do wrong to the general public *and* to limit the right of individuals, thus restraining the free flow of commerce. . . .[52]

The quest for an explanatory intent does not involve psychoanalysis. The question is not: "Why did A really do what he did?" but simply: "What was A really doing? Was he competing or was he suppressing competition?" "To what kind of activities may one most reasonably attribute the formation and growth of Company B—to technological imperatives, vigorous competition, and 'satisfied customers,' or to anticompetitive manipulations?" The attempt is simply to provide a logical ordering and interpretation of the objective record, out of which there may emerge a reasonable, summary description and appraisal of a course of action, in order to ascertain whether it falls within the acts condemned by law.

Most individual business acts, merging, agreeing, or competing, on their face provide, at best, no more than equivocal evidence of their underlying character or aim. Accordingly, it would be the height of folly either to sanction or to proscribe them per se. Suppressing competition cannot be defined as clearly as sneezing. It can only be inferred from a complex series of actions and consequences.[53]

A state medical association expels some doctors for "a breach of medical ethics." A publishing company controlling a morning and an evening newspaper refuses to accept advertising in either one separately. Another newspaper refuses to run certain advertisements at all. A number of cement manufacturers quote identical delivered prices. An individual glucose manufacturer accepts a single distant basing point of a major competitor as the basis for its own pricing. A chain store reduces its margins in a par-

[52] 221 U.S. 1, 58 (1911). Stress supplied. The new Sherman Act has altered this doctrine essentially by changing the "and" which we have italicized to "or" and by weakening the necessity, implied in the foregoing quotation and what follows it, of demonstrating a substantial achievement of monopoly power.

[53] Situations are conceivable in which the determination even of whether a person sneezed or made a derogatory sound might require an inquiry into intent!

ticular locality, at a particular time. A soap manufacturer circulates among its salesmen a list (which does not *look* black) of dealers to whom they are no longer to sell. A pipeline company owned by an oil refiner establishes minimum tenders. A motion picture exhibitor refuses to show the films of an independent producer on weekends. A manufacturer of machines for fabricating concrete blocks buys out a competitor. A company manufacturing taxicabs obtains control over a large number of taxi operators in three cities. A man standing in front of a bank which is being robbed whistles loudly when a policeman comes into view.

How does one decide when to exonerate, when to condemn these acts or courses of conduct? The logical test, it might appear, would be an evaluation of their objective consequences. Where the act itself is not plainly objectionable, this is the only possible test. But the consequences are often impossible to trace, as we have argued. Second, there are no scientific standards for drawing the line between desirable and undesirable consequences, even where they are traceable. By how much must group medical practice be discouraged before we condemn the medical association? How far must the margins of independent refiners be squeezed to make the action of the integrated refiner reprehensible? At what point does the market share of a merging firm become excessive? How much of a market may be closed to outsiders by vertical integration before the expansion becomes undesirable? How can one tell whether a competing newspaper might not have been born if it had not had to contend with a large established competitor charging advertisers a unit rate? Finally, it may be desirable in certain circumstances to prohibit such actions, regardless of whether there are demonstrable, or even probable, evil economic consequences.

The inescapable conclusion is that, from a practical standpoint, the criterion of intent alone "fills the bill" for a sensible antitrust policy in many of these cases. Why did the loiterer whistle? Why was the doctor dismissed? What was the purpose of the list which may have made it black? Was the lower price offered in good faith to meet competition? Why did one firm buy out another? In this connection the court may be justified in considering the relative efficiency of integrated and nonintegrated operations, but only in order to ascertain intent. The purpose of the investigation should not be to see whether particular acts of integration did or would reduce costs; businessmen should be free to merge (within limits) if they think they can cut costs and should have their judgment subject to appraisal only by the market. They should be free to charge a favorable combination rate for a combined service if they think such a rate fairly mirrors the economies of integration. What the government may ask is whether the act was reasonable: were the companies merging in order to compete better, in acceptable ways, or less; were they competing or monopolizing in selling a package service at a low price?

The point is not to ascertain whether the business units in question were driven by some sort of collective Oedipus complex but simply to find out what they were doing. Was the loiterer helping to rob the bank? Were the cement companies or the manufacturer of concrete-block machines systematically suppressing competition? Was the chain store or the refiner or the newspaper publisher exerting its leverage to squeeze out competitors?

At the risk of repetition, it seems necessary to meet explicitly two related misunderstandings that have contributed to the general dissatisfaction with intent as a basis for antitrust. The first concerns the meaning of intent, the general belief that it simply describes a state of mind. The second concerns the kind of evidence required to determine it, the general belief that it must be inferred mainly from evidence of psychological motive. Both conceptions are essentially incorrect. People (and, following the familiar fiction, businesses) must be assumed at law to have intended what they did. Intent is therefore inferred mainly from the objective record of overt actions, policies, and results, though admittedly evidence of what the defendants thought, or said, they were doing may assist in the interpretation of actions. As for the substance of intent, there is certainly a psychological element. Conspiracy, for example, involves a meeting of minds. But the primary test of whether defendants conspired to fix prices or to boycott must be whether in fact they did so, effectuating the conspiracy by a meeting of bodies, or by other objective, collaborative behavior. (How then does one handle the phenomenon of monopolistic yet nonconspiratorial oligopoly pricing? It may be that the law is defective because it cannot reach such market situations without evidence of collusion. Our espousal of the traditional definitions of illegal restraint or monopolizing is based on the conviction that this animal, bearing the arresting name of "pure, non-collusive, oligopolistic parallelism of action" is a much rarer species than most people think.) The evidence of intent is mainly objective behavior; and its content is a description of what the defendants were doing.

Thus a host of actions, themselves individually unexceptionable, may form together a consistent pattern, explicable and condemnable solely on the basis of the general policy (intent) which they seem to mirror. Only if it is a fact that the man's whistle was part of a broader plan can his participation in the robbery legitimately be inferred. Only as part of a price-fixing conspiracy may an individual act of price reporting or freight absorption be objectionable. Only as part of a systematic attempt to monopolize their particular markets can a rational basis be found for condemning the refusal of a theater to handle certain films, the reduction of a fabricating margin by a vertically integrated firm, or a business machine company's acquisition of a competitor's patents or plants. Justice Holmes said, almost a half-century ago, "The plan may make the parts unlawful." [54] A more recent decision holds, in the same vein:

> While it must be admitted that not all of these acts are prohibited, nevertheless, we must view them in the broad panorama of other acts and their association with each other to note, not only the effect —but to pierce the veil for evidence of intent. . . . It is clear then that the intent . . . to dominate this industry by monopoly is obvious and the result of the . . . conspiracy was to restrict competitors which latter is illegal under the Sherman Act.[55]

[54] *Swift and Co.* v. *U.S.*, 196 U.S. 375, 396 (1905). In a later case he agreed with the government that "the intent alleged would convert what on their face might be no more than ordinary acts of competition . . . into a conspiracy of wider scope. . . ." *Nash* v. *U.S.*, 229 U.S. 373, 378 (1913).

[55] *U.S.* v. *Besser Mfg. Co.*, 96 F.Supp. 304, 313 (1951).

The quest for a unifying and underlying intent is in most of these cases unavoidable, even though the statute seems to say, simply and objectively, "these things you may not do." [56]

Supplementary Economic Criteria

It does not follow that an intent (as the psychologist might use the term) to suppress competition is or should be either a sufficient or in all cases a necessary basis for condemnation. Intent unaccompanied by overt action cannot enter into judgment in the present life. It must be accompanied, first, by the power (actual or imminent) to restrain or exclude and, second, by some evidence that the power has been or, barring interference, will be exercised. Thus, in Sherman Act cases the courts will usually appraise the power of the defendants, to help determine the character and probable results of their actions. But where the objectionable nature of the act is clear, they ordinarily make no "systematic economic assessment of market power." [57] As Judge Taft put it, fifty-five years ago, "The most cogent evidence that they had this power is the fact, everywhere apparent in the record, that they exercised it." [58]

Objective consequences (or their lack) are surely relevant as well. Indeed where, in certain cases, the evidence of power and its exercise is clear, and where the consequences are both sufficiently manifest and plainly objectionable, it has not and should not have been necessary to demonstrate a "specific" illegal intent.[59] This was, of course, one purpose of the Clayton Act, as far as the practices therein specified were concerned.

But where the external evidence both of actions and results is equivocal—and we have argued that it is inevitably so in many

[56] Even the familiar criminal offenses cannot be defined except in terms of intent. See *Morrisette* v. *U.S.*, 342 U.S. 246 (1952).

[57] See Adelman's argument to the contrary and the reply by Dirlam and Kahn in 61 *Jour. Pol. Econ.* 436 (1953).

[58] *U.S.* v. *Addyston Pipe & Steel Co.*, 85 Fed. 271, 292 (1898).

[59] See the *Alcoa, Griffith,* and *United Shoe Machinery* decisions, in Chap. 3, below. All three decisions were forced closer to the adoption of a simple market structure test by earlier decisions (of the respective District Courts in the first two, of the Supreme Court in 1913 and 1918, in the last) which had refused to find an intent to monopolize except in unequivocally immoral and predatory actions.

cases—an investigation of intent is and always has been essential. As Justice Hughes observed:

> Good intentions will not save a plan otherwise objectionable, but knowledge of actual intent is an aid in the interpretation of facts and prediction of consequences.[60]

Or as Justice Lurton stated more positively:

> Whether a particular act, contract or agreement was a reasonable and normal method in furtherance of trade and commerce may, in doubtful cases, turn upon the intent to be inferred. . . . Of course, if the necessary result is materially to restrain trade . . . the intent with which the thing was done is of no consequence.[61]

Thus economic considerations are by no means irrelevant in the rule of reason. Power and consequences are considered, and rightly so. But they are not decisive. Mere unexercised power to exclude, the mere exclusion of competitors which occurs when a supplier consolidates with a customer, the mere power to influence price, remain and should remain free from condemnation. And the relevant consequences to be appraised are those implied in the traditional legal criterion: the mutual suppression of rivalry or the exclusion or threatened exclusion of competitors (by unfair methods).

Thus the crucial inquiry under the rule of reason is into the character of the act. In borderline cases this requires an imputation of intent. Having assisted in this determination, the rule of reason has fulfilled its legitimate function.

Acts that investigation reveals fall into the category of unreasonably collusive or unfairly exclusive tactics must, in a free enterprise system, be condemned. This is the only "workable" rule of antitrust. These acts cannot be condoned simply because there is no clear evidence they have actually impaired the "workability" of competition in the market or contributed to a poor economic performance, narrowly construed.

In Chapters 5 to 8 below, we shall attempt to show that application of this standard will not ordinarily produce a result that violates the requirements of effective competition.

[60] *Appalachian Coals, Inc.* v. *U.S.*, 288 U.S. 344, 372 (1933).
[61] *U.S.* v. *Reading Co.*, 226 U.S. 324, 370 (1912).

CHAPTER 3

The Path of the Law: Business Size and Integration in Monopoly Cases

THE purpose of this chapter and the one that follows is to answer the question, "How new are the new Sherman and Clayton Acts?" How far have recent interpretations actually gone in altering the historic legal criteria we described and defended in Chapter 2? As we have already pointed out, the infatuation of economists and lawyers with the rule of reason has grown as they have become convinced that the ardor of the courts has been cooling. Therefore we will be particularly interested in seeing to what extent and in what ways the courts have really been whittling away at the rule of reason as traditionally defined. Only then can we assess the criticism that the law now harasses vigorous competitors and proscribes economically beneficial business practices and policies that make competition perhaps less pure but also more effective.

The only satisfactory way to do so is to examine each of the leading recent cases in the round. It may help the reader, in threading the legal maze, if we set forth our general view at the outset. Our conclusion, with some qualifications, is that the recent decisions conform to the essential purposes and philosophy of the law and still accept the guidance of the traditional legal criteria of monopolizing and unreasonable restraint. The qualifying rule of reason has been weakened; and that rule admittedly brought economic considerations, notably the competitive impact of the business structure and practices under scrutiny, to bear in antitrust proceedings. Yet this dilution has helped restore the vigor of the laws in condemning *what they have always condemned:* the accumulation of market power by unreasonable methods and its unreasonable exercise, in short, collusion, coercion, and exclusion.

There is no simple, logical way of grouping the controversial cases. Least of all would it be useful to take up each statutory provision separately. Under the rule of reason, enunciated in the 1911 *Standard Oil* case, an important test of the presence or absence of an intent to monopolize (under Sec. 2 of the Sherman Act) was the accomplishment of an unreasonable restraint of trade, in contravention of Section 1. Similarly, the *American Tobacco* and *Paramount* decisions of 1946 and 1948 found in price-fixing (and other) conspiracies, illegal under Section 1, part of the evidence sustaining a charge of monopolization, even though several separate companies rather than true monopolists were involved. Price discrimination and exclusive arrangements have helped convict companies sometimes of Clayton Act violations (Secs. 2 and 3), sometimes of illegally restraining trade or monopolizing (under Secs. 1 or 2 of the Sherman Act), sometimes of employing unfair methods of competition (under Sec. 5 of the Federal Trade Commission Act), and usually of some combination of these. Conversely, the prohibition of "monopolizing" in Section 2 of the Sherman Act has been applied to authentic monopolies, to integrated businesses with little monopoly power, to oligopolists acting as though they were engaged in simple, Section 1, price-fixing conspiracies, and to suppliers obtaining long-term full requirements contracts from their customers. Similarly attenuated standards of competitive impact of trade practices and of integration alike have been applied in cases under Sections 1 and 2 of the Sherman Act and Sections 2 and 3 of the Clayton Act.

Therefore we will group the leading cases according to the preponderant economic element in each, though the developments are closely interrelated and many of the cases might with almost equal logic have been shifted from this category to that.

In this chapter we discuss the cases in which the primary element was the size, market power, and integrated structure of the defendants; most were monopoly (Sec. 2) cases, though many involved also Section 1 restraints, and all were concerned in some measure with questionable competitive tactics. Second, in Chapter 4, we turn to cases focusing primarily on the business practices themselves—notably, exclusive dealing, full requirements contracts, and price discrimination. These again, as we shall see, were by no means confined to Clayton or F.T.C. Act proceedings.

Monopolizing as the Enjoyment of a Monopoly

As we have demonstrated in Chapter 2, the "old" Sherman Act was not intended to attack the mere enjoyment of monopoly power. Rather, the stigma of monopolizing has attached, traditionally, to the unreasonable acts incident to attempts to acquire or maintain substantial monopoly power. The economic assumption implicit in accepting such a law as the charter of a competitive system is that if these actions are prevented, no serious monopoly problems will arise.

It was in Judge Hand's decision in the *Alcoa* case, according to most accounts, that the rule of reason was frankly jettisoned in favor of a test framed exclusively in terms of market structure. After resolving the complex issue of how best to measure the company's share in the national aluminum market by selecting the combination of figures which yielded the highest possible percentage, Hand then apparently disregarded standards of reasonableness: 90 per cent control "is enough to constitute a monopoly"; "having proved that 'Alcoa' had a monopoly . . . the plaintiff had gone far enough"; and it would be "absurd" unconditionally to condemn price-fixing conspiracies "and not to extend the condemnation to monopolies."[1] At a later point the opinion pays its respects to the traditional doctrine that mere size is no offense ("the successful competitor, having been urged to compete, must not be turned upon when he wins") and accepts the necessity for considering the mitigating if not exonerating possibility that monopoly might have been "thrust upon" the company. But Hand met this hurdle merely by stating that (*a*)

[1] *U.S.* v. *Aluminum Co. of America,* 148 F.2d, 416, 424, 427, 428 (1945).

no one attains 100 per cent control of domestic production unwittingly, and (*b*) Alcoa "effectively anticipated and forestalled all competition" by steadfastly increasing its capacity to meet all demands. Although offered as evidence of illegal intent, mere increase in productive capacity is indistinguishable from vigorous competitive conduct; at most it proved that Alcoa did not reach and hold its position against its own will. If such actions were reprehensible, it could only have been because the outcome—the monopoly position—was itself illegal.[2]

If the *Alcoa* decision stands, any other single-firm monopoly that the courts henceforth encounter, if persisting, as did the monopoly enjoyed by the Aluminum Company of America, for thirty-five years beyond the expiration of controlling patents, will be held *ipso facto* illegal. Does this represent a revolutionary legal shift from the famous *U.S. Steel* case dictum that "mere size is no offense"? We think it does, within the rather narrow limits of pure monopolies.

True, in the old *Steel, Harvester,* and *Can* cases, where the companies were exonerated, the courts were heavily influenced by the fact that the defendants were not pure monopolists: "The Corporation did not achieve monopoly . . . and it is against monopoly that the statute is directed. . . ." [3] So Judge Hand expressly restricted application of his diluted rule of reason to companies accounting for a preponderant part—something like 90 per cent—of the national supplies of a physically distinct product. Therefore it might appear that the *Alcoa* decision was en-

[2] *Ibid.*, pp. 429–432. "No intent is relevant except . . . [the] intent to bring about the forbidden act" (p. 432). But the "act" was the enjoyment of 90 per cent of the market. See also Adams, "The Aluminum Case: Legal Victory—Economic Defeat," 41 *Amer. Econ. Rev.* 917 (1951).

There is a clear implication of the same attitude in the earlier *Pullman* case. In effect, Judge Goodrich said there that a monopoly is a monopoly; the problem of drawing the line enters somewhere below 100 per cent market control. *U.S.* v. *Pullman Co.*, 50 F.Supp. 123, 134–135 (1943). Nevertheless in his appraisal he insisted on looking "at the whole picture." And in this picture was a conscious purposeful program for obtaining and then cementing this monopoly control by mergers, exclusive agreements, and the like.

[3] *U.S.* v. *U.S. Steel Corp.*, 251 U.S. 417, 444 (1920).

tirely consistent with those earlier cases turning on the rule of reason. However, we must remember that, in each of the earlier cases, the defendants had originally been put together by mammoth mergers that left them with preponderant shares of total national production; had they retained those market positions the courts might have been able to condemn them for monopolizing, "not as a result of normal methods of industrial development, but by new means . . . resorted to in order that greater power might be added than would otherwise have arisen had normal methods been followed. . . ."[4] These words of Chief Justice White in 1911 defined monopolizing as consisting in an unreasonable course of conduct, involving a consistent effort to obtain or maintain market control by methods other than those of normal competition. The grounds on which Judge Hand chose to condemn Alcoa, on the contrary, seem to embrace within the term the mere enjoyment of monopoly power, even if attained entirely as a result of efficiency, foresight, and technological progressiveness.

However, Judge Hand's *Alcoa* decision is not so revolutionary as it seems, for two important reasons. First of all, his condemnation of monopolies as such is explicitly confined to classic, single-firm monopolies. Perhaps Hand's measures of Alcoa's market position, both the particular divisor and dividend which yielded the 90 per cent quotient and the identification of market control with percentage shares in a given product, represent "dubious economics."[5] But the deficiency is in economics, not in the law. Significantly, Mason, who has voiced these criticisms, offers no better economic measure. None is available. The figure of 90 per cent was as indicative as any other of the fact that one company had a very substantial range of discretion in the pricing and the rate of development of an entire industry. To be sure, other metals, imports, and scrap substantially restricted the monopoly power of the sole domestic producer of virgin aluminum. But no monopolist has a completely inelastic demand except within extremely narrow limits. Except for imports, which constituted, in Judge Hand's computation, the 10 per cent of sales not subject

[4] *Standard Oil Co. of N.J.* v. *US.*, 221 U.S. 1, 75 (1911).

[5] Mason, in 62 *Harv. Law Rev.* 1273–1274 (1949).

to Alcoa's control and which were subject to cartel arrangements restricting sales in the United States, Alcoa had the primary power to determine how rapidly aluminum made its way in competition with other metals.[6]

Our reasons for rejecting the implication that interproduct competition, however real, eradicated Alcoa's monopoly may well be applicable also to the argument of the District Court in throwing out a monopoly case against du Pont in cellophane.[7] The court stressed the variety of other packaging materials with which cellophane was in direct competition and the necessity for du Pont's reducing its prices if it was to capture a large volume of business. First of all, cellophane is in some measure unique. More important, neither consideration of the court was relevant to the central issue: whether du Pont monopolized the production of cellophane by unreasonably excluding others from its production.

The second and more important reason for questioning the revolutionary character of the *Alcoa* decision is that the *Aluminum Company really had monopolized the aluminum ingot market* in the traditional sense. Hence it was not incumbent on Judge Hand to find a precise measure of the company's monopoly powers before convicting it under the antitrust laws. The economic assumption of the Sherman Act is that fair competition in finding and satisfying customers will not alone create a serious monopoly problem. Nothing in the historical panorama of the aluminum industry disproves this assumption. In the background can be discerned activities of Alcoa obviously designed to rid itself in one way or another of competitors. Alcoa bought out the Cowles Brothers and their critical Bradley patent in 1903; its bauxite and power purchase contracts carried rigidly exclusive clauses, designed to prevent others from using the facilities (these

[6] On the limited substitutability of secondary ingot and scrap, see 148 F.2d 416, 422–424; C. Muller, *Light Metals Monopoly,* p. 21 and Chap. 1 *passim,* and Wallace, "Aluminum," in W. Y. Elliott *et al., International Control in the Non-ferrous Metals* (hereafter cited as Elliott), p. 258 n. 87.

[7] *U.S.* v. *E. I. du Pont de Nemours and Co.,* Civil Action No. 1216, Findings of Fact, Conclusions of Law and Opinion of Chief Judge Paul Leahy, Wilmington, Delaware, Dec. 14, 1953, Findings 123–149, 163–170.

clauses were annulled by a consent decree in 1912); it acquired at least one imminently threatening domestic competitor in the 1920's; it subjected fabricators to a price squeeze; it brought foreign producers into its family through direct and indirect understandings.[8]

Hence, although the company's head start and capable management might alone have sufficed to discourage or destroy competitors, there is ample evidence that Alcoa did not rely merely on these blameless competitive superiorities in reaching and maintaining its monopolistic position. So there was ample evidence to support a finding of monopolizing in the traditional sense, even though Judge Hand did not appear to lean heavily upon it in reaching his decision. His failure to do so is a fact of great legal importance; yet it was undoubtedly such activities that he had in mind when, in the face of a District Court decision absolving the company of illegal intent, he said that no one obtains and maintains such a monopoly as Alcoa's unconsciously or unintentionally. Alcoa's actions had clearly betrayed an intent to keep the American market its exclusive preserve by whatever methods were required.

The *Alcoa* case illustrates the defect of applying considerations of intent in the sense of mere psychological motive to the complicated historical record of a giant corporation. It supplies the most compelling argument for a simple market structure test. But an examination of the way in which Alcoa obtained, retained, and used its market power supports rather than vitiates the basic antitrust premise. The record does not lend support to the contention of some economists that Alcoa's monopoly position was a simple and inevitable consequence of today's "monster technology" and of success in the competitive struggle: "We cannot have 'old-fashioned' intra-industry competition . . . without reasonably expecting somebody to win or nearly win that competition. . . . [In consequence, the antitrust laws threaten] to throttle the very thing the policy pretends to promote." [9] It

[8] See Wallace, *Market Control in the Aluminum Industry,* pp. 380–395; 148 F.2d 416, 436–438; Stocking and Watkins, *Cartels in Action,* pp. 224–273; Muller, Chaps. 2–6.

[9] Levitt, in 42 *Amer. Econ. Rev.* 893–895 (1952). See the persuasive state-

therefore supports the logic of an antitrust policy prohibiting monopolizing rather than the possession of monopoly power itself; the latter policy would always be subject, correctly, to the criticism that the government was "turning upon the successful competitor."

Our conclusion that the *Alcoa* decision did not destroy either the legal sway or the economic logic of applying the rule of reason even to pure or almost pure monopolists is clearly supported by the recent decision against the United Shoe Machinery Company. Here again the mere fact of preponderant market position, extending over a period of fifty years, weighed very heavily in the court's decision. Yet, while following the *Alcoa* precedent in placing a very narrow interpretation on the "intent to monopolize" requisite for Section 2 conviction, Judge Wyzanski plainly predicated his condemnation of United Shoe on his finding that the company had not attained and maintained its "overwhelming strength" solely by virtue of its "ability, economies of scale, research, natural advantages, and adaptation to inevitable economic laws." Rather, its "own business policies," i.e., its actions, while not inherently predatory or immoral, had "erected" substantial "barriers to competition": "They are contracts, arrangements, and policies which . . . further the dominance of a particular firm. In this sense, they are unnatural barriers; they unnecessarily exclude actual and potential competition; they restrict a free market." [10] His conclusion seems completely justified that United's rigid policy of leasing rather than selling its machines, and of inserting contractual provisions in the leases to penalize the use of competitors' machines, had the effect of unreasonably excluding potential competitors. In the *Cellophane* case, not only did the court find a complete absence of predatory tactics but it held expressly that acts—"monopolistic behavior such as that followed by Alcoa"—not good or bad results, were the basic test of illegality.[11] The acquittal of du Pont was therefore consistent with the convictions of Alcoa and United.

---

ment on the opposing side of Lee Loevinger, "Antitrust and the New Economics," 37 *Minn. Law Rev.* 550–551 (1953).

[10] 110 F.Supp. 295, 343–345 (1953).

[11] *U.S.* v. *E. I. du Pont de Nemours and Co.*, Findings 340–532, and p. 348.

Judge Hand's virtual per se condemnation of Alcoa as a monopolist did not extend to the company's vertical integration. Perhaps it should have. Alcoa tied together a domestic monopoly in aluminum, protected for a time by patents, control of extensive bauxite deposits and power sites, and large operations in the more competitive fields of fabrication. Whether accomplished by exclusive purchase contracts or by financial integration, the tie-ins made it more difficult for prospective competitors to engage in the production of ingot. And they exposed fabricators to a squeeze, either because of their inability to command adequate supplies of ingot in time of shortage, or because Alcoa compressed the margin between its ingot and product prices. The two kinds of squeeze are in some measure alternatives. In the late 1920's and early 1930's it was the price squeeze that forced sheet rollers to close down; ingot production was the profitable operation. In the recent defense boom, the low price of aluminum ingot relative to the costs of new construction and additional power apparently made reduction less profitable than fabrication; but for that very reason, integrated producers were reluctant to sell, and nonintegrated fabricators could not get the necessary ingot to take advantage of the wide margins.[12] In either event, monopoly positions at certain levels subsidized competition and reinforced monopoly power at other levels.

The trial judge found not illegal intent but merely prudent business motivations in Alcoa's vertical integration. Judge Hand declined to hold this finding "clearly erroneous," except for finding in the price squeeze on rolling mills prima-facie evidence of illegal intent. Even for the latter, Wallace demonstrates there need have been no specific intent to injure or to exclude; the competitive difficulties of nonintegrated fabricators were the consequence primarily of the varying pressures of competition in Alcoa's different operations. Was it an evidence of predatory intent or merely a statement of the facts when Alcoa officials warned two utensil manufacturers contemplating construction of their own rolling mills that future ingot shortages would naturally

[12] See Dewey Anderson, "Aluminum for Defence and Prosperity," pp. 22–23; Celler Comm. *Aluminum,* pp. 3, 5, 7, 22.

shut down their projected mills before Alcoa's own? [13] Given the market structure in aluminum ingot, there were good reasons for holding the vertical integration itself objectionable. Here we encounter another version of the plausible case an economist might make for outlawing monopoly power itself.

Yet it was not necessary even here for the law to condemn integration or market power per se on the one hand, or to require specific evidence of predatory intent on the other. The decision could have turned on the traditional test of monopolization, the evidence of what the defendants did. Alcoa had the power to exclude. It maintained this power by something more than "normal methods of industrial development." It exercised its power, with the result that competitors, actual and potential, were seriously squeezed.[14] Because the power and the exclusion were the consequence not merely of the kind of competition the Sherman Act was supposed to promote, but of explicit company policies, an illegal intent was inferred so far as the squeeze on fabricators was concerned, and might equally have been inferred from other aspects of the company's history already discussed. The test of intent is not a test of the purity of a company's motives, but an evaluation of its conduct.

Monopolizing as the Possession of Oligopoly Power—Cigarettes and Movies

The *American Tobacco* decision of 1946 [15] seemed to strengthen the new Sherman Act's flat prohibition of monopoly power in two ways. First, it upheld a jury's finding of conspiracy among three separate companies to fix prices and to monopolize, even though the record contained no direct evidence of collusion among the defendants. But there is strong reason to believe that

[13] See Wallace, pp. 437–440; also 374–395 and Chap. 18 *passim*.

[14] It would be unfair to imply that Alcoa continually and flagrantly starved its customers of supplies or squeezed their margins. This would have been a stupid policy for a company that was interested in expanding the use of aluminum and was never prepared to do all the fabricating itself. See, e.g., Wallace, p. 430.

[15] 328 U.S. 781 (1946).

the rigid and noncompetitive price leadership practiced by the Big 3 required no collusion, overt or covert, but followed naturally from an independent and rational pursuit of oligopolistic interest.[16]

Illustrated here is one extremely controversial aspect of the new Sherman Act—its dilution and broadening of the offense of conspiracy. The boundaries of conspiracy have been extended at both ends, in opposite directions as it were. At one end there has been the increasing resort to allegations of "implied" or "presumptive" conspiracy. At the other end, typified by the *Yellow Cab* and *A & P* cases, which are discussed below, even employees or subsidiaries of the same company are held to have conspired with each other.[17] In its least novel form, the conspiracy among competitors of the *American Tobacco* variety merely involves a heavy reliance on circumstantial evidence drawn from the behavior of the defendants to prove the existence of a restrictive agreement between them. This was the nature of one of the charges not only in the *American Tobacco* but also in the *Paramount Pictures* case.[18] However, the increasing tendency to infer conspiracy from noncompetitive market behavior, without proof of actual agreement, proceeds naturally from a contention that there has been a meeting of bodies, to the claim that there has been a meeting of minds, and finally to the claim that it is illegal for each individual seller to act in a noncompetitive fashion in the knowledge that his competitors are doing the same. If members of a trade association exchange price information and, on the basis of this better knowledge of the market, price more uniformly thereafter, or if an oligopolistic industry falls into a pattern of noncollusive price leadership, a conspiracy may be inferred, though no real agreement has been reached. So, in its extreme version, conspiracy becomes "conscious parallel action," in which there is no claim of formal agreement. "Conscious par-

[16] See W. H. Nicholls, *Price Policies in the Cigarette Industry, passim.*

[17] See James A. Rahl, "Conspiracy and the Antitrust Laws," 44 *Ill. Law Rev.* 743 (1950).

[18] *U.S.* v. *Paramount Pictures, Inc.,* 334 U.S. 131, 142 (1948). See pp. 69, 72–73, below.

allel action" was explicitly adopted as a substantive offense in the *Rigid Conduit* case. The Supreme Court affirmed this part of the charge by a 4 to 4 vote.[19] Even the requirement implied by the word "conscious," that to violate the law each defendant must have acted in the knowledge that others were doing the same, may represent only a meaningless gesture of retaining the conspiratorial meeting of minds, since evidence of "parallel action," nothing more, may suffice. In such cases, the connection between the defendants may seem too remote to justify a conspiracy charge.

A second oligopolistic characteristic of the cigarette industry that the court declared illegal was the mere joint possession by the Big 3 of the "power to exclude"—evidence of actual exclusion of competitors was unnecessary, it held—provided the power was accompanied by an intent jointly to use it. Here again, the "jointness" was demonstrated entirely by circumstantial evidence. Moreover, Justice Burton's opinion specifically recognized the heavy advertising expenditures of the Big 3 as one evidence and source of monopoly power, correctly, most economists would say.[20] These findings seemed therefore to go far in bringing normal oligopoly behavior, hence oligopoly itself, within the compass of the antitrust laws.

In the three movie decisions of 1948 the Supreme Court seemed to confirm the vulnerability of an oligopolistic market structure. The *Griffith* case is in many ways the most interesting, because the court was faced there (as in the *Alcoa* case) with a District Court's findings of fact exonerating the defendants on all counts. The judge had found nothing to criticize in a chain of theaters using its bargaining power to obtain master agreements under which the several members of the chain exercised the right of pre-emption in selecting films, obtained lengthy clearances

[19] The second count of the Commission's order alleged violation of Sec. 5 of the F.T.C. Act because of "concurrent use of a formula method of making delivered price quotations with the knowledge that each did likewise." *Triangle Conduit & Cable Co., Inc.* v. *F.T.C.*, 168 F.2d 175, 181 (1948), affirmed in *Clayton Mark & Co.* v. *F.T.C.*, 336 U.S. 956 (1949).

[20] 328 U.S. 781, 797 (1946).

over competitors, made inroads on the latter's business, and continually bought out competitive theaters. The Supreme Court, therefore, was forced (partly under the pressure of the accompanying *Schine* case [21], where the facts were similar and the lower court findings the opposite) virtually to hold the market structure itself in violation of Section 2. They could not, by the traditions of legal courtesy, reject the lower court's "findings of fact" that there was no illegal intent. But its legal reasoning could be challenged. "It is . . . not always necessary," Justice Douglas said, following Judge Hand's reasoning in the *Alcoa* decision, "to find a specific intent to restrain trade or to build a monopoly. . . . It is sufficient that a restraint of trade or monopoly results as the consequence of a defendant's conduct or business arrangements." [22]

The Griffith chain embraced theaters both in towns where its theater was the only one and in competitive towns, and it bargained with distributors for exhibition rights in all theaters as a group. Since the distributor had to offer his pictures to Griffith if he was to have any audience at all in the one-theater towns, he was forced to give the chain valuable advantages over competitors in the other towns. Thus, as the almost inevitable consequence, it would seem, of their geographic integration, the Griffith defendants used the leverage of local monopolies in one-theater towns to obtain unfair competitive advantages in the others. The Supreme Court majority held that such a situation conferred monopoly power; and, citing the *Alcoa* doctrine that "no monopolist monopolizes unconscious of what he is doing," they found in the ways in which the chain bargained evidence of an intent to exercise that power sufficient to meet the test of the *Tobacco* case.

Thus, the court came close to condemning, per se, horizontal integration embracing a monopoly market. Any type of integration almost inevitably confers such an advantage over nonintegrated competitors in one or another of the markets in which the integrated firm operates. The theater in a one-theater town plays the same role as the patent monopoly in the *International*

[21] *Schine Chain Theaters* v. *U.S.,* 334 U.S. 110 (1948).
[22] *U.S.* v. *Griffith,* 334 U.S. 100, 105 (1948).

Salt case, discussed below: any use of the leverage to extend the monopoly area is illegal.

In the *Paramount* case, as in *Alcoa,* and *Griffith,* the Supreme Court majority was forced by certain negative findings of fact by the District Court to approach condemning a market structure itself, under Section 2 of the Sherman Act. The lower court had found that the five major motion picture producers and distributors neither sought nor enjoyed a "national monopoly in exhibition." Speaking for the Supreme Court, Justice Douglas focused his attention instead on individual exhibition markets, notably the first-run field in the largest cities, which the Big 5 did dominate, and on the inherent advantages in access to first runs enjoyed by the exhibition houses of the vertically integrated producers. Relying then on the *Griffith* doctrine that a "specific intent" to monopolize need not be proven "if monopoly results as a necessary consequence of what was done," the Supreme Court set aside the lower court's exculpation of the defendants on the monopoly charges and granted the divestiture remedy.[23]

The Supreme Court decisions in the cigarette and movie cases unquestionably strengthened the antitrust laws. But their novelty has been exaggerated. *All of them depended essentially on the actual employment of collusive and exclusive tactics.* First, strong circumstantial evidence convinced the lower courts that the big cigarette manufacturers and motion picture producers and distributors had in effect conspired to eradicate price competition among themselves. Apart from the absence of direct evidence, the decisions on this score therefore represented no advance over *Trenton Potteries* or *Socony-Vacuum.* One may explain each item of circumstantial evidence in the *Tobacco* case in terms of an independent recognition and scrupulous pursuit of oligopolistic self-interest. Yet the course of conduct was so punctilious (witness the conscientious refusal of each of the Big 3 either to enter any tobacco market unless the others were represented or to fill any orders at its unchanged and still nominally prevailing price the instant the leader announced an increase as well as decrease; witness their systematic policing of retail prices to avoid any discrepancies between their products in either direc-

[23] 334 U.S. 131, 166–174 (1948).

tion) as to render the drawing of lines between such oligopoly behavior and collusion entirely academic.[24]

Nevertheless, the authors would still contend that here, as in the use of a basing-point system, discussed in Chapter 4, instances of genuinely independent oligopolistic behavior producing a monopoly result are extremely rare. For this reason, we have no objection to an inference of collaboration from the scrupulous avoidance of competition exhibited by the cigarette companies.

Yet we recognize that by accepting the crime of "implied conspiracy," inferred exclusively from circumstantial evidence, we come very close to sanctioning an appraisal of the economic record. The case is strong for openly evaluating the economic results, therefore, and eschewing completely the legalism of lumping what (so far as the record shows) may be only "conscious parallel action" under the ancient crime of conspiracy. But the advocates of economic tests in such situations supply completely divergent recommendations. Some would openly judge the results and, if they are indicative of monopoly (whether conspiratorial or consciously parallel), condemn the market structure that produced them. Others, mainly among the new critics, imply at least that "conscious parallel action" and "implied conspiracy" are to be dropped, and nothing put in their place. The second approach is surely indefensible on economic grounds. If the antiquated legal catchwords are to be abandoned in the name of workable competition, the only alternative is to delegate to some agency the duty of surveying the entire economy, judging each market by economic tests, and devising whatever remedies are required for workable competition. Here at least is a consistent proposal for abandoning the concept of conspiracy where the evidence is entirely circumstantial.

Our own preference would be roughly for the path the law has actually taken: a recognition that conspiracy in concentrated markets does not necessarily require many overt acts; that one may have to look at the price record for evidence instead. But the

[24] See Nicholls, p. 399; also Stocking and Watkins, *Monopoly and Free Enterprise,* pp. 136–166. However, cf. W. Baum, *Workable Competition in the Tobacco Industry* (unpublished dissertation, Harvard University, 1949), Chaps. 3–7.

evidence to be sought is still evidence of behavior—were they acting like competitors or like conspirators?—rather than evidence to permit an economic appraisal of the market results. If we mistake him not, this view is close to that of Handler.[25] It is also the view of the Supreme Court:

> The crucial question is whether respondents' conduct toward petitioner stemmed from independent decision or from an agreement, tacit or express. To be sure, business behavior is admissible circumstantial evidence from which the fact finder may infer agreement. . . . But this Court has never held that proof of parallel business behavior conclusively establishes agreement or, phrased differently, that such behavior itself constitutes a Sherman Act offense.[26]

Second, it is probably not true, as several observers have triumphantly concluded, that the Supreme Court in the *Tobacco* case condemned the mere joint and noncollusive power to raise prices.[27] Nor did it authorize attacks on the unexercised power to exclude. Had it done these things, the legality of all oligopolistic markets would, truly, have been jeopardized.

The issue before the Supreme Court in the *Tobacco* case was simply this: Is actual evidence of exclusion of competitors necessary to establish a Section 2 violation? The court said it was not; the government had to prove only that the companies had conspired to obtain and maintain the power to exclude competitors *and* had demonstrated an intent to use it.[28] But how does one establish intent to exclude except by showing actual resort to

[25] In 6 *The Record* 61–68 (1951).

[26] *Theater Enterprises, Inc.* v. *Paramount Film Distributing Corp.*, 74 Sup.Ct. 257 (1954).

[27] Eugene V. Rostow: "The essence of the offense under Section 2, Justice Burton said, is whether 'power exists to raise prices or to exclude competition when it is desired to do so.'" "Problems of Size and Integration," *Business Practices under Federal Antitrust Laws, 1951 Symposium,* p. 121.

[28] The question whether it was necessary to look beyond a determination that the defendants had conspired to obtain the power to raise prices had been clearly settled years before, and did not have to be reconsidered. Rostow's quotation from the majority opinion is of course accurate, but it is an isolated dictum that, considered in its context, gives no support for the implication that the court held illegal the mere power of oligopolists to raise prices, in the absence of a conspiracy. See Baum, pp. 329–331.

exclusive tactics? Entirely in keeping with the traditional concept of monopolizing, the court summarized the evidence of the illegal actions of the cigarette companies, which established the requisite intent to drive out competitors. The antitrust laws proscribe actions, not economic or psychological situations. Intent must be sought in overt actions.

Suppose instead that the law required an economic evaluation of the market structure or pricing performance of the cigarette industry. The Supreme Court based its findings of an exclusionary intent partly on the drastic price reductions of early 1933, on the ground that they were "directed at the competition of the 10-cent cigarettes." This finding was not unreasonable, considering the flagrant price rises of mid-1931, the pressure on retailers to keep the differential between major and economy brands down to 3 cents, and the simultaneous increase in prices once the interlopers had been cut back to size. But would it have been fair to condemn the big companies for their mere power over price (demonstrated in 1932) in view of the reductions into which they were forced by their competitors (in 1933) and the permanent decline in their share of the market? Only a consideration of intent—neither blanket condemnation nor endorsement, nor tests of short-run economic performance—can fulfill the inescapable function of differentiating vigorous competition from predatory price cutting in quest of monopoly.

The movie cases of 1948 provide even more instances of extreme competitive disadvantage imposed upon independents by virtue not only of the structure but also of the monopolizing actions of the large firms. In the *Paramount* case the Supreme Court held the five integrated producers guilty of monopolization on the basis of a lengthy record of unreasonable clearances, pooling agreements, formula deals, master agreements, block booking and discrimination among exhibitors, all tinged with conspiracy and all at the expense of unaffiliated theaters. In *Griffith*, it found monopsony power exerted to obtain unfair competitive advantages, at the expense of exhibitors whose deficiency was one of bargaining power only.[29] It did not strike at any and all busi-

[29] See, for example, "What's Playing at the Grove?" 38 *Fortune* 95–98 and ff. (Aug. 1948).

ness arrangements that might have the incidental consequence of excluding competitors from some area of the market. It rejected in *Paramount* the government's claim that, in the peculiar circumstances of the motion picture industry, vertical integration was inherently objectionable. It made it clear in *Griffith* that the inescapable monopoly power of a movie house in a one-theater town does not violate the law. It condemned power over price only insofar as it was found to be the product of collusion, and the power to exclude only after showing that the defendants had actually exerted it, just as they had in the *Tobacco* case.

Monopolizing without Achieving Monopoly

The 1945–1948 cases which we have just discussed raised high hopes among those who saw in them a new Sherman Act because they seemed to bring the law nearer to outlawing overriding monopoly and even oligopoly power as such. But the courts went further. They began also to suggest the possibility of condemning companies merely for controlling some "appreciable" portion of interstate commerce. The conception of monopolizing suggested by these cases was much more disturbing to economists than the one in *Alcoa,* because the "any part" of commerce which might be "monopolized" was not defined in economically realistic terms. In consequence, a company might be held to have monopolized without ever having really achieved any monopoly power at all.

The *A & P* decisions [30] condemned a company which had, by virtue of its size, aggressive bargaining, and integration, helped to introduce strong competition into the distribution of grocery products. As we shall see, the conviction hinged essentially on abuses of power, in the traditional sense. But the courts did not always differentiate the economically beneficial and legally "reasonable" from the undesirable and unreasonable aspects of A & P's organization and tactics and their consequences. In particular, the opinions demonstrated some tendency to criticize (*a*) the quest of bargains and discounts justified by the performance

[30] *U.S.* v. *The New York Great Atlantic and Pacific Tea Co., Inc.,* 67 F.Supp. 626 (1946), 173 F.2d 79 (1949), and Civil Action No. 52–139, filed Sept. 15, 1949; Consent Decree, Jan. 19, 1954.

of functions; (*b*) efficient vertical integration (including manufacturing and operation of a buying organization that attempted to obtain from suppliers fees or discounts equivalent to the charges of brokers whose services it circumvented and that resold some of its products to independent jobbers), on the ground that the "profits" earned therefrom illegally "subsidized" retail competition; (*c*) any regional discrepancies in margins charged by a big and powerful company, whether promotional, defensive, or predatory, all in the absence of anything approaching convincing evidence of undesirable market consequences.[31]

A & P thus represents an extension of the logic of the movie decisions. In both the defendants enjoyed a strategic superiority over their competitors, by virtue of their size and the geographic dispersion of their operations. The existence of that power, combined with some evidence of an intent to exercise it—found, in *A & P,* in coercive bargaining for discriminatory discounts and in operating on unusually low retail margins in selected market areas to "put the heat on" competitors—was held sufficient to sustain a charge of monopolizing. The only market consequences considered were the handicap imposed on competitors in particular local markets; the court did not consider whether competition had been rendered more or less effective as a result.[32]

A similar disregard for the over-all market consequences of strategic advantages exercised by an integrated firm was suggested in the Supreme Court's first *Yellow Cab* decision. There the court held that if the evidence demonstrated an intent to monopolize, the mere fact that the vertical integration of taxicab manufacturing and operating companies shut competing manufacturers out of an appreciable market would be sufficient to condemn the arrangement as a conspiracy to monopolize under Section 2 of the Sherman Act.[33] Vertical integration inevitably forecloses com-

[31] See Adelman, in 63 *Q. Jour. Econ.* 238 (1949); also Galbraith, Chap. 10.

[32] See the exchange between Adelman and the writers in 61 *Jour. Pol. Econ.* 436 (1953)—"Dirlam and Kahn on the A & P Case," and "A Reply."

[33] "And § 2 of the Act makes it unlawful to conspire to monopolize 'any part' of interstate commerce, without specifying how large a part must be affected. . . . The complaint in this case deals with interstate purchases of replacements of some 5,000 licensed taxicabs. . . . That is an appreciable

petitors from the custom of the integrated purchasers. Taxicabs are sold in a nation-wide market, and only a very small portion of that market was here affected (particularly since most taxicabs are nothing more than specially painted passenger automobiles). By defining "any part" of interstate commerce as nothing more than a volume of business large enough to satisfy a *de minimis* requirement and by extending the doctrine of conspiracy to the organizers of a proprietary consolidation,[34] the decision seemed to condemn all vertical integration, contingent on the necessary demonstration of intent. However, subsequent proceedings have shown that the latter condition is truly a substantial one, so far as vertical integration is concerned.

In the same way, the *International Salt* case (which we discuss at greater length in Chapter 4) in effect found all patent tie-ins in violation of both Section 1 of the Sherman Act and Section 3 of the Clayton Act, without regard to whether they substantially reduced competition in the tied-in field as a whole. After declaring that "it is unreasonable, *per se,* to foreclose competitors from any substantial market," the Supreme Court inferred a sufficient effect on competition from the mere fact that "the volume of business affected by these contracts cannot be said to be insignificant or insubstantial and the tendency of the arrangement to accomplishment of monopoly seems obvious. . . ."[35]

The "any part" of interstate commerce, deemed sufficient in the *Yellow Cab* case to condemn vertical integration (if improperly motivated), is obviously the same thing as the "not insignificant volume of business" from which henceforth patent tie-ins may no longer legally foreclose competitors.

Were the greatly diminished standards of competitive impact accepted in the foregoing cases applied to all vertical integration

---

amount of commerce under any standard. . . ." 332 U.S. 218, 225–226 (1947).

[34] "The fact that these restraints occur in a setting . . . [of] a vertically integrated enterprise does not necessarily remove the ban of the Sherman Act. The test of illegality under the Act is the presence or absence of an unreasonable restraint. . . . The corporate interrelationships of the conspirators . . . are not determinative of the applicability of the Sherman Act." *Ibid.*, p. 227.

[35] 332 U.S. 392, 396 (1947).

and not merely to such unreasonable actions as were engaged in by International Salt and A & P, the new Sherman Act would indeed have discarded the rule of reason. In fact they were not, as a detailed examination of the vertical integration aspects of the *A & P, Columbia Steel,* and second *Yellow Cab* cases will show.

Vertical Integration and the Persistence of the Rule of Reason

The antitrust laws have almost always applied a more rigorous standard to associations and agreements among competitors than they have to the formation or activities of financially consolidated, integrated companies enjoying just as great or greater market power. The double standard appeared in the contrasting treatment accorded the first two groups of business defendants whose cases reached the Supreme Court. The consolidation was held beyond the reach of antitrust because it was a combination of manufacturing properties, affecting interstate commerce only indirectly; the price-fixing association was illegal per se because it restrained commerce directly.[36] The *Standard Oil* decision of 1911, which finally established that the law could reach mergers in industry, at the same time set forth the rule of reason, under which thenceforth the courts proceeded to condemn the weakest efforts at price fixing, while blessing the most powerful business combinations. In *Appalachian Coals,* the Supreme Court explicitly rejected this dual approach.[37] Yet summary condemnation of loose associations seeking in any way to influence price, whatever their market power, and hence the double standard were resurrected by the *Socony-Vacuum* decision of 1940, particularly by the sweeping language of the opinion.[38] Judge Hand's decision in the *Alcoa* case represented the second attempt to adopt a consistent treatment of monopoly power, regardless of the form of the defendants; but even this forthright attack on

[36] *U.S.* v. *E. C. Knight Co.,* 156 U.S. 1 (1895) and *U.S.* v. *Trans-Missouri Freight Assn.,* 166 U.S. 290 (1897).

[37] 288 U.S. 344, 376 (1933).

[38] See Handler, *A Study of the Construction and Enforcement of the Federal Antitrust Laws,* T.N.E.C. Monograph No. 38, pp. 30–34, 46–47, 84–86.

monopoly was, as we have seen, limited to true monopolies in the classic sense.

The new criticism of antitrust springs largely from the conviction that the courts have now adopted the same condemnation of mere size and integration as such that *Socony-Vacuum* applied to all agreements seeking to influence price, regardless of the presence or absence of market power. Probably no single case has been more responsible for this belief that the double standard has been eradicated, and with it any sensible rule of reason as well, than the criminal and civil suits against A & P. Certain dicta of the courts and certain aspects of the case considered in isolation do seem to justify this impression. To a slight extent, therefore, the effect of the decisions must be to make it more difficult in the future for large, integrated firms to bargain hard with suppliers or to meet the prices of their competitors in different retail markets.

Nevertheless, even a hasty perusal of Judge Lindley's opinion, or of the appeals court decision that summarized it, should satisfy any fair reader that the impression is essentially an illusion. No doubt the A & P Company would have escaped prosecution had it not been large, integrated, and aggressive. But these characteristics were not what convicted it. It was convicted of monopolizing: the court found in the evidence a consistent course of action and policy involving flagrant abuse of bargaining power and strategic position. Certainly this is what the courts *thought* they were attacking. The opinions are replete with clear-cut disavowals of hostility to size and integration alone. According to Judge Lindley, the government had contended, and would have to prove "that the size of A & P, its integration . . . were so *employed* as to bring about inevitably unreasonable advantages. . . . The charge is that defendants have so *utilized* their power and integration as unreasonably to restrain commerce." [39]

Judge Lindley's own analysis of A & P's operations centered on the company's "headquarters profits," their sources and use. Scattered references to the "subsidization" of retail operations in general by these "profits," and in particular those referring to the "profits" from manufacturing, appear to betray a basic hos-

[39] 67 F.Supp. 626, 642 (1946) (stress supplied); see also 630–631, 638.

tility to vertical integration itself. But the discussions consist almost entirely of a demonstration that all but the "profits" from manufacturing were tainted in their source, being the product of coercive bargaining, and all were deliberately misused at the retail level.[40]

It is only because so much of the comment on the *A & P* case has misinterpreted the decisions that something more than a brief summary is necessary here. A quantitative breakdown of the District Court opinion shows clearly where the heaviest stress was placed. The factual analysis of the defendant's operations covers twenty-eight pages, distributed in the following manner:

1. Twelve pages describe the pressures on suppliers, of many kinds and under many pretexts, to obtain buying prices not merely lower than quoted but, explicitly, consistently less than were charged competitors. Less than three pages are devoted to the company's persistent efforts to continue to receive the equivalent of brokerage after 1936. Though these efforts, like the others, involved the wielding of buying power to obtain preferential advantage, they deserve some sympathy, since as we shall see in Chapter 4, they represented in part (though by no means entirely) [41] economically legitimate efforts to evade discrimination imposed on integrated retailers by Section 2(c) of Robinson-Patman. The remaining nine pages clearly describe a systematic quest of discriminatory concessions bearing no relationship to savings in cost or the performance of function.[42]

2. The next nine pages (of the twenty-eight) are devoted to

[40] Thus, significantly, Judge Lindley has very little to say about manufacturing operations themselves, which were certainly unexceptionable, considered in isolation. The only portions of these discussions which may without question be criticized on economic grounds are the very few, isolated statements implying that manufacturing or other headquarters profits, *untainted* in their source, might have been suspect merely because they permitted *generally* low retail margins.

[41] See pp. 168 and 239–241, below.

[42] For example, with regard to the so-called advertising allowances: "The contracts were specific as to what should be paid but vague as to performance." 67 F.Supp. 626, 650. "The allowance was not based upon service rendered but rather on quantity purchased." *Ibid.*, 651. Another subsection is entitled "Alleged allowances for pretended services to suppliers." *Ibid.*, 653.

the practices of A & P's buying subsidiary, the Atlantic Commission Company, which acted also as broker for the trade. Here again the court's condemnation is directed in part against activities springing from vertical integration itself: ACCO's efforts to get the equivalent of brokerage, its sales to A & P's competitors and the "inevitable" effect of the "profits" therefrom to give A & P an "unfair" competitive advantage. But the major portion by far of the discussion centers on ACCO's abuse of its monopsonistic and monopolistic powers. These policies took three forms: (*a*) ACCO tried persistently to get discriminatory buying advantages unrelated to the performance of functions or saving of costs, and often succeeded; (*b*) it persuaded and coerced produce growers and shippers to sell to or through it exclusively (thus giving it truly unfair advantages in the selection of quality products for A & P and quasi-monopolistic power in the brokerage business), and (*c*) it put pressure on jobbers (dependent upon it both for supplies and for patronage because of its huge purchases in less than carload lots for A & P's account) to buy only through it, even, in some cases, to pay it "brokerage" on produce that they had in fact obtained from someone else.[43]

3. The remaining eight pages deal with retail policies, citing instance after instance of predatory local price cutting, operating individual stores and regions in the red, and so on. In these pages the court nowhere explicitly attacks A & P's over-all low retail margins or its meeting of competition. Its condemnation of the chain's retail policies is always heavily influenced by (*a*) the citation of numerous individual instances of manifestly predatory

[43] In the words of the lower court, the latter "odorous unjustified transactions can not be excused in any manner. . . . The incidents are illuminating as to the extent to which others dealing with Acco . . . were willing to go either in fear of losing its patronage or in order to cultivate its good will" (p. 658). Again, "One can only conclude that Acco's intention was to bring about a situation whereby growers and shippers relied more and more on Acco's facilities and advice, all of which served to increase Acco's advantageous preferential relationship, its business as selling broker and as buying broker and its resultant profits at the expense of A & P's retail competitors . . ." (p. 659). Compare the foregoing account with Adelman's implication that the court indiscriminately attacked any and all profits on resales to competitors, in 63 *Harv. Law. Rev.* 54 (1949), and 63 *Q. Jour. Econ.* 250–251 (1949).

conduct (e.g., "turning the heat" on selected competitors, particularly new stores) and (*b*) the "subsidization" (the term was employed by A & P's own officers) of such selective competition by headquarters profits themselves tainted in their source.[44]

It seems impossible to doubt that the courts conscientiously tried to apply a rule of reason and to differentiate mere size and integration from abuse of the power that they conferred. What was lacking was evidence that A & P had achieved any substantial monopoly power in the retail grocery business by these tactics—even in those localities, all of them small towns, in which the company enjoyed a very large share of the market.

The question therefore remains whether the *A & P* decisions demonstrate a conflict between the requirements of equity in competition and of effective competition. The rule of reason as applied to big business before 1946 took into consideration market results; it required a convincing demonstration that the effectiveness of market competition was jeopardized by the defendants. The mere unfair disadvantaging of competitors did not ordinarily suffice for conviction. As long as this was so, the antitrust laws did not threaten the vitality of impure markets, where competition may be fostered by big buyers bargaining hard with suppliers, or by integrated retailers cutting margins, even if selectively. Whether or not the *A & P* decisions have actually jeopardized the competitiveness of retail markets is discussed at the relevant points in Chapters 5, 7, and 8. There remains the question of how far they weakened the rule of reason. It can be concluded with confidence that the courts' belittling of the market consequences of A & P's integration and bargaining techniques by no means eradicated the rule of reason or the double standard. That the company had power and exercised it there is no doubt. Here we have one of the two necessary elements to violation of Section 2, as elaborated in the *Griffith, Paramount,*

[44] See 173 F.2d 79, 86–87 (1949); also C. Fulda, "Food Distribution in the United States," pp. 152–173. Judge Lindley's exposition, incidentally, documents numerous instances of "recoupment"—where margins were deliberately raised in less intensely competitive areas in order to help finance selected reductions in others. Cf. Adelman, in 63 *Harv. Law Rev.* 58–59 (1949). On the economics of "recoupment" and the meaning of operating units "in the red," see pp. 212–215, below.

Schine, and *American Tobacco* cases. Was there an intent to monopolize as well? Again by the tests developed in these cases, there unquestionably was. The company was trying to displace particular competitors; it planned, by wielding its extraordinary bargaining power, to put its rivals in a permanently inferior competitive status.

If there is any condemnation per se in the *A & P* case, it is of local discriminatory price cutting and systematic extraction of price concessions, which the integration of the company merely assisted. No move against A & P was made simply because it set up central buying offices, a nation-wide vegetable-purchasing organization, grocery-manufacturing plants, or a chain of retail stores. It was only a particular use of these facilities that was found objectionable. Therefore it is wrong to conclude that the *A & P* decision condemns integration in the same way, let us say, that *Trenton Potteries* condemns price fixing.

The new Sherman Act, like the old, attacks vertical integration only when it represents a device for unreasonably extending monopoly power from one stratum to another. The major element of novelty is that now the act requires very little in the way of a demonstration of market consequences, where a course of conduct may clearly be characterized as betraying an intent to monopolize. The same summary condemnation does not any more than in the past extend to actions that cannot so easily be characterized in this fashion. Thus even under the new Sherman Act, there seems no reasonable basis for condemning A & P's manufacturing operations.

The first *Yellow Cab* decision applied the standard of "not insubstantial amount" to a vertical integration "conspiracy"—but only contingent on a demonstration of an intent to monopolize. After trial of the facts, the lower Court concluded:

> From the evidence it appears . . . that the stock relationships which developed among the defendants were not part of a design to compel the purchases of CCM cabs and were not accompanied by an intent to control commerce in the sale of cabs to any of the four cities under consideration. The affiliations which occurred were occasioned by other business factors.[45]

[45] 80 F.Supp. 936, 942 (1948).

The Supreme Court sustained this verdict, exonerating the defendants, by a 5 to 2 vote.[46]

In the *A & P* and first *Yellow Cab* (as well as the earlier *G.M.A.C.*[47]) cases, the defendants were charged with conspiracy, in spite of the fact that they were a group of commonly owned companies and their officers, in effect a single operating entity. Here, in contrast with the "presumptive conspiracy" cases such as *American Tobacco,* the criticism is that the relationship between the defendants was too close to justify condemnation as a conspiracy.

The reason the enforcement agencies have pressed for both these extensions of the idea of conspiracy is clear. Under the antitrust laws it is illegal merely to agree with competitors to fix a price or to boycott certain suppliers or customers; it is not necessarily illegal for an individual firm to do these things. Section 1 of the Sherman Act outlaws contracts, combinations, or conspiracies in restraint of trade—all of which require more than one party—rather than restraint of trade itself. The law thus hinges on the method or form of price fixing or refusals to deal, not the economic results—which may be more serious when the act is committed by a single powerful firm than by a group of weak firms. Here we encounter again the familiar double standard, already described. To the extent therefore that the government can establish a charge of conspiracy, for example between a parent company, its officers, and subsidiaries, it can more readily establish a per se offense. It becomes less necessary to demonstrate serious market consequences, or to prove illegal intent, such as would be required in proceeding, subject to the rule of reason, against a single corporate defendant under Section 2.

[46] 338 U.S. 338 (1949).

[47] *U.S.* v. *General Motors Acceptance Corp.,* 121 F.2d 376 (1941). For more recent applications, based in part on *Yellow Cab,* see *Kiefer-Stewart Co.* v. *Joseph E. Seagram & Sons, Inc.,* 340 U.S. 211, 215 (1951); *Timken Roller Bearing Co.* v. *U.S.,* 341 U.S. 593 (1951); see also the separate complaints of the F.T.C. against Distillers-Seagrams, Ltd., and Schenley Industries, Inc., and their respective subsidiaries, under Sec. 5 of the F.T.C. Act, Docket Nos. 6047 and 6048, Sept. 24, 1952; Consent Settlements, March 8, 1954.

The second *Yellow Cab* decision indicates that the consequences of extending to the actions of financially integrated firms the conspiracy doctrine of the first *Yellow Cab* case have not been as extreme as was originally feared. On the one hand, it is obviously possible for separate individuals or companies to accomplish by joint action a more extensive and less reasonable restraint than might follow from the acts of one alone; and there is no question that the government has long been able to attack such actions as conspiracies to restrain trade, even though they *eventuate* in close-knit consolidations.[48] On the other hand, until the law condemns the mere formation or normal subsequent activities of every consolidation—which by its very nature reduces competition, actual or potential, within the market areas thus enclosed—the fact that its organizers or managers may under certain circumstances be charged with conspiracy involves no economic catastrophe. While therefore it seems foolish to have sustained conspiracy charges against the officers and subsidiaries of A & P, under Section 1 of the Sherman Act, the conviction was not a per se one; the demonstration of power to exclude, accompanied by an intent to use it, sufficed under the new Sherman Act to convict the company under Section 2 as well.

One might suppose from reading the Supreme Court opinions alone that the conviction of the Timken Co. carried the conspiracy doctrine to the ridiculous extreme of a per se condemnation of integration. So far as these opinions show, the company was apparently guilty of nothing more than "conspiring" to divide world markets with its English and French subsidiaries. Had the parties been separate departments of Timken rather than legally separate entities, it appears the arrangements between them would have escaped censure.[49] The distinction would seem to represent a triumph of form over substance. The facts of life in international trade, the strong considerations impelling Timken to organize legally separate local companies to do business in these countries, argue that it would be unreasonable to apply to such an arrangement merely incidental to geographic integration the same summary condemnation as was applied, for example, to the comprehensive division of world markets between

[48] See *U.S.* v. *Reading Co.*, 253 U.S. 26 (1920).

[49] 341 U.S. 593, 606.

du Pont and Imperial Chemical Industries.[50] Nevertheless the *Timken* decision was in no sense an attack on joint ventures or geographic integration, per se. The critical finding of the lower court, which the Supreme Court sustained, was that the central purpose of the arrangements, including the acquisitions of the British and French companies in the first place, was "to create a world-wide cartel in antifriction tapered bearings." The case disclosed a long record of rigid divisions of territories and price fixing among the predecessors of the combine, and between them and outside firms as well. Significantly, the members of the combine did not behave like a single firm. During World War II American Timken refused to encroach on the territory of its British "partner" by supplying Australia with bearings, or helping the Australian Government construct a plant, even though British Timken was unable to do so.[51] It is difficult to understand why a truly integrated enterprise would have been unwilling to let its American branch take on business that its British branch was unable to handle.

The *Columbia Steel* decision established beyond all question that in the absence of a record of monopolizing, or, conversely, in the presence of legitimate competitive reasons for the acquisition of a customer, vertical integration is not invalid merely because it shuts competitors out of 3 per cent of a market. However, the court recognized that "legitimate" intent would not exonerate mergers with truly substantial market consequences: an individual acquisition is illegal, it said, if it "results in *or* is aimed at unreasonable restraint." Therefore it grappled conscientiously with the economic facts to see whether Columbia's acquisition of Consolidated would have "the effect . . . [of] unreasonably restrict[ing] the opportunities of competitors to market their product." [52] Nor did the Supreme Court minority quarrel with the majority's conception of the law, or with its economic assump-

[50] *U.S.* v. *Imperial Chemical Industries, Ltd.,* 100 F.Supp. 504 (1951); see also Stocking and Watkins, *Cartels in Action,* pp. 438–465.

[51] 83 F.Supp. 284, 288–311 (1949); see also Oppenheim, "Foreign Commerce under the Sherman Act—Points and Implications of the Timken Case," 42 *Trade Mark Bulletin* 4, 12–14 (1952). On the case for applying a special rule of reason in such cases, see pp. 272–274, below.

[52] 334 U.S. 495, 527, 524 (1948).

tion that mere substantiality of dollar volume does not suffice to demonstrate an undesirable economic impact of vertical integration.

> In determining what constitutes unreasonable restraint, we do not think the dollar volume is in itself of compelling significance; we look rather to the percentage of business controlled, the strength of the remaining competition . . . the probable development of the industry, consumer demands, and other characteristics of the market. We do not undertake to prescribe any set of percentage figures by which to measure the reasonableness of a corporation's enlargement of its activities by the purchase of the assets of a competitor. The relative effect of percentage command of a market varies with the setting in which that factor is placed.[53]

Thus Justice Douglas' dissent did not contend that it would or should have been illegal for any firm, in any circumstances, to acquire Consolidated:

> The result might well be different if Consolidated were merging with or being acquired by an independent west coast producer for the purpose of developing an integrated operation. The purchase might then be part of an intensely practical plan to put together an independent western unit of the industry with sufficient resources and strength to compete with the giants of the industry.[54]

What is questionable about the *Columbia Steel* decision, and what the Supreme Court minority criticized, is its finding of fact concerning, first, the intent underlying the acquisition and, second, the substantiality of the resultant restraint. As for the first, the majority's exposition of the "legitimate business reasons" for the merger is not very satisfying. Essentially, it accepted at face value and endorsed without question U.S. Steel's contention that it *had* to *control* an outlet for its Geneva output (in con-

[53] *Ibid.*, pp. 527–528. See the clear statement of this legal criterion in the *Reading* case, 226 U.S. 324, 370 (1912). The one criterion omitted from the foregoing quotation is the one of intent: "whether the action springs from business requirements or purpose to monopolize." *Ibid.*, p. 527. Under the new Sherman Act this consideration is alternative to the other; if the intent is to exclude, the action is objectionable if any appreciable dollar volume is affected.

[54] *Ibid.*, p. 539.

trast, the minority condemned the merger precisely because it was a "purchase for control" in avoidance of competition).

It is impossible to make the second appraisal, of economic consequences, except in terms of the size, origins, and already substantial power of U.S. Steel, and the pattern of limited competition that has for decades characterized the steel industry.[55] In these circumstances, the cause of competition would probably have been served better by preventing this merger. Unfortunately, the blessing that the Attorney General had conferred on the disposal of the Geneva plant to U.S. Steel had almost inevitably confined the *Columbia* case to the narrower question of the legality of the one subsequent acquisition. Although the majority mentioned the long history of acquisitions by U.S. Steel, offered by the government to support its charge that the purchase of Consolidated was only one link in a chain of "monopolizing," it turned its attention immediately, without ever really appraising that record, to the intent underlying the Consolidated merger alone. It found the merger to be a reasonable supplement to the Geneva purchase.[56]

Yet, given even the limited issue, the court might still have interpreted the facts differently.[57] In particular, it might well have concluded that the social drawbacks of permitting the company to acquire rather than to construct a controlled outlet more than offset "the legitimate business reasons" for choosing the former course. Certainly the Federal Trade Commission should henceforth make precisely this kind of appraisal of the relative economic merits of mergers versus expansion by the construction of new facilities in enforcing the amended Section 7 of the Clayton Act.[58]

Justices Black and Reed, dissenting in the second *Yellow Cab* case, would have relieved the government of the necessity of demonstrating a "specific intent" to monopolize, while retaining

55 See Adams, *The Structure of American Industry,* Chap. 5.

56 334 U.S. 495, 532.

57 For the evidence, not presented to the court, that the acquisition of Consolidated was a direct and heavy blow to Kaiser, see Note, "Vertical Forestalling under the Antitrust Laws," 19 *U. of Chicago Law Rev.* 591–592 n. 62 (1952).

58 See the suggestion of Clark, p. 42, above, and pp. 282–283, below.

the greatly attenuated requirement of competitive impact that had been accepted in the *International Salt* and first *Yellow Cab* decisions:

> I think that the trial court erred in holding that a formed intent to suppress competition is an indispensable element of violations of the Sherman Act.
>
> In the *United States* v. *Griffith* . . . we said: "It is . . . not always necessary to find a specific intent. . . . It is sufficient that a restraint of trade or monopoly results as the consequence of a defendant's conduct or business arrangements. . . . To require a greater showing would cripple the Act. . . ."
>
> . . . Since the trial court went on the assumption that subjective intent to suppress competition is an essential ingredient of Sherman Act violations, it did not make specific findings as to whether the freedom of the taxicab companies to buy taxicabs had been hobbled by the defendants' business arrangements, regardless of compulsion or intent to destroy competition.[59]

Since vertical integration by merger ordinarily hobbles the freedom of choice of one or both of the merging firms, this statement appears to call for complete abolition of the rule of reason applied to such acquisitions—even though Justice Reed had written the majority opinion in *Columbia Steel* the preceding year.

However, a good case can be made for upholding the government's complaint against the taxicab combination, even under the rule of reason. Here as in *Columbia Steel* we have the phenomenon of mergers for "legitimate business reasons" which may none the less be economically undesirable, even though it is difficult to prove a substantial resultant impairment of the force of competition in the market as a whole. The rule of reason does not preclude, on the contrary it requires, asking what socially beneficent considerations might justify a manufacturer of taxicabs acquiring control of a number of operating companies, with monopolies in their local markets. This too is part of the investigation of intent.

In view of his attitude in the *Columbia Steel* case, it cannot be deduced that Justice Reed would outlaw all vertical integration by merger simply because he joined with Justice Black in

[59] 338 U.S. 338, 343 (1949).

the second *Yellow Cab* dissent. He must have felt that this was a clearer case of obtaining financial control merely to sew up a market. His distinction between the two cases presumably hinged, in short, on his interpretation of the intent underlying each.

It is of course dangerous to try to supply a unified rationalization of a host of Supreme Court decisions, even with an unchanging court. Yet lawyers and businessmen cannot avoid asking why the court held 6 to 1 for the government in the *Griffith* case and one month later exonerated Columbia Steel by a 5 to 4 vote. Or why, since Justice Black's dissent raised the question, did two justices (Vinson and Burton) who had voted to overturn the District Court and condemn Griffith decide a year and a half later to sustain the lower court's verdict in favor of Yellow Cab? Only one reason (consistent with judical consistency) suggests itself: the *Griffith* case involved manifestly exclusive tactics; an integrated theater chain *used* its bargaining power and market leverage to obtain unfair advantages over competitors. In *Columbia* and *Yellow Cab,* any handicaps imposed on competitors were merely the incidental consequence of integration by merger. The line between these cases delineates the rule of reason in the antitrust laws.

These comparisons of leading recent monopoly cases involving business size and integration epitomize both the novelty and the continuity of recent antitrust doctrine. Its rule of reason requires relatively little showing that unreasonable competitive acts of large or integrated defendants have had a serious impact on competition. This is new. It requires less of a showing of predatory motivation than used to be necessary to condemn a company enjoying something like a pure monopoly. But the new Sherman Act still adopts as the test of legality the reasonableness or unreasonableness of the acts committed, the policies followed, whether by actual monopolies, or by highly competitive firms using a strategic foothold to bargain coercively, or by companies in between in the market spectrum. And attainment of market position by pleasing customers, or merging in order to please customers better, qualifies still as a reasonable act. Senator Hoar, the main framer of the Sherman Act, defined monopoly as "the sole engrossing to a man's self by means which prevent other men from engaging in fair competition with him." [60] The conception of "sole engrossing" has been changed; it is no longer necessary to enjoy a real monopoly in the classic sense; but the rest of the definition is as descriptive of the law today as it was sixty years ago.

[60] Quoted by Mason, note 3, Chap. 2, above.

CHAPTER 4

The Path of the Law: Exclusive Arrangements and Price Discrimination

EXCLUSIVE dealing, full requirements contracts, package deals, and price discrimination, because in some circumstances they may make for more rather than less effective competition, can never be unqualifiedly condemned under the antitrust laws. Yet, as competitive techniques they may quite clearly be the instruments of unfairly or excessively limiting the market opportunities of the firms against whom they are used. It has been the historic role of the rule of reason to weigh these possible effects against each other before reaching a decision. The new critics of antitrust, in judging exclusive arrangements and price discrimination, would have the courts disregard entirely any criteria of fairness and consider only the probable effect upon competition, broadly considered.[1]

Flouting both the historic rule of reason and the pleas of the new critics, the *A & P,* first *Yellow Cab*, and *International Salt* decisions, as we have seen, condemned the use of market leverage that merely put competitors at a disadvantage, regardless of any other broader, and possibly beneficial economic consequences. Other recent decisions have followed much the same line in con-

[1] Lockhart and Sacks, in 65 *Harv. Law Rev.* 913 (1952); K. F. Curran, "Exclusive Dealing and Public Policy," 15 *Jour. of Marketing* 133 (1950); see also Watkins, *Public Regulation of Competitive Practices,* pp. 209–228

demning price discrimination, exclusive dealing, and full requirements contracts without assessing their over-all economic effects. (We ignore temporarily the indications that the antitrust authorities are already in the process of reversing this trend.)

It is mainly in the interpretation of the qualifying clause of Sections 2 and 3 of the Clayton Act, "where the effect . . . may be to substantially lessen competition or tend to . . . create a monopoly in any line of commerce," that the change has been effected. In the first twenty-five years of the Clayton Act, this clause was interpreted as requiring a demonstration that the practices in question would probably, if unchecked, weaken competition in the market regarded as a whole. As we shall see, the alteration of the wording of the clause in Section 2 by the Robinson-Patman amendment of 1936 has modified this burden of proof, making it much easier than before to attack price discrimination. One cannot be sure just where interpretation begins and legislative policy ends. However, a similar process has been going on in Section 3 cases as well. In consequence, the clause may be said now to read, in effect, that the specified practices are illegal "where the effect may *possibly,* now or in the future, be to weaken the force of competition in some not insubstantial portion of the market, sectional or national, by putting some *competitors* of the seller or the buyer at a disadvantage."

It was in the *Morton Salt* case of 1948 that the new interpretation was most clearly established, so far as Section 2 was concerned. The Federal Trade Commission had ordered the company to stop offering its customers discounts increasing progressively with the quantities of cases of salt that they purchased. The largest discount, for which only five retail chains could qualify, permitted the recipients to resell salt at a price below their smaller competitors' invoice cost. Morton Salt's strongest defense was that the Commission had failed adequately to show injury to competition, actual or potential.

Speaking for the Supreme Court, Justice Black sustained the Commission. He held first that it was not necessary for the Comission to prove that injury to competition had actually resulted; the purpose of the Clayton Act is to "nip in their incipiency" acts that may, if unchecked, have this harmful effect. As for the requisite intensity of the threat to competition, he held the view that while the use of "may" in the qualifying clause was not intended to outlaw actions having a "mere possibility" of harming competition, all that had to be demonstrated was a "reasonable possibility" thereof.[2]

Essentially Black justified this reasoning on the ground that it was the explicit purpose of the Robinson-Patman amendment to strike at the practice of large buyers securing advantages over smaller competitors merely by virtue of the size of their purchases. It did so, he said, by narrowing the required demonstration of competitive impact from a showing of "general injury to competitive conditions" to one of "injury to the competitor victimized by the discrimination." The quantity discounts resulted in price differentials sufficient to influence resale prices. Since as a result the smaller buyers "might have been handicapped in competing with the more favored . . . purchasers, . . . the Commission was justified in finding that competition might have thereby been substantially lessened or have been injured within the meaning of the Act." [3]

So a "reasonable possibility" of injury to competition exists whenever some customers of manufacturers buy goods substantially more cheaply than other customers with whom they are in competition. As Justice Jackson pointed out in his dissent, it is difficult to visualize any discrimination between competing buyers which does not result in illegal injury to competition under such an interpretation.

The Federal Trade Commission, which for years had shown signs of hostility to price differentiation in any form, understandably seized upon the apparent invitation of *Morton Salt*. In many instances thereafter it confined its "economic findings" to a bare statement of the words of the statute and of the fact that a price discrimination had occurred the effect of which *might* be substantially to lessen competition among sellers or buyers. In some instances it purported to find a sufficient impairment of competition in the fact that a seller had, by offering selective discounts,

[2] *F.T.C.* v. *Morton Salt Co.*, 334 U.S. 37, 46, and Justice Jackson's dissent, 56–58 (1948).

[3] *Ibid.*, pp. 49–50.

taken customers away from his competitors or prevented them from taking customers away from him.[4]

There is more to the rule of reason, so far as Section 2 is concerned, than the necessity for demonstrating a substantial effect on competition. We therefore return at a later point in this chapter to a summary description of the path of the law in price discrimination cases—to the narrow interpretations placed by the Commission upon both the good-faith meeting of competition and the cost-saving defense, to the attempts of the courts and Congress to preserve some of the substance of these defenses, and to the clear evidence that a reconstituted Commission is now in the process of reversing these trends.

The leading decision under Section 3 of the Clayton Act that seemed to weaken the rule of reason was *Standard of California.* Its novelty is suggested by the fact that the Supreme Court held for the government by a 5 to 4 margin. The primary issue, as in *Morton Salt,* concerned the competitive impact of Standard's full requirements contracts. In contrast with its *Morton Salt* and *International Salt* decisions, the court, through Justice Frankfurter, set out to require the government to assume the heavier burden of "some sort of showing as to the *actual* or *probable* economic consequences of the agreements. . . ."[5] However, it found "the qualifying clause of § 3 . . . satisfied by proof that competition has been foreclosed in a substantial share of the line of commerce affected."[6] The "proof" consisted in the mere demonstration that Standard's exclusive supply contracts covered 16 per cent of the retail gasoline outlets and 6.7 per cent of the total gasoline sales in the western area. This was a somewhat heavier requirement than sufficed in the other two cases: a percentage share of the market actually affected was found to be substantial, rather than an absolute volume not insignificant. But the court declined to appraise economic consequences. It ex-

[4] *Curtiss Candy Co.,* 44 F.T.C. 237, 268–269 (1947); *Minneapolis-Honeywell Regulator Co.,* 44 F.T.C., 351, 397 (1948); 191 F.2d 786 (1951), *certiorari* denied, 344 U.S. 206 (1952). But see *Spark Plug* cases, Docket Nos. 3977, 5620, and 5624, Findings, July 10, 1953.

[5] 337 U.S. 293, 302 (1949) (stress supplied); see also pp. 305–308.

[6] *Ibid.,* p. 314.

plicitly refused to consider whether the requirements contracts might have been economically beneficial or might have intensified rather than reduced competition in the market—as dissenting Justices Jackson, Vinson, and Burton held it should have—on the ground, first, that the Clayton Act was not intended to require the same proof of market consequences as the Sherman Act and, second, that it would be extremely difficult to evaluate these results. In short, the decision seemed to say that all full requirements or exclusive dealing contracts covering any "substantial" share of commerce are *ipso facto* illegal, because by their very nature they exclude competitors from that segment of trade which they cover.[7]

The *Richfield* decision merely extended the *Standard of California* prohibition, on much the same grounds, to another of the "Big 7" on the West Coast. The contracts at issue involved thousands of service stations and sales running over $40,000,000 annually. This absolute volume was held sufficiently "substantial," without reference to the fact that it probably amounted to less than 3 per cent of total gasoline sales in the area.[8] (Incidentally, this was just about the share of the western rolled steel market that U.S. Steel was permitted to sew up by its purchase of Consolidated.) The main formal difference between the two cases concerned Richfield's defense of the exclusive dealing contracts with the 1,343 dealers (about 45 per cent of the total) who were its own lessees. These, it contended, were not independent businessmen but, in effect, its employees; it had "created" their business and could therefore hardly be suppressing pre-existing competition in confining their sales to its own products. Judge Yankwich dismissed this argument on the ground that by all the traditional tests the lessees were independent businessmen, assuming all the usual responsibilities and risks. He held that

[7] See Louis B. Schwartz, "Potential Impairment of Competition," 98 *U. of Penn. Law Rev.* 10 (1949); also H. Thomas Austern, "The Supreme Court and Section 3 of the Clayton Act," *1950 Symposium,* pp. 43–51; Adelman, *1951 Symposium,* p. 145.

[8] *U.S.* v. *Richfield Oil Corp.,* 99 F.Supp. 280 (1951); sustained, *per curiam,* 343 U.S. 922 (1952). Judge Yankwich apparently considered it unnecessary to discuss the percentages of the market affected by these contracts.

Richfield could not in certain connections choose the form and obtain the benefits of leasing (avoiding social security and chain store taxes and the direct responsibility for retailing) while at other times supporting a claim it was really only doing business with itself, depending on which legal fiction served its purposes.

Certain decisions subsequent to *Standard of California* seem to have gone even farther in condemning all exclusive dealing and full requirements contracts. And here again, as in the case of that other key decision in "the new Clayton Act," *Morton Salt,* the Federal Trade Commission seized upon a favorable precedent to launch a series of suits apparently without serious consideration of the general economic consequences of the practices. Only in December 1953, with its remand of the *Maico* case, did the Commission, in a reversal of position, insist that evidence of economic consequences be introduced. The hearing examiner had refused to admit in evidence even a showing that competitors were in fact excluded, on the theory that such evidence was unnecessary to sustain the complaint.[9]

It is easy to understand how the language of *Standard of California* and *Morton Salt,* as of subsequent decisions based upon them, have given rise to fears that exclusive arrangements and price discriminations are henceforth to be condemned per se. This is true even if, in the light of the circumstances of each case, the decision itself was fully compatible with the rule of reason.[10] Only by examining the leading recent decisions, one by one, can we fully appraise the validity of these fears.

The "exclusive practices" cases have all involved attempts by sellers with market power of one kind or another to set off some or all of their customers as an exclusive preserve, closed to competitors. The techniques have varied widely: International Salt, with patent control on salt-dispensing machinery, tried to extend its monopoly domain to unpatented salt used in conjunction with the machines; American Can, with almost 50 per cent of the United States production of can-closing machinery, leased only to those who purchased its cans and tried to induce

[9] Docket No. 5822, Remand, Dec. 15, 1953.

[10] Thus the dissent in *Morton Salt* was directed much more against the language employed by the majority than against the decision itself.

customers to agree to take all their cans from it under five- to twenty-year full requirements contracts; J. I. Case, a leading manufacturer of farm machinery, insisted that its dealers give its products "adequate representation," which it interpreted as giving their primary if not exclusive attention to its own line of products; the Times-Picayune Publishing Company, with a monopoly in the morning newspaper field in New Orleans, refused to make its columns available to certain advertisers unless they purchased space also in its afternoon publication, which faced an independent competitor; four leading distributors of advertising films for exhibition in theaters signed contracts with theaters to exhibit their films exclusively; Standard of California and Richfield forbade service stations handling their products to sell those of competitors also; a number of manufacturers, producers of busses, gasoline, and tires, purchased stock in two holding companies controlling numerous bus lines in return for ten-year contracts of exclusive supply.

In each of these cases, the F.T.C. or the courts had to decide whether the practices employed, with the purpose or effect of excluding competitors from some business, were reasonable or unreasonable by the standards of one or another of the antitrust laws. In evaluating these decisions, we will have two major questions to ask. The first, essentially legal question—How much remains of the rule of reason?—is the subject of this chapter. The second—Can the attenuated rule of reason that remains still play its historic economic rule of differentiating the practices which make competition more effective from those which tend to destroy or distort it?—we reserve for Part II.

It may help the reader if we anticipate our conclusion on the legal question. As we read the law in these cases, innocence or guilt does not even now depend upon whether competitors were incidentally excluded by contracts issuing from a process of fair competition. The question is whether power has been exerted in such a way as to impose a serious and unfair handicap. Only if requisite power and intent are present, i.e., if the objectionable character of the action is established, does the law strike down contractual or proprietary arrangements which do no more than exclude competitors from a "not insubstantial" percentage share of the market. At the same time, not one of the cases says this clearly, and this failure, plus the far weaker demonstration of contracompetitive impact now required, admittedly represents a considerable attenuation of the rule of reason.

Patent Tie-ins as Monopolizing Techniques

In the *International Salt* case, the objectionable character of the act itself was clear. International used its monopoly power in one sphere to force lessees to deny their patronage to competitors in another market. There has been relatively little objection to this decision. Yet the same economic criticisms might have been leveled against it as against *Standard of California* or *Richfield*. The court did not inquire how substantial a monopoly power International Salt's patents gave it in the supply of machines or whether competition in the entire market for salt was really significantly affected by the tie-ins.[11] The reason was doubtless that the intent was so clearly to exclude, and the opposition of the law to such abuses of governmentally conferred monopoly privilege was of very long standing.[12] But these are the traditional legal distinctions, not economic assessments of either market power or consequences.

However, Justice Jackson's opinion appeared, when taken together with that of Justice Murphy in the first *Yellow Cab* case, to condemn all integration or exclusive arrangements involving a "not insubstantial" volume of business, regardless of intent or consequences. Some observers have placed this interpretation on his statement, "It is unreasonable, *per se*, to foreclose competitors from any substantial market." [13] But the interpretation is unjustified. There are only two reasonable constructions one may place upon Jackson's dictum. He may not have meant what

[11] For example, see Lockhart and Sacks, in 65 *Harv. Law Rev.* 942–954 (1952), whose severe strictures against the *Standard of California* decision for its failure to ask these broader economic questions do not extend to patent tie-in cases.

[12] *Motion Picture Patents Co.* v. *Universal Film Manufacturing Co.*, 243 U.S. 502 (1917).

[13] Adelman, in *1951 Symposium*, p. 143.

he said; the facts of the case required no such broad and sweeping declaration. Alternatively—and in view of his votes to exonerate Standard of California, Columbia Steel, and Yellow Cab in the second case, this seems the more likely interpretation—he could not have meant by "foreclosing" the incidental exclusion of competitors involved in every full requirements contract or in every vertical merger. He could have meant only deliberate exclusion by exercise of coercion.

The latter construction has an interesting historical precedent; the dispute over the rule of reason before 1912 was entirely analogous. Justices Peckham, Taft, and Harlan, who rejected the rule of reason on the ground that Congress had prohibited all restraints of trade, did not thereby condemn all contracts or all partnership agreements, which, as Justice Holmes pointed out back in 1904, inevitably "restrain trade" in a sense.[14] Rather they defined restraints of trade as embracing only those contracts having the primary purpose and effect of eliminating or weakening competition in the market. In precisely the same way Jackson's conception of "foreclosing" almost certainly embraced only the exclusion that is deliberate, collusive (as in *Fashion Originators' Guild*,[15] which he cites to support his dictum), or coercive (*International Salt*).

In *International Salt* the court did consider the positive economic justification offered for the tying provision and, in so doing, suggested a reconciliation of the legal proscriptions and the requirements of workable competition:

> Of course, a lessor may impose . . . reasonable restrictions designed in good faith to minimize maintenance burdens and to assure satisfactory operation. . . . But it is not . . . argued, that the machine is allergic to salt of equal quality produced by anyone except International. . . . It is admitted that, at times, at least, competitors do offer such a product. They are, however, shut out of the market by a provision that limits it, not in terms of quality, but in terms of a particular vendor.[16]

In short, restrictive provisions that are reasonably required for the protection of the legitimate interests of one or both of the

[14] *Northern Securities Co.* v. *U.S.*, 193 U.S. 197, 410 (1904).

[15] 312 U.S. 457 (1941).

[16] 332 U.S. 392, 397–398 (1947).

contracting parties may still be upheld.[17] Again the deciding question is really one of the underlying intent; only thus can the act be properly defined.

Exclusive Dealing Imposed by Dominant Firms

It is doubtful that the *Standard of California* decision establishes exclusive dealing itself as an undesirable act. The unreasonable course of action is the imposition of exclusive dealing by dominant firms in such a way as to ensconce them in the market. Consider the language of Section 3 of the Clayton Act, under which Standard of California's full requirements contracts were outlawed:

> It shall be unlawful for any person . . . to lease or make a sale or contract for sale . . . or fix a price . . . or discount [there]from . . . on the condition . . . that the . . . purchaser thereof shall not use or deal in the goods . . . of a competitor . . . of the . . . seller, where the effect . . . may be to substantially lessen competition or tend to create a monopoly. . . .

A sale or lease requires a buyer or lessee as well as a seller or lessor, but it is against the latter only that the prohibition is directed. Why? Because the purpose of Section 3 is to preserve the buyer's (lessee's) freedom of choice and in this way to protect the access to the market of competing sellers. So it was Standard, not its dealers, who was attacked. It was Standard that drew up the prescribed contracts; dealers had to sign them if they wanted to sell Standard's products.[18]

In appraising the competitive impact of these contracts, Justice Frankfurter considered the extent to which such a marketing system limited dealers' freedom of choice. He found it re-

[17] See Richard W. McLaren, "Related Problems of 'Requirements' Contracts and Acquisitions in Vertical Integration under the Anti-trust Laws," 45 *Ill. Law Rev.* 151 (1950).

[18] The District Court opinion steadfastly refers not so much to the contracts themselves as to Standard's adoption of them, to Standard's pressure on its customers. 78 F.Supp. 850, 857–859, 886 (1948). Note the statement by the Supreme Court in an analogous case (see p. 101, below): "No theater owner (lessee) is a party to this proceeding. The cease and desist order binds only respondent." *F.T.C.* v. *Motion Picture Advertising Co., Inc.*, 344 U.S. 392, 395 n. 3 (1953).

stricted the individual dealer considerably more than the limitations at issue in the 1923 *Sinclair* case, where dealers were not permitted to put competing brands of gasoline in leased pumps. In contrast with the *International Salt* decision, he measured not the absolute amount of commerce involved but the percentage of the market affected. The share was unquestionably substantial and economically significant. He concluded that the use of such contracts, not only by Standard but by its six leading competitors, might reasonably be interpreted as having had the effect of enabling "the established suppliers individually to maintain their own standing and at the same time collectively, even though not collusively, to prevent a late arrival from wresting away more than an insignificant portion of the market." [19] The contracts thus represented an instrument of policy, with the effect if not the purpose of exclusion over a wide market area. So, the opinion concludes, "Standard's use of the contracts creates just such a potential clog on competition as it was the purpose of § 3 to remove. . . ." [20] Obviously the effects of the contracts on competition would have been quite different had not exclusive dealing (in gasoline at least) been a condition of all of them and had not similar contracts been employed by all of the Big 7.

Justice Frankfurter's opinion is admittedly susceptible to the interpretation that it outlaws all full requirements contracts employed by a big firm, no matter what the *quid pro quo* or the alternatives available to buyers or rivals. However, one may reasonably conclude instead that what was forbidden in *Standard of California* and *Richfield* was a dominant company's using its market power to impose full requirements contracts, as a condition of sale, on dealers lacking reasonable alternatives to do business on a nonexclusive basis, where also competitors were seriously handicapped as a result.[21] If this interpretation is cor-

[19] 337 U.S. 293, 309 (1949). See also *Signode Steel Strapping Co.* v. *F.T.C.*, 132 F.2d 48 (1942), for a similar consideration of the parallel restrictive practices of other dominant firms besides the defendant.

[20] 337 U.S. 293, 314.

[21] This is definitely Frankfurter's present interpretation of his *Standard* opinion. In his dissent in *Motion Picture Advertising* he contrasts the facts with those in the *Standard* case: "In the Standard Oil case we recognized the

rect *Standard of California* was not revolutionary. The evidence of market power, actually exerted, with the effect [22] of creating a serious potential impediment to competition surely sufficed to satisfy even the traditional rule of reason, though the court did not hinge its decision upon such evidence with sufficient clarity. Because of their size, the public acceptance of their brands, the uniformity of their market practices, and their direct financial control of numerous retail outlets, each of the Big 7 on the West Coast was obviously in a position to insist on exclusive handling. All thus imposed on the industry a pattern of retailing gasoline that, the court pointed out, gave the individual dealer virtually no opportunity to acquire gasoline on a nonexclusive basis, probably entrenched the position of each, and posed substantial obstacles to new entrants.

The *Standard* and *Richfield* precedents do not, should not, and in actual practice cannot, prohibit a voluntary choice of exclusive handling by dealers who are offered a substantial freedom of choice to do business in other ways. A seller, even a very big one, may still be able to contract to supply a customer's full requirements, if so requested.

Does the recent *Motion Picture Advertising Service* decision, significantly with Justice Frankfurter dissenting, deny this interpretation of the *Standard* decision? Here the Supreme Court voted 7 to 2 to uphold an order of the Federal Trade Commission condemning exclusive exhibition agreements between the four leading producers and distributors of advertising films and their theater customers as unfair methods of competition under Section 5 of the F.T.C. Act. The defendants had exclusive contracts with three-fourths of the theaters showing such films. But

---

discrepancy of bargaining power and pointed out that the retailers might still insist on exclusive contracts if they wanted. . . ." (In fact, his statement in the earlier decision was not nearly so clear on this point.) 344 U.S. 342, 402.

[22] Judge Yankwich's final findings of fact were that "the intent, purpose and effect of the exclusive supply provisions" are to exclude. 78 F.Supp. 850, 888 (1948). In the *Richfield* case, the same judge speaks of the defendant's "coercive" tactics. 99 F.Supp. 280, 295–296 (1951). In both he considered evidence of intent as well as effect because the complaints were brought under the Sherman as well as the Clayton Act.

the majority of both the Commission and the Supreme Court ignored the contention that no coercion was involved in obtaining the contracts of exclusive supply, that on the contrary theater owners actively requested them.[23] Though the Commission did in its order give heed to the desires of the customers, prohibiting only exclusive screening agreements extending more than one year, it failed to show how, by merely acceding to requests for longer-term full requirements contracts (if this is all they did), the distributors could be said to have competed unfairly. The Supreme Court was strongly swayed by the view that an expert body like the Commission should be the one to decide on the basis of the particular circumstances of each case whether a particular competitive practice is unfair. Doubtless the Commission, as now reconstituted, will do more in the future than it did in the *Motion Picture Advertising Service* case to justify such confidence.

Not only have the new Commission's first major decisions in exclusive dealing cases justified this expectation. They have, like its first formal action in the *Pillsbury Mills* case,[24] also dispelled the fear that it would go too far in the opposite direction, looking beyond the character of the act to require proof of "unworkable competition" in a poor economic performance, before issuing a cease-and-desist order. The Commission required Dictograph Products, Inc., one of the three leading manufacturers of hearing aids, to discontinue its rigid insistence on exclusive dealing by its distributors. The latter comprised an estimated 22 per cent of the total number of full-time distributors in the business. In the light of the evidence that competitors were disadvantaged (and distributors unreasonably coerced) by the policies foreclosing them from a substantial share of the market, the Commission's opinion paid no attention to the defendants' claim that exclusive representation assured the public of better service.[25] In the same vein, where all evidence of com-

[23] See the dissenting opinions of Commissioner Mason and Justices Frankfurter and Burton and the opinion of the Circuit Court overruling the Commission. F.T.C. Orders 5495–5498, Nov. 5, 1950; 194 F.2d 633 (1952); 344 U.S. 392, 402 (1953).

[24] See p. 283, below.

[25] *Dictograph Products, Inc.*, Docket No. 5655, Decision, Sept. 14, 1953; see also the exclusive dealing portions of the *Spark Plug* decisions.

petitive impact was excluded from the record, the Commission refused to sustain a hearing examiner's decision prohibiting the Maico Company from insisting on exclusive dealing. The examiner based his rejection of economic evidence on *Standard of California;* but the Commission held that the economic data which the Supreme Court said in that decision that it was "ill-suited" to appraise are the very kinds of evidence that the Commission was set up to consider. Thus the F.T.C. is apparently prepared to see whether distributors have been coerced and competitors seriously handicapped, without engaging in tortuous appraisals of market performance.

Tie-ins and Requirements Contracts as Devices to Maintain or Extend a Dominant Market Position

The first important decision following *Standard of California* held American Can guilty of violating Sections 1 and 2 of the Sherman and Section 3 of the Clayton Act by (*a*) tying-in leases of can-closing machinery and sales of cans and (*b*) selling cans under five-year requirements contracts.[26]

Unlike Standard of California, American did not flatly refuse to sell on a nonexclusive basis. Why then should the contracts it employed have been considered objectionable? The court conceded that some of American's tactics in soliciting the contracts were undistinguishable from ordinary methods of competitive salesmanship:

> Certain practices, as defendant claims, represent no more nor less than "ordinary business practices, such as the extension of credit, the servicing of leased machinery, the equalization of freight rates and similar activities one would expect to find in any industry in which competitors are seeking to serve the needs of their customers and keep their good will."

It solicited and obtained the requirements contracts largely by the offer of numerous competitive inducements, including the lease of machines at favorable rates:

> The devices took many forms: defendant provided discounts in ancillary contracts; defendant paid large sums of money to obtain

[26] *U.S.* v. *American Can Co.,* 87 F.Supp. 18 (1949). The facts cited below, unless otherwise indicated, are taken from Judge Harris' opinion.

business of its customers; defendant furnished equipment, in addition to closing machines, at nominal rentals; defendant paid large claims when it appeared propitious and good policy; defendant purchased can-making equipment from its customers at inflated values in order to obtain can business. . . .[27]

But it was impossible to appraise these practices without considering American's position in the industry over the years. This the court did conscientiously. It cited the finding of the original (1916) antitrust decision that the company enjoyed monopoly power and that the gigantic financial agglomeration which gave rise to that power, and the company's practices in its formative years, evinced an attempt to monopolize. It pointed out that American accounted for 40 per cent of the national production and 46 per cent of national sales of cans, and controlled 54 per cent of the can-closing machines available for lease; in individual market areas and in particular types of cans its dominance was even greater. In the light of these facts, and only after a painstaking appraisal of the entire course of American's business dealings, Judge Harris concluded that the tie-ins and requirements contracts (binding customers to purchase all their requirements of virtually "every conceivable type of container" for five years—indeed up to twenty years in earlier contracts) and the methods employed to obtain them represented something quite different from forthright, bona fide competition. They bore an unmistakable odor of monopolizing:

> The incidents, when examined realistically and not as mere abstractions, are deeper than the typical run-of-the-mill, day-to-day business transactions. They represent a studied, methodical and effective method of retaining and acquiring by refined, gentlemanly and suave means, plus an occasional "commercial massage," the dominant position which American has had and maintained for at least a generation on and over the canning industry.[28]

[27] *Ibid.*, pp. 27, 28. Standard, too, had used "competitive inducements"; it assisted its dealers in numerous ways which were certainly regarded by both parties as a *quid pro quo* for being a "Standard" dealer. But the courts disregarded the blandishments in the *Standard* case; they condemned the contracts themselves.

[28] *Ibid.*, p. 28; see also p. 29.

Judge Harris therefore required American thenceforth to offer its can-closing machines for sale as well as lease, prohibited the tie-in of leases with can requirements contracts, and limited requirements contracts thereafter to one-year duration. This decision did not represent a condemnation of American's integration, its offer of the machine-can package, or its sales under requirements contracts. If American—along with its only important competitor, Continental Can, which employed identical tactics—had merely made these packages available to canners as one alternative, with the other alternatives likewise available on terms fairly mirroring their respective costs, there could have been no objection to the practice.

The fact that a condemnation of tie-ins is not a condemnation of integration provides the simple answer to the Supreme Court's unfortunate *Times-Picayune* decision in 1953. Here the defendant, a publishing company, required purchasers of general display and classified advertising to take space in both its morning *Times-Picayune* (the only morning newspaper and the most important newspaper in New Orleans) and in its evening *States,* which competed with the city's only other newspaper, the evening *Item.* The defendants contended that their two publications were really separate editions of a single newspaper. Yet a substantial volume of evidence, including assertions by the company's own executives in soliciting advertising, argued to the contrary. Although many of the publishing operations became joint after the *Times-Picayune* acquired the *States* in 1933, the tie-in was not an inevitable, "natural" single package, but in part at least a policy decision adopted "to slow the *Item* down," in the words of one defendant.[29] Many advertisers obviously did not consider the package a single product until they were forced to do so: before adoption of the unit rule less than half as many classified advertisers and something less than two-thirds as many general display advertisers bought space in the *States* as in the morning paper. Afterward, of course, the percentage rose at once to close to 100.[30]

On what grounds, after the *International Salt* and *Griffith* opinions, could five justices of the United States Supreme Court

[29] 105 F.Supp. 670, 678 (1952).

[30] 345 U.S. 594, 616, 618 (1953).

have overturned the verdict of the District Court that such a tie-in in itself violated Sections 1 and 2 of the Sherman Act? (Griffith was condemned merely for tying together its monopoly and nonmonopoly theaters in bargaining for films, without regard to any market consequences other than the disadvantaging of competitors.) The main reason was their finding that the defendants did not enjoy the "dominant position" which alone makes tie-ins illegal per se: "The essence of illegality in tying agreements is the wielding of monopolistic leverage. . . ."[31] Since the morning newspaper's sales of general display and classified advertising were only 40 per cent of the total New Orleans lineage and would have been only 6 ⅔ per cent less if all papers were of equal size, the Supreme Court concluded the company's power full short of the necessary "dominance."

This computation compounded three errors (listed in ascending order of importance):

1. Justice Clark, speaking for the court, said that the relevant market in this case was the one where newspapers compete for advertisers, not readers. Accordingly, he computed the share of the morning newspaper, the *Times-Picayune,* in advertising lineage, not in circulation. But the one does not follow from the other. As Clark himself said, what a newspaper does in the advertising market is to sell its readership to the buyers of advertising space. Its importance to advertisers, then, is the size of readership; this measures what it has to sell. The *Times-Picayune* had 46 per cent of the combined circulation of the three newspapers, not 40 per cent. The latter proportion, its share of combined advertising lineage, was *necessarily lower because of the unit rule itself;* under that rule, no one could buy space in the morning paper without buying it in the *States,* though the latter's circulation was much lower. So even if the *Item* closed up shop entirely, giving the Times-Picayune Publishing Company a complete monopoly, the morning newspaper could not possibly have obtained over 50 per cent of the relevant advertising business!

2. If the correct computation was of the position of the defendants in the entire New Orleans newspaper market, morning

[31] *Ibid.,* p. 611.

and evening taken together, certainly Justice Clark should have added together the lineage of the two papers bound together by the unit rule. This would have given him a "dominant" market share of 78 per cent.

3. But the court's simple, glaring error was to add together the "tying" and the "tied-in" markets in its calculation. It was the position of the *Times-Picayune* in the morning field that provided the leverage. This share was 100 per cent, the same as the share of the Griffith chain in towns where it owned the only theater, the lever in that case. Clark justified his consideration of the morning and evening fields as a single market on the ground that the service sold to advertisers was a uniform, undifferentiated, "fungible customer potential," rather than two distinct products:

> No dominant "tying" product exists (in fact, since space in neither the Times-Picayune nor the States can be bought alone, one may be viewed as "tying" as the other); no leverage in one market excludes sellers in the second, because for the present purposes the products are identical and the market the same.[32]

He might have seen through this spurious contention merely by looking at the consequences of the unit rule, which he so tortuously appraised later in order to see whether the effects of the restraint on competition had been substantial. He would have seen that the immediate result of imposing the rule was to pull the lineage of the *States* up to that of the *Times-Picayune,* and not the other way around, raising it by 100 per cent in the case of classified and almost 50 per cent in the case of general advertising. Any advertiser who wanted to reach a morning audience now had to patronize the evening *States* as well. This must have been precisely what the defendants had in mind in imposing the rule.

The court should certainly have concluded, as Judge Harris did in *American Can,* that the insistence on a combination package deal by so dominant a seller appreciably reduced the buyers' range of alternatives and unfairly constricted the market opportunities of other, nonintegrated sellers without regard to their

[32] *Ibid.*, p. 614.

relative efficiency or to the economic merits of the arrangements. The *Griffith* decision held it unnecessary to find a "specific intent" to monopolize or to appraise market consequences of package bargaining of this sort. In the *Times-Picayune* decision, a scant five years after that high point in the new Sherman Act, we find the rule of reason of 1920 rejuvenated in all its glory. But certainly the rule of reason does not preclude finding a practice illegal whose intent is plainly to use a dominant position in one field to obtain an unfair competitive advantage in another. The most unfortunate implication of the *Times-Picayune* decision is that the court will henceforth have to be convinced of substantial deleterious effects on existing competitors before it will condemn a tying device which has nothing to be said in its favor and which (as Justice Clark ingenuously admits at the outset of his opinion) has undoubtedly been effective in discouraging competitive entry into the 90 per cent of newspaper markets where undiluted, 100 per cent monopoly is the rule.[33]

Voluntary and Mutually Beneficial Exclusive Arrangements

Although the District Court found that the use of "strong competitive persuasions" by American Can to induce customers to sign five-year full requirements contracts represented an unreasonable device to sew up the market, it recognized that some exclusive arrangements might serve the mutual interests of the contracting parties without unreasonably foreclosing others from the market. In this industry full requirements contracts assure the canner the necessary quantities whatever the unpredictable pack may require and provide the can manufacturer with a reasonable *quid pro quo* for standing ready to provide all his customers' needs. Therefore one-year contracts were sanctioned as meeting the need without unreasonably excluding competitors. Later, in the case of the distributors of motion picture advertising films, the Trade Commission permitted similar arrangements.

These instances of willingness to permit exclusive supply ar-

[33] *Ibid.*, pp. 604, 622; see comment, "Local Monopoly in the Daily Newspaper Industry," 61 *Yale Law J.* 948, 951, and *passim* (1952).

rangements which are not the product of coercion and which are beneficial to both parties without unreasonably excluding competitors suggest that the earlier *Bausch & Lomb* decision still stands. That case involved a contract between Bausch & Lomb and the Soft-Lite Lens Company, under which the former manufactured and ground pink-tinted lenses exclusively for distribution by the latter, which sold them under its trade name. The government contended that the undertaking by Bausch & Lomb neither to sell such lenses to others nor to distribute them itself in competition with Soft-Lite violated the Sherman Act, Section 1. An evenly divided Supreme Court sustained the District Court's exoneration of this arrangement, lending its support to Judge Rifkind's application of the rule of reason:

> These arrangements were developed through arm's length negotiations. . . .
>
> The restraining covenant is for the protection of the purchaser who is spending large sums to develop his good will and enlarge the public patronage of a relatively new article of commerce. The arrangement, though not a partnership in legal form, is functionally a joint enterprise. . . .
>
> Others have entered the pink tinted lens field. . . .
>
> Nothing in the evidence indicates that Bausch & Lomb enjoyed a monopoly in the manufacture of glass for lenses, whether pink or otherwise. On the contrary, the evidence is clear that other manufacturers of lenses have had access to pink glasses from other sources and that the success of Soft-Lite has stimulated emulation and competition. . . .
>
> Throughout the period mentioned there has been competition between untinted and tinted lenses, as well as in the various tints of lenses and among the distributors of pink tinted lenses. . . .[34]

In short, the agreement did not involve the use of market power by a dominant seller to exclude competitors. It was not anticompetitive either in intent or in effect.

[34] *U.S.* v. *Bausch & Lomb Optical Co.,* 45 F.Supp. 387, 391, 398–399 (1942); 321 U.S. 707 (1944). Since the government had contended that the exclusive arrangement was contaminated by a price-fixing agreement, which both courts condemned, it is conceivable that in the absence of the latter the Supreme Court's exoneration of the former might have been more nearly unanimous.

Similar considerations induced a Federal District Court in 1951 to dismiss the government's charge against the J. I. Case Company. This case illustrates how complex the task often is of distinguishing between competition and exclusion.

Most farm machinery is sold through dealers, each of whom is the exclusive local representative of a single full-line manufacturer and, for the most part, handles the line of only one manufacturer. Although the exclusiveness is neither tight—only a minority, and perhaps a small one, of dealers handle no competitive equipment whatsoever—nor embodied in binding contracts, the exclusive agency–exclusive dealing pattern is typical nevertheless, particularly as far as the full line is concerned.[35] The Department of Justice launched three civil suits in 1948, against International Harvester, John Deere, and Case, to break up this pattern; when it lost the one against Case, the only one which went to trial, it dropped them all.

There are several related points on which the positions of the Department of Justice and the District Court diverged in *J. I Case*. They differed in their interpretation of the facts; they did not agree on how many clear-cut instances of coercion and how much in the way of competitive impact are required to demonstrate an illegal restraint; and they held different conceptions of how far the antitrust laws go or should go in decreeing a regime of pure competition.

The government contended that it was the general policy of J. I. Case to have its dealers handle its products exclusively. Judge Nordbye agreed the evidence showed "that Case has been intent . . . on obtaining dealers who will devote the major part of their activities to the Case line. . . ." [36] The Department of Justice said that the company's field representatives continually exerted pressure on the retailers, backed by the threat of contract termination, to drop competitive lines. It cited 108 dealers as having been subjected to "specific acts of coercion and pressure" of this kind. The District Court conceded that, in some "relatively few" cases, it appeared there had been "flagrant at-

[35] F.T.C., *Report on Manufacture and Distribution of Farm Implements* (1948), pp. 113–114, 126–127, and *passim*.

[36] *U.S.* v. *J. I. Case Co.*, 101 F.Supp. 856, 861 (1951).

tempts to coerce and put pressure on a few dealers to give up competing lines as a condition for obtaining a Case contract or to obtain a renewal. . . ." [37] These policies and pressures, the government contended, had caused contracts with a "substantial" and increasing number of dealers to be accompanied by understandings that they would be exclusive, and therefore they effected an unreasonable restraint of trade.

> The largely successful elimination of competitive long lines from the hands of 3700 Case dealers, and the steady pressure to eliminate, also, competitive short lines imposes a substantial restraint upon a large segment of interstate commerce and is violative of Section 1 of the Sherman Act.[38]

These understandings also violated Section 3 of the Clayton Act, it argued, regardless of whether they were secured by coercion:

> Where the effect is to exclude competitors from selling to large numbers of the Case dealership organization, defendant Case is not immunized from the antitrust laws merely because in many instances the oral understanding . . . was thought to be mutually beneficial. . . . The decision of the Supreme Court in the Standard Oil of California case did not turn upon evidence of coercion. . . .[39]

In short, it contended that the market must be free of even voluntary contractual constraints; at every moment everyone must be free to contract with everyone else.

The court, on the other hand, saw no legal objection to exclusive dealing as such, whether secured by contractual stipula-

[37] *Ibid.*, pp. 864–865. The government claimed that with respect to almost none of the 108 instances of alleged coercion did the company bring to the stand the territorial representatives responsible, and in 28 it offered no controverting evidence of any kind; that there was no evidence that the home office ever took to task the branch managers or salesmen responsible for admitted acts of coercion and inducement to handle Case products exclusively. (In 1948 it was the industry's frequent, or general, practice to refer all such complaints back to the very district representatives about whom the dealers were complaining. F.T.C., *Report on . . . Farm Implements,* pp. 126, 136, 151.) *U.S.* v. *J. I. Case Co.,* Motion by Plaintiff for Amendment of Findings of Fact and Conclusions of Law and of the Judgment, Dec. 27, 1951 (mimeo.), pp. 10–13, 20–24.

[38] *Ibid.,* Brief for the U.S., June 15, 1951, Sec. III A, par. 5.

[39] Motion of Plaintiff for Amendment, p. 18.

tion or understanding. The manufacturer has the right to select distributors according to whether or not they give its products "fair representation" and are "sold, so to speak, and enthusiastic about its line"; therefore the manufacturer may reasonably withdraw its machines from a dealer who divides his loyalties and attention between two full lines, in both selling and servicing this complicated machinery. But the purpose of these policies of selection and rejection must not be to effect a monopoly; the methods may not be "unreasonably coercive"; and there must be no strong likelihood that the effect of the policies will be to weaken competition in the final market, regarded as a whole.[40]

Jude Nordbye found that Case's actions fell within these rather vague boundaries of legitimacy. He disputed the government's dismissal, as mere window dressing, of Case bulletins advising salesmen and regional representatives not to be "overzealous" and to avoid "dictating" to or "coercing" dealers with respect to the lines they carried (while at the same time assuring them they could insist on adequate representation). While he agreed that "the home office executives were inclined to leave the problems of dealership largely to the branch managers and at times may have accepted their decisions without a thorough investigation when controversies arose as to competitive lines being carried by dealers," nonetheless, he concluded that "the executives of the company adhered to and fairly endeavored to sustain the policies enunciated in the bulletin referred to. . . ."[41] He attributed exclusive handling of Case's products and handling of the full line not to pressure by the manufacturer in the great majority of instances, but to a mutual recognition that sound business practice demands it, and held that arrangements thus arrived at are legally unexceptionable.

There was no showing that Case policies had had any substantial deleterious effect on competition, actual or potential. Over 70 per cent of its dealers carried competitive products, though few carried another full line. There was no testimony from competing manufacturers that these policies had excluded

[40] 101 F.Supp. 856, 863, 865.

[41] *Ibid.*, pp. 861–862.

them from markets.[42] On the contrary, the court found that most towns within reasonable distance of potential customers have dealers representing nearly every full-line and many short-line manufacturers. It found, in short, that workable competition prevailed: "The evidence reflects that there is healthy competition among all farm machinery manufacturers." [43]

The antitrust laws do not and should not require pure competition. They do not and should not prohibit voluntary decisions to seek out stable and mutually beneficial exclusive buyer-seller relationships, so long as most competitors can find their way to most ultimate consumers, except insofar as they may be hindered by irremediable handicaps like those arising out of unequal access to capital. If a company can convince a court that it has not constructed unreasonable barriers against the entry of competitors, it should be permitted to distribute its products as it pleases.

At the same time, it is difficult to escape the feeling that the court may have slighted the particular rationale of the Clayton Act. Section 3 creates a strong presumption in favor of freedom of choice on the part of the buyer and, correspondingly, freedom of competitive access to the market. Judge Nordbye conceded that it protects a dealer against "undue coercion" to drop the lines of a competitor; he conceded also that in some instances Case representatives had exercised such coercion.

A decree in equity prohibiting coercive pressure for exclusive dealing might have forced Case thereafter to be a good deal more scrupulous than it actually had been in keeping its field representatives from overstepping the bounds of reasonable salesmanship.[44] Defining precise bounds of reasonable salesmanship

[42] The government pointed out that such evidence would have been difficult to obtain for the years 1944–1948, when the bottleneck in the industry was supply, not market outlets.

[43] 101 F.Supp. 856, 866.

[44] See the court's concessions of some of the government's allegations, on p. 111, above. The threat of treble-damage suits perhaps makes it more difficult to suggest a finding for the government in order to guard against future abuses by individual subordinates. However, a finding that Case had violated the law could have been cited as prima-facie evidence in subsequent damage suits only with respect to the general allegations, not with

or of "unfair labor practices" must be left in large measure to the extralegal processes of negotiation and compromise. A decree might have contributed to the development of such a system of business jurisprudence, perhaps by inducing Case to set up formal grievance machinery for airing the complaints of dealers allegedly subjected to excessive pressure. In consequence the ability of smaller short-line competitors to reach the market would surely have been enhanced.

Full Requirements Contracts as a Quid Pro Quo

American Can was following a widespread practice when it offered its customers special inducements to make it worth their while to enter an exclusive relationship. (When supplies are short, on the other hand, it is the customer who tries, by similar inducements, to get preferential access to supplies.) [45]

The *National City Lines* decision [46] seems much more clearly than *American Can* to indicate that such practices and arrangements may be unequivocally illegal under either the Sherman or Clayton Act so long as a few million dollars of sales are involved.

In this case, Firestone Tire and Rubber, General Motors, Phillips Petroleum, Mack Manufacturing, and Standard of California were convicted of conspiring to monopolize "certain portions of interstate commerce" under Section 2 of the Sherman Act, because they had jointly furnished capital to two bus-line holding companies in exchange for ten-year exclusive supply contracts for petroleum products, busses, and tires. In

---

respect to the "evidentiary" allegations of specific injury to each of the 108 dealers cited in evidence. See Roy W. McDonald, "Proof of Conspiracy: The Prima Facie Rule," *1952 Symposium,* pp. 68–69

[45] See the proposed loan of $28,000,000 from General Motors to Jones and Laughlin, in exchange for "an assured supply of steel until the loan is paid off" (*Business Week,* Dec. 16, 1950, pp. 111–112) and the contract in which Phillips Petroleum gave the Barium Steel Corp. a share in its crude oil and gas leases, reportedly in exchange for supplies of scarce steel. *N. Y. Herald Tribune,* June 14, 1951, p. 41, col. 3.

[46] *U.S.* v. *National City Lines,* 186 F.2d 562 (1951); *certiorari* denied, 341 U.S. 916 (1951).

testing whether the exclusive arrangements with forty-six bus lines in forty-five cities amounted to a monopoly of "any part" of interstate commerce, within the meaning of Section 2, the effect on competition was established by analogy to *Yellow Cab*. Sales to bus- (taxicab-) operating companies, amounting in 1946 to over $11,000,000 (replacement for 5,000 cabs), from which competitors were excluded by the contracts (vertical integration), met the test of "noninsubstantiality" even though they amounted to a negligible percentage of the total national or regional sales of the companies or products in question. The only "market" monopolized was a group of financially consolidated customers. But whereas Yellow Cab was ultimately exonerated because the lower court found no evidence of illegal intent, similar evidence (indicating that it was the bus companies who had been in financial straits and had approached the suppliers for assistance) proved unavailing in *National City Lines*. Likewise unavailing was the offer of proof that the practices in question were widespread and that the arrangements were in the best interests of the bus companies.[47] Why?

The condemnation hinged largely on the finding of conspiracy. The supplier defendants were separate firms, each of whose individual subscriptions to the bus companies' stock were apparently predicated on an understanding that the others were doing the same. But the question arises whether a common course of action planned by noncompeting firms [48] makes offensive acts that might escape censure if committed by each individually. Moreover, the Supreme Court was willing to entertain a charge of conspiracy against Checker Cab, its organizers and subsidiaries; they were exonerated only when the purpose of the "conspiracy" was found to have been reasonable.

The different conclusions in the two cases can really be ex-

[47] 186 F.2d 562, 572–573.

[48] Since each supplier received an exclusive contract, the plan obviously had no room for direct competitors. Each of the two oil companies obtained the exclusive contract for bus companies operating in its own market area. The indictment might then have charged an illegal division of market territories between Phillips and Standard, but it did not.

plained only in terms of the double standard, which requires a more specific demonstration of intent to monopolize for close-knit consolidations than for agreements between separate (even noncompetitive) firms. In *National City Lines,* the exclusive contracts and their inevitable effect were held themselves to constitute sufficient evidence of an intent to exclude.[49]

National City Lines epitomizes the tendency of the courts to obliterate the distinction between the Sherman and Clayton Acts, while weakening the rule of reason applied to both. With *International Salt* and *Standard of California* greatly reducing the required demonstration of competitive impact (under Section 3 of the Clayton Act); with the former declaring it also illegal per se (under Section 1 of the Sherman Act) to foreclose competitors from any substantial market; and with the first *Yellow Cab* opinion finding that such foreclosure might constitute monopolization of "any substantial part" of the national market (under Section 2 of the Sherman Act), the way was paved for applying any and all of these statutory provisions to condemn tie-ins or exclusive dealing by any big company, despite the Supreme Court's attempt in *Standard of California* to limit the reduced burden of proof to Clayton Act cases. Thus American Can was condemned under Sections 1 and 2 (Sherman) and 3 (Clayton), Richfield under 1 (Sherman) and 3 (Clayton), and National City Lines under 2 (Sherman). The language of the Clayton Act probably did not cover the loan-exclusive-supply tie-in of the National City Lines. Nevertheless, because of the *Yellow Cab* precedent, under the Sherman Act, an even more limited proof of consequences sufficed to convict than was required, under the Clayton Act, in the *Standard* case. So the Clayton Act's prohibition of specific practices, regardless of intent, was incorporated into Section 2 of the Sherman Act, with the diminished standard of substantiality of effect of the first *Yellow Cab* case. Yet there was no incorporation of the saving proviso in *Yellow Cab* requiring evidence of an intent to monopolize (beyond the mere intent to do what was done).

Nevertheless, the rule of reason was not ignored. The defendants' course of action might reasonably have been character-

[49] 186 F.2d 562, 571.

ized as demonstrating an intent to gain assured customers by other than normal competitive methods.[50] A group of companies joined, through an intermediary, in a program to purchase control of a number of potential customers, in exchange for the intermediary's promise to divert to them for ten years all the patronage of the subsidiaries thus acquired. It is surely one of the traditional purposes of the antitrust laws to prevent the exercise of financial power for the primary purpose of sewing up markets. Vertical integration motivated solely by this purpose would likewise be suspect, and rightly so. It does not follow, then, that a supplier must henceforth deny a customer's free, uncoerced, and uninduced request for a full requirements contract, or that isolated transactions exchanging financial assistance for contracts of supply would violate the law. One might reasonably contend, however, that the law requires more substantial ancillary economic evidence of market power used as a lever and of market consequences than the Antitrust Division provided in *National City Lines.*

Exclusive Dealing and Requirements Contracts—Conclusion

The fact that buyers and sellers find exclusive contractual relationships sufficiently satisfactory to enter into them does not necessarily make them socially acceptable. The mutual economic advantages in such arrangements do not justify a seller's insisting on them. Since the effect of the arrangements, and their purpose, is to make entry difficult, the presumption of antitrust must be against them, even in the absence of clear-cut evidence of harmful effects on economic performance, and in favor of easier entry.

The legal appraisal of requirements contracts or exclusive dealing should turn therefore on whether or not they issue from the exertion of appreciable market or financial power, with the

[50] This evaluation is implicit in the Appellate Court's description of the plan. 186 F.2d 562, 565 (1951). On the other hand, the only intent which it held relevant (in keeping with *Alcoa* and *Griffith* and in striking contrast with second *Yellow Cab,* see pp. 86–88, above) was the intent to "bring about the forbidden act," i.e., merely to execute the contracts themselves.

effect of excluding competitors from a substantial market.[51] The more flagrant the exclusive tactics, the more clearly they betray an intent to exclude, the less stringent should be the test of economic consequences. The prime question is whether the exclusion, i.e., the *act,* is unreasonable, or stems merely from socially acceptable methods of vying for customer patronage and from the free decision of the buyer or dealer. If the former, the only relevant test of competitive impact is whether competitors have been subjected to an appreciable handicap.

These criteria do not require that all exclusive arrangements be outlawed. Where exclusive dealing helps a new firm to gain a foothold, it clearly does not represent the use of appreciable bargaining power unreasonably to foreclose competitors from a substantial market.[52] The use of exclusive dealing by small manufacturers as a means of breaking into a market represents one of the most defensible uses of the practice. Obviously none of the recently outlawed arrangements that we have discussed could have been justified on these grounds. Such a determination of the facts admittedly implies a market structure test and explains our periodic references in the foregoing discussion to the fact that the seller was a "dominant firm." But the application of the test cannot be rigorous: economics alone provides no scientific yardstick for drawing the line between the "unreasonable" exercise of "substantial" market power and the uncoercive adoption of a "reasonable" exclusive relationship. The

[51] See the similar, though not identical argument in Comment, "Vertical Forestalling under the Antitrust Laws," in 19 *U. of Chicago Law Rev.* 617–619 (1952).

[52] See, in addition to the *Bausch & Lomb* case, p. 109, above, *B. S. Pearsall Butter Co.* v. *F.T.C.*, 292 Fed. 720 (1923) and *Exelsior Motor Manufacturing & Supply Co.* v. *Sound Equipment, Inc.*, 73 F.2d 725 (1934).

The Supreme Court employed identical logic in rejecting the effort of the I.C.C. to extend full common carrier status to a products pipeline. *U.S.* v. *Champlin Refining Co.*, 341 U.S. 290 (1951). Pointing out that the Hepburn Act was passed because the dominant oil companies had used pipelines to exclude independents from the market, and that common carrier pipeline transportation was already available in Champlin's area to all independents who desired it, the court majority refused to bring under the act the line of an independent "whose presence fosters competition in markets heavily blanketed by large 'majors.' " *Ibid.*, p. 298.

primary purpose is still to define the act, not to evaluate market structure or performance.

Where, as in *Sinclair*,[53] *Pick* v. *General Motors*,[54] and *J. I. Case*, the courts can be convinced that exclusive dealing is essential to protect the good will attaching to a manufacturer's product, they will not condemn what is a necessary instrument for conducting competition. These considerations are relevant in applying the traditional criterion of reasonableness under the Sherman or Clayton Acts: the intent, in such cases, is to compete rather than to exclude. Competition of this kind could not raise an inference of reasonable probability of harm to competition.

In contrast, the contractual provisions at issue in *Standard of California, Richfield, American Can, International Salt,* and even *National City Lines* were, on their face, manifestly exclusionary. Nor were they necessary; most economically legitimate benefits could have been achieved without the imposition of restrictive, exclusive clauses. Their condemnation therefore required a far lighter demonstration of competitive impact than in, say, the vertical integration cases, *Columbia Steel* and *Yellow Cab*.

Price Discrimination

Unlike the developments in antitrust law elsewhere, those involving price discrimination are overshadowed by statutory changes that have in some measure altered the original character of the law itself. The Robinson-Patman Act is one of the most tortuous legislative pronouncements ever to go on the statute books. It attempts to deal explicitly with minute details of business practice, such as cost accounting, the use of demonstrators, advertising allowances, and brokers, in order to bolster its broad and multitudinous purposes. Numerous qualifying clauses set up innumerable permutations and combinations of hypothetical legal situations involving relations of subsections to each other, so that, even before the Federal Trade Commission had time to undertake enforcement activity, various authorities including Representative Wright Patman himself had no difficulty what-

[53] *F.T.C.* v. *Sinclair Refining Co.*, 261 U.S. 463 (1923).

[54] 80 F.2d 641 (1935), affirmed *per curiam* 291 U.S. 3 (1936).

ever in writing treatises on the meaning of this one amendment to a single section of the Clayton Act.

It would therefore be impossible, and in view of the purpose of this book and the volume of literature on this specialized subject undesirable, to attempt in a few pages to reconsider all the possible implications of the Robinson-Patman Act. Our analysis is confined to tracing the development of those elements which are said to be typical of the new Sherman Act in all its aspects: the tendency of the Commission and the courts to adopt pure competition as a standard; to outlaw certain practices per se, regardless of intent or general consequences; to circumscribe the activities of large, integrated firms. We reserve for Part II a detailed consideration of the economic consequences of the cases, which the commentators have relatively neglected in favor of a welter of vague charges of "soft competition," based on textual analyses of sometimes ineptly phrased court and Commission opinions.

The *Morton Salt* decision, as we have seen, appeared to relieve the F.T.C.[55] of the responsibility of finding, before the Commission condemned it, that a price discrimination would probably impair competition. The same line of reasoning made the mere possibility of injury to competitors as valid a basis for condemnation as injury to competition generally. Section 2(a) of the act outlaws discrimination whose effect may be merely "to injure, destroy, or prevent competition with any person who either grants or knowingly receives the benefit of such discrimination. . . ." Since impact on a particular competitor is easier to hypothesize than effect on an industry, it appeared after *Morton Salt* that the road was open for the Commission to eliminate virtually all price discrimination. Two obstacles stood in the way. Section 2(b) of the Robinson-Patman Act provides that a prima-facie case can be rebutted by a showing that a discrimination was made in good faith to meet an equally low price of a competitor. And in Section 2(a), concessions that merely reflect

[55] By agreement between the Commission and the Department of Justice, enforcement of all but the moribund criminal Section 3 of the Robinson-Patman Act has been left to the former agency.

differences in cost of manufacture, sale, or delivery are excepted from the category of illegal discriminations, even if competition is injured. The latter provision is entirely in keeping with the underlying assumption of all the antitrust laws, described in Chapter 2, that the true economies of large-scale operations (in contrast with the bargaining or strategic advantages) are not likely to threaten the survival of competition. (At the same time, the Robinson-Patman Act does not accept this assumption with complete confidence. Section 2(a) also authorizes the F.T.C. to fix maximum permissible quantity discount limits, regardless of cost justification, where it finds that purchasers able to qualify for larger discounts on cost grounds are so few "as to render differentials on account thereof unjustly discriminatory or promotive of monopoly." Also it permits only discounts justified by differences in cost of "manufacture, sale, or delivery," mainly because cost savings of other kinds are too difficult to measure.)

The Commission in the *Standard of Indiana* case attempted to reduce the good faith defense to a procedural vestige. The defense would suffice only to rebut the prima-facie case against a discrimination, it argued; a price discrimination that was demonstrated by "affirmative proof" to have injured or prevented competition, even if only with individuals, could be prohibited, whether or not it was in response to an offer of a competitor. The Supreme Court overruled the Commission on the point in 1951, even though, as the dissenting opinion pointed out, there is strong evidence that the framers of Robinson-Patman did not intend to have the good faith defense perpetuate undesirable patterns of discrimination.[56] The spate of bills introduced in every Congress since 1948, inspired first by the *Cement Institute* decision but thereafter by *Standard of Indiana* also, seeking first to revive the good faith defense and then to

[56] *Standard Oil Co.,* 41 F.T.C. 263, 281–282 (1945). The Supreme Court held that the Robinson-Patman Act did not "cut into the actual core of the defense. That still consists of the provision that wherever a lawful low price of a competitor threatens to deprive a seller of a customer, the seller, to retain that customer, may in good faith meet that lower price." *Standard Oil Co.* v. *F.T.C.,* 340 U.S. 231, 242 (1951).

make sure that no future Supreme Court will change its mind, suggests that the effort of the F.T.C. to emasculate this protective clause was bound to fail.

However, the status of the good faith defense is still by no means clear. The Supreme Court decision in *Standard of Indiana* merely sent the case back to the Commission to decide whether Standard's discounts did in fact represent a meeting of competition in good faith. The Commission has now decided that they did not. It says that a company cannot justify giving a discount over a long period of time to favored customers: the good faith defense applies only to meeting isolated, individual competitive offers.[57] Similarly, in the earlier *Minneapolis-Honeywell* case, even though conceding that the defendants had to grant the lower prices to individual customers in order to keep their business, the Commission denied that the good faith defense permitted continuously discriminatory pricing.[58] Having rescued the clause itself, the Supreme Court will doubtless have to decide one day whether, under the F.T.C.'s interpretation, any discrimination can qualify for its protection.

The Commission has had considerable success in diluting the cost-saving defense. In very few cases have proffered cost justifications been accepted. The Morton Salt Company failed to get support even for its discounts on carload deliveries, which obviously save money compared with smaller shipments.[59] In the

[57] *Standard Oil Co.,* Docket No. 4389, Modified Findings, Jan. 16, 1953, p. 18.

[58] In two instances it rejected the defense because it appeared that Honeywell had been bludgeoned into granting the discounts in order to induce customers to stop selling burners equipped with its devices at a higher price than those equipped with competitive controls. 44 F.T.C. 351 (1948), Dissent of Commissioner Mason, p. 402. The Commission eventually lost the *Honeywell* case in the courts, see p. 133, below, but only on the ground of insufficient injury to competition.

[59] The majority of the Circuit Court of Appeals, which overruled the F.T.C., said, "The quantity carload discount . . . was related by substantial and uncontroverted evidence to the cost of the sale and delivery. . . ." 162 F.2d 949, 957 (1947). The Supreme Court said, instead (and the minority did not contradict it), that the defendants had failed to offer a cost justification; the sole issue before the court was the competitive impact of the discrimination. 334 U.S. 37, 48 (1948).

Standard of Indiana decision, a cost-saving defense was rejected because it did not come up to the Commission's standards of cost accounting; it appeared to have been concocted only as an afterthought, for the purposes of the case. The fact remains that the favored customers performed certain wholesaling functions and therefore did save Standard some expense. In general, the Commission has rejected other cost defenses for the same reason —that they did not support directly the particular discrimination in question.

The severity with which the F.T.C. has treated cost-saving defenses creates a dilemma for a company that sells on a price list embodying established quantity discounts. In view of the Commission's position that the good faith defense applies only to sporadic discounts, such a seller probably could not use a good faith defense either. However, the Commission has shown a much more reasonable attitude toward discount schedules based on conscientious cost appraisals before the fact.[60]

As the Commission interpreted the law until recently, therefore, it appeared to have scuttled the rule of reason in favor of a blatantly per se approach to a practice that, in a milder age, would have been considered on its merits and in terms of its consequences.

The clamor aroused by the substantive views of the price discrimination decisions was heightened by an unfortunate administrative incompetence of the Federal Trade Commission. Its findings were often of little help in interpreting the facts or in assessing the validity of the contentions of the defendants in each case. Its orders frequently did little more than restate the vague language of the act, thus providing defendants with no more certain guide to future action than they had enjoyed in the past.[61]

When we turn, however, to the actual decisions, it is not clear

[60] See, for example, its *Minneapolis-Honeywell* decision, 44 F.T.C. 351 (1948), in which it accepted the cost-saving defense of some of the discounts at issue.

[61] See the opinion even of the Supreme Court majority in *Morton Salt,* 334 U.S. 37, 53–54 (1948), and the dissent of Justice Jackson in *F.T.C.* v. *Ruberoid Co.,* 343 U.S. 470, 482 (1952).

that they represent such a substantial deviation from the mainstream of legal doctrine as has often been represented. It is significant that even the dissenting justices agreed with the majority in the *Morton Salt* case that the quantity discount schedule other than the ten-cent concession on carload lots was illegal and unquestionably tended to lessen competition substantially.

It is the basing-point cases which have probably occasioned more hostile criticism than any other phase of the Commission's campaign against price discrimination. Yet, all of them except *Corn Products*[62] have turned correctly on the charge of conspiracy (under Sec. 5 of the F.T.C. Act "unfair competition" has now come to embrace restrictive agreements that suppress competition) or on a consideration of intent, in the form of an assessment of the good faith defense. Their condemnation of "conscious parallelism" is their only novel element.

The *Corn Products* decision was based on considerably more substantial proof of injury to competitors than sufficed in the later *Morton Salt* case. The rejection of the good faith defense in the companion *Staley* case[63] was justified by the same fact that has been crucial in all the others: delivered prices were matched industry-wide in order to eliminate price competition. Thus price discrimination was not the heart of any except the *Corn Products* case. It was novel to apply Section 2 to the use of price discrimination as a means of eliminating price competition between a group of defendant sellers, in contrast with the more familiar objects of attack, predatory price cutting or differentials in favor of big buyers. But the terms of the statute were clearly applicable; here was price discrimination that undoubtedly had the effect of lessening competition. In any case, this novelty must not obscure the fact that Section 5 was the primary basis of action in most of the basing-point cases, and that Section 1 of the Sherman Act would have done just as well.

The important point is that these decisions did not find price discrimination in the form of varying mill nets (by freight absorption) in violation of the Clayton Act. It is difficult to see how Justice Black, speaking for the Court in the *Cement Institute*

[62] *Corn Products Refining Co.* v. *F.T.C.*, 342 U.S. 726 (1945).
[63] *F.T.C.* v. *A. E. Staley Mfg. Co.*, 324 U.S. 746 (1945).

case, could have deduced from the *Staley* decision a rule forbidding "a seller to use a sales system which constantly results in his getting more money for like goods from some customers than he does from others." [64] The *Staley* opinion indicates that there is no illegal injury to buyers unless their *delivered* prices are continuously higher than those of competitors who are geographically less well situated:

> It does not follow that respondents may never absorb freight when their factory price plus actual freight is higher than their competitors' price, or that sellers, by so doing, may not maintain a uniform delivered price at all points of delivery, for in that event there is no discrimination in price.[65]

The leading treble-damage cases involving basing points or freight equalization have likewise turned, like *Corn Products* and *Staley,* on discrimination in delivered prices, not justified by cost.[66] In any event, the Supreme Court explicitly denied that the F.T.C.'s order in the *Cement* case could be construed as "bar[ring] an individual cement producer from selling cement at delivered prices such that its net return from one customer will be less than from another, even if the particular sale be made in good faith. . . ." [67] Despite the loud outcries that this decision had created great "confusion" among businessmen about the legality of individual, independent freight absorption, only three out of the fifty-five cement companies bound by it expressed the belief that the order forbade this practice, and thirty-seven advised the F.T.C. of their definite intention to absorb freight.[68] The Commission's explicit refusal to classify differing net receipts at the point of manufacture as price discriminations in the *National Lead* decision of 1953 should dispose once and for all of the hypothesis that the *Corn Products, Staley,* and

[64] *F.T.C.* v. *Cement Institute,* 333 U.S. 683, 725 (1948).

[65] 324 U.S. 746, 757 (1945).

[66] *Russellville Canning Co.* v. *American Can Co.,* 87 F.Supp. 484, 491–494 (1949), reversed 191 F.2d 38 (1951), and *Bruce's Juices* v. *American Can Co.,* 87 F.Supp. 985, 991 (1949), affirmed 187 F.2d 919 (1951).

[67] 333 U.S. 683, 727.

[68] Robert A. Wallace and Paul A. Douglas, "Antitrust Policies and the New Attack on the Federal Trade Commission," 19 *U. of Chicago Law Rev.* 697 (1952).

Cement decisions, taken together, outlawed differential mill net prices charged either by a single firm or an industry.[69] There is no threat in these decisions to freight absorption *employed as an instrument of competition.*

Of course, the collusive adoption of any pricing system is illegal. Hence, it was not unreasonable of the Commission to find that the glucose, steel, cement, and rigid steel conduit manufacturers were not competing in good faith when they systematically avoided all rivalry in their price quotations. The glucose industry had employed a single basing-point system for many years as a method of avoiding price competition.[70] It would be pointless to reiterate here the history of several decades of collusive efforts of the cement industry to the same end.[71] In steel and rigid steel conduit, similarly, the systems were highly developed techniques of avoiding price rivalry.[72]

These observations do not deny that real ambiguities in the law persist. In particular, the line may not be easy for an individual seller to draw between the precise matching of the delivered price of his competitors, which is required if he is to avail himself of the good faith clause (a ridiculously restrictive requirement), and the avoidance of "conscious parallelism." [73] The Supreme Court held in *Standard of Indiana* that a seller

[69] Docket No. 5253, Opinion of the Commission, Jan. 12, 1953, pp. 6–7.

[70] *In re Corn Products Co.,* Docket No. 5502, Memorandum to the Trial Examiner and Proposed Report and Findings as to the Facts, June 6, 1950, especially pp. 7–16. It was because of Staley's complete acceptance of Corn Products' Chicago basing point, without deviation, charging the full phantom freight where the customer was nearer its own Decatur plant than the Chicago base, that the Supreme Court unanimously denied its plea of good faith. 324 U.S. 746, 757 (1945).

[71] Stocking and Watkins, *Monopoly and Free Enterprise,* Chap. 7; see also Earl Latham, "Giantism and Basing Points: A Political Analysis," 58 *Yale Law J.* 383 (1949).

[72] See, e.g., Seager and Gulick, *Trust and Corporation Problems,* pp. 246–251, on the question whether the steel companies were competing in good faith in following Pittsburg Plus. See also *Triangle Conduit & Cable Co., Inc.,* v. *F.T.C.,* 168 F.2d 175 (1948); *American Iron & Steel Institute,* 48 F.T.C. 123 (1951).

[73] See pp. 66–67, above; also Austern, "Inconsistencies in the Law," *1951 Symposium,* pp. 158–159.

could meet only "the lawful lower price" of a competitor in a discriminatory manner. The requirement that a seller convince himself of the legality of the price he must meet (which may depend in turn on whether his competitor has done the same in meeting the price of some third party) may impose an impossible burden on him and in effect deny him the protection of the good faith clause.[74] However, this qualification was probably inserted in deference to the *Staley* decision; that company was not competing in good faith when it slavishly followed Corn Products' basing-point system. This is precisely the problem of the rule of reason—to differentiate bona fide competition from explicit or implicit collusion. As long as it would be harmful to competition to ban freight absorption or any other kind of discrimination per se, one must apply the test of intent: What was the company really doing when it absorbed freight, competing or avoiding competition? We have seen no evidence that the Commission or courts applied it incorrectly in the basing-point cases. We know of no instance where the Commission has proceeded against an individual firm for absorbing freight.[75]

Lawyers defending basing-point systems have asserted that under the "conscious parallelism" doctrine any two sellers quoting the same discriminatory price are vulnerable to an adverse order under Section 5 of the Federal Trade Commission Act or Section 2 of the Clayton Act. The dilemma is a real one, but its existence is a necessary part of a policy of maintaining competition. Especially as elaborated in *National Lead*,[76] the doctrine

[74] See note 56, above, and Austern, in *1951 Symposium*, pp. 166–168.

[75] See also Stocking, "The Law on Basing Point Pricing: Confusion or Competition," 2 *Jour. Public Law* 20 and *passim* (1953).

[76] In this case, the Commission appeared to be making it very difficult for conscientious unconscious parallelers. It inferred the existence of a price-fixing conspiracy mainly from the fact that the defendants followed a zone-pricing system, producing uniform delivered prices, and the fact that some of them sold their products through agents, to prevent resale price cutting. It then proceeded to prohibit not merely further conspiracy, but conscious parallelism itself: each of the defendants was ordered to stop quoting prices pursuant to a zone-delivered price system with the effect of systematically matching other sellers' delivered prices. Docket No. 5253, Order, Jan. 12, 1953, pp. 2–3. See also the dissenting opinion of Commissioner Mason and pp. 128–129, below.

has two parts. It requires the defendants to refrain from collusion. It insists that they act like price competitors. This last is difficult, perhaps impossible, to enforce. But it is hardly consistent for self-proclaimed advocates of hard competition or workable competition to attack the Commission when, in desperation, it refuses to countenance the continued employment by a tightly knit industry of a method of systematically avoiding price competition. Moreover, is not the Commission justified, in our free enterprise system, in refraining from formulating detailed prescriptions of acceptable pricing patterns? The success of its cement order [77] testifies to the fact that the ingenuity of American business is just as great in devising alternatives to illegal pricing systems as in constructing the systems themselves.

The novelty in the conscious parallelism doctrine, as actually applied, has been greatly exaggerated. Long ago, in the trade association cases of the 1920's, the Supreme Court inferred price-fixing conspiracy from the actions of sellers who had admittedly collaborated in certain ways. As Justice Stone said, in the *Interstate Circuit* case:

> It taxes credulity to believe that the several distributors would, in the circumstances, have accepted and put into operation with substantial unanimity such far-reaching changes in their business methods without some understanding that all were to join, and we reject as beyond the range of probability that it was the result of mere chance.[78]

A similar conclusion was entirely justified by the evidence of the cement and rigid steel conduit industries. Even in *National Lead,* the condemned pricing pattern was not the simple consequence of noncollusive oligopoly. Commissioner Mason, dissenting, considered the direct evidence of conspiracy flimsy, and it was. Yet he did not dispute the majority's contention that the defendants had discussed a zone pricing system and consignment selling at meetings held to formulate an N.R.A. Code, had exchanged maps of freight equalization zones, and that these dis-

[77] See release of the Attorney General, Aug. 27, 1953, announcing the dropping of the antitrust suit against the cement industry on the ground that the pricing practices of the industry had greatly improved.

[78] 306 U.S. 208, 223 (1939).

cussions had contributed to the subsequent adoption of these practices. His major quarrel with this evidence was that it was inappropriate for the government to "prosecute in '53 for what it spent millions in '33 to accomplish. . . ." [79] None of this is to deny, as we shall point out in Chapter 7, that the primary cause of the noncompetitive pricing pattern was the industry's structure itself—notably the dominant position of National, built up by a long series of mergers over the period 1899–1930.

In what case, then, has really pure conscious parallelism, without exchanges of price information, freight books, freight equalization zone maps, and other methods of collaboration been condemned? If the answer is "none," as we believe is the case, the inference of anticompetitive agreement from uniform pricing that could not possibly be the consequence of either coincidence or bona fide price competition represents a real procedural strengthening of the law but hardly a revolutionary substantive alteration that conflicts with the requirements of hard competition. It represents a procedural strengthening in two ways: it reduces the need for direct evidence of conspiracy, which may be increasingly difficult to find as businessmen become more sophisticated about leaving evidence around and as the pattern of noncompetitive pricing becomes habitual. And it increases the effective range of remedies; in an industry which has settled upon a consistent noncompetitive pattern of pricing, it may be futile to prohibit only future collaboration; instead it may be necessary to forbid each individual seller to follow the system thereafter.[80]

The proceedings against the A & P Company by the Antitrust Division and against Automatic Canteen Company by the Federal Trade Commission [81] struck down discriminatory tactics as old as the antitrust laws themselves. A & P's local price discrimination would have been as illegal under the old Clayton (if not Sherman) as under the new Sherman Act. Nor was it an

[79] Docket no. 5253, Dissenting Opinion, Jan. 12, 1953, p. 9.

[80] See Stocking, in 2 *Jour. Public Law* 2–4 (1953) and the Commission's *National Lead* Opinion, Jan. 12, 1953, pp. 9–12.

[81] 46 F.T.C. 861 (1950); reversed on Sec. 2(f), *Automatic Canteen Co. v. F.T.C.*, 346 U.S. 61 (1953).

unheard-of extension of the boundaries of antitrust to make illegal the exertion of pressure on suppliers by A & P and Automatic Canteen to get discriminatory concessions. In his classic treatise on *Unfair Competition,* published in 1915, W. H. S. Stevens discusses as a matter of course the possible illegalities of coercion by a big buyer.[82] Discriminatory rates secured by powerful shippers were the most important single evil that Congress sought to curb when it passed the Interstate Commerce Act in 1887. Hence we can scarcely subscribe to the theory that the antitrust authorities were fabricating a novel offense, or that the Robinson-Patman Act represents a dangerous deviation from historic antitrust policy in moving against either of these two types of price discrimination. The only significant issue, which we discuss in Part II, is whether the threat to competition inherent in these practices was sufficiently serious to warrant condemnation, in view of the desirability of having buyers large and small bargain for low prices to pass on to the consumer.

Technically, the Automatic Canteen case differed from the others mentioned so far because it was brought under Section 2(f) rather than 2(a) of the Robinson-Patman Act—a section directed against the buyer who knowingly induces or receives illegal discounts, rather than the seller. Some lawyers have pretended that the Commission was taking the position in this case that every buyer violates Section 2(f) if he accepts a discount the seller cannot justify.[83] The Supreme Court, which reversed the Commission and the Circuit Court, seemed to fear a similar consequence: that, as interpreted by the Commission, Section 2(f) would require the *buyer* to prove cost saving by the *seller.*[84] In leaving the reader with the impression that here was another instance of the Federal Trade Commission threatening to impose an impossibly unfair burden on any and all businessmen inter-

[82] See his Chap. 7.

[83] Austern, in *1951 Symposium,* p. 165, and Madison, in *1952 Symposium,* p. 111 n. 16.

[84] The court decided it would place an intolerable burden on the buyer to require him to rebut the prima-facie case under Sec. 2(f), as sellers must do in Sec. 2(a), by proving that the discounts were justified by cost savings—even though, as the minority pointed out, Sec. 2(b) seems to stipulate such a procedure.

ested only in buying economically, the majority of the court ignored the flagrantly coercive tactics of the defendants. As Commissioner Mason had pointed out, speaking for the Commission (and not himself alone!) the officers and agents of Automatic were not only fully aware they were getting discriminatory discounts but, like A & P, insisted on them. It does not seem reasonable to suppose that in other cases, the F.T.C. would impose (or would be permitted by the courts to impose) arbitrary burdens of proof even on dominant buyers who had made good faith efforts to ascertain that their lower prices (if not made in response to competitive offers) were justified by lower costs.[85]

There were, however, two cases where the Commission took unreasonable advantage of the temptation offered by *Morton Salt;* in both it has been reversed. Evidence of illegal competitive impact at the selling level was deduced in the *Minneapolis-Honeywell* case from the mere fact that a dominant competitor succeeded in getting and holding customers by offering quantity discounts. The Commission also seemed to take the view in this case that any discount large enough to be worth giving or getting is sufficiently injurious to competition among buyers to bring it afoul of the law.[86] In its treatment of functional discounts in the *Standard of Indiana* case (as in several earlier cases), the Commission held that the allowances to which a buyer is entitled depend upon the role he plays as a seller rather than upon the upstream functions he performs (except to the extent that he can demonstrate a cost justification). Thus, integrated wholesaler-retailers of gasoline in competition with other (nonintegrated) retailers were to be permitted only the retailers' discount on that part of their purchases sold at retail, regardless of the wholesaling functions they performed. The Commission did insert a proviso in its order permitting discounts that make only due allowance for

[85] This was precisely the conclusion of the lower court. 194 F.2d 433, 439 (1952).

[86] See note 58, above. Particularly frivolous was the Commission's objection to Honeywell's basing its discounts in contracts negotiated yearly in advance on the buyer's estimated purchases (based primarily on purchases in the preceding year), which sometimes permitted customers during a single year to get discounts larger than proved to be justified as the year progressed.

cost saving. But even apart from the difficulty of making a cost defense that will satisfy the Commission, the order still denies to integrated jobbers whatever discounts the market will allow.

In addition to selling at retail themselves, some of Standard's wholesaler customers sold to price-cutting retailers; to prevent the resultant "injury" to other retailers, the Commission put itself in the ridiculous position of ordering Standard to require its wholesalers to police their retail customers.[87] There was an alternative; Standard might have been required to make gasoline available at equal rates to anyone with the same facilities (i.e., performing the same upstream function) as the favored jobbers.

The F.T.C. is not necessarily required by the Robinson-Patman Act to limit functional discounts to demonstrable cost saving. It could equally well decide that there is no price discrimination when a company charges a different price for gasoline f.o.b. marine terminal or tank car than it charges for gasoline delivered in a tank wagon after being stored in a bulk plant. If instead the Commission interprets the Robinson-Patman Act as requiring every functional discount to meet the requirement that it mirror cost savings and nothing more, it is assuming the power to regulate practically every price in the economy. The Commission's fundamental error, repeated in its latest modified findings, was to contend that Standard was discriminating simply because there was a difference between its tank-wagon price to conventional service stations and its jobber prices, or between *its* tank-wagon price and the one charged by its independent wholesaler customers to *their* retail customers.

Without going into the subtleties of the brokerage section (2c) of the Robinson-Patman Act,[88] we can find a parallel be-

[87] See Note, "The Swinging Door—or How to Obey One Antitrust Law by Violating Another," 59 *Yale Law J.* 158 (1949). In its modified order of 1953, the F.T.C. eliminated the resale price maintenance requirement and ordered Standard to reduce its tank-wagon price (to its retailer customers) if it discovered that a wholesaler customer was undercutting it on sales to other retailers. For a similar proposed order see the *Sylvania* case, F.T.C. Docket No. 5728, Initial Decision, Dec. 9, 1953.

[88] We have argued elsewhere, in "The Integration and Dissolution of the A & P Company," 29 *Indiana Law J.* 9, n. 28 (1953), in "Antitrust Law and the Big Buyer: Another Look at the A & P Case," 60 *J. Pol. Econ.* 130–

tween the handicap it imposes on the vertically integrated buyer and those the Commission sought to impose in *Standard of Indiana*. In the latter, the F.T.C. exhibited no interest in the possibility that independent wholesalers might be offering effective competition to the conventional distribution system by cutting the spread between refinery and final customer. And in recent cases where it has applied Section 2(c), prohibiting groups of retailers from collecting from suppliers the brokerage they save them by purchasing direct, it has impeded aggressive groups of buyers attempting to buck a stratified distribution system.[89]

However, in both the courts and the Commission itself the tide is clearly turning, and we shall consider in Chapters 7 and 8 the question whether it may not have carried some legitimate values out to sea. The fate of the *Minneapolis-Honeywell* decision on appeal suggests that the F.T.C. must make a convincing showing at least of potential effect on competitors of seller or buyers.[90] The Supreme Court's reinvigoration of the good faith clause in *Standard of Indiana,* while by no means clarifying the issue, further mitigates the apparent trend toward the blanket prohibition of price differentiation per se. A majority of the Commission would now clearly reverse its long campaign against the pricing policies followed by Standard of Indiana. A similar relaxation of the former opposition to price differentiation between different classes of customers as a method of competition is indicated by the final decision of the pre-Eisenhower Commission in the *Spark Plug* cases, which rejected the staff's contention that competition was injured by differences between prices charged

---

131 (1952), and in 61 *J. Pol. Econ.* 445 (1953) that the brokerage clause had some justification in a program of preventing unfair price discrimination.

[89] See the *Carpel Frosted Foods* and the *Independent Grocers Alliance Distributing Company* decisions, Docket No. 5482, Dec. 13, 1951, and Docket No. 5433, March 17, 1952; the latter was sustained, 203 F.2d 941 (1953).

[90] Of the members of the Supreme Court, only Justice Black, it appears from his dissent (though the dismissal of *certiorari* turned on the finding that the petition had not been timely), was entirely prepared to accept the Commission's flimsy evidence of injury to competition. 344 U.S. 206, 214 (1952), cf. p. 217. See also the opinion of an F.T.C. trial examiner virtually repeating *Morton Salt,* in the *Purex* case, May 11, 1954.

to auto manufacturers on original equipment and to distributors for replacement plugs.[91]

Finally, Chairman Howrey has appointed a committee to study the cost-saving defense in the hope of developing cost-accounting standards that businessmen may actually be able to use in fixing their discounts and defending them before the Commission.[92]

Conclusion

In this chapter, as in the one preceding, we have attempted to determine the extent to which the antitrust enforcement agencies have deviated from the historic path of the law, from the assessment of business practices required by the rule of reason. Certain practices have come to be summarily condemned—notably collusive and predatory price discrimination, discounts coercively extracted by big buyers, and exclusive arrangements whose major purpose is to shut out competitors. However, these practices might legitimately have been attacked by the Federal Trade Commission or the Department of Justice even within the context of the old Sherman Act. Chief Justice White would probably have found them unreasonable in 1911, though he would doubtless have insisted on more convincing evidences of market consequences than now suffice to condemn.

[91] *Champion Spark Plug Co.,* Docket No. 3977, and companion cases against Electric Auto-Lite Co. and AC Spark Plug Co., Docket Nos. 5624 and 5620, Findings, July 10, 1953.

[92] In December 1953, a hearing examiner dismissed the four-and-one-half-year-old complaint against B. F. Goodrich after Commission attorneys had stipulated that all the disputed discounts were justified by cost except those covering ½ of 1 per cent of the total sales. Docket No. 5677, Initial Decision, Dec. 10, 1953. Similarly, the *Sylvania* Initial Decision foreshadows the Commission's willingness to accept cost analyses that justify rather substantial concessions to big buyers. It illustrates, too, the absurdity of the Robinson-Patman requirement that unless the cost justification is perfectly matched by the discrimination, all price differences must be erased. Although a survey revealed that in many cases price differences were less as well as more than the higher cost of marketing tubes to the Sylvania distributors, the examiner required that all sales to Philco for resale should henceforth be made at prices identical with those charged the small distributors. Nevertheless, the way is left open for Sylvania to adopt a price list that exactly mirrors the cost difference. Docket No. 5728, Dec. 9, 1953.

On the other hand, insofar as the Federal Trade Commission has shown hostility to price discrimination as a bona fide method of competition, as in the *Minneapolis-Honeywell* and *Standard of Indiana* cases, it has definitely deviated from the historic rule of reason, though the obscurities of the Robinson-Patman Act are partially responsible. Likewise essentially anticompetitive is the Commission's hostility to functional discounts in those cases where the vertically integrated recipients take advantage of their combination of functions to cut prices.

As far as exclusive dealing and related practices are concerned, there has been some disposition on the part of the courts to push them into the category of per se offenses, again with the F.T.C. until recently following enthusiastically. But the heart of the offense is, as it has always been, the employment of exclusive tactics, not the voluntary adoption of reasonable contractual relationships which happen incidentally to "exclude" competitors.

Thus there is no necessary conflict in the law as it has developed with respect to tie-ins and full requirements contracts, on the one hand, and vertical integration on the other. The act of integrating vertically, even if by merger, is not necessarily an act of foreclosing, as Justice Jackson used the term in the *International Salt* decision. The underlying intent is seldom clearly exclusionary. It may have other, socially acceptable purposes and consequences. Only if market leverage is exerted to force the transaction or, after the merger has occurred, to put competitors at an unreasonable disadvantage is a similar condemnation legally or economically justified.

Critics of the *Columbia Steel* and second *Yellow Cab* decisions, on the one hand, and of *Standard of California* and *National City Lines,* on the other, join in a plea that it is inconsistent to permit a firm to do by financial acquisition what it may not do by contract.[93] The criticism has considerable force. It supports the

[93] See the dissent of Justice Douglas in the *Standard* case; and Adelman, "Not the incidence of objectionable market control, but the adventitious possibility of forcing a situation into a familiar legal mold, controls our antitrust policy." 61 *Harv. Law Rev.* 1349 (1948). Our own argument is, precisely, a defense of these "familiar legal molds" on both ethical and economic grounds.

logic of the 1950 amendment to Section 7 of the Clayton Act or of proposed amendments to prohibit market structures deemed excessively monopolistic.

But in obscuring the distinction between "exclusion" by integration and exclusion by contracts imposed by dominant sellers who refuse to do business in any other way, the critics, whether of the right or left, ignore the fact that investment, involving the inevitable risks of ownership, cannot be equated at law with the exclusion resulting from coercion. Nor are the economic aspects of the two phenomena the same. If big business is to be denied the right to produce for its own needs or do its own marketing, to make use of some by-product idea or material in a new field, or simply to enter some new market, the consequences may very well be economically undesirable. Such integration is a prime source of economic progress and effective competition. On the other hand, it is extremely doubtful that a similar economic defense exists for the achievement of differential advantages by the coercion of suppliers into granting discriminatory preferences or of customers into accepting exclusionary arrangements. We discuss these economic questions more fully in Part II.

From the point of view of those who would apply economic tests to all antitrust issues, we have been guilty of advocating a double standard. The different treatment accorded by the Supreme Court to *Standard of California* and *Columbia Steel* is a reflection of that double standard. But from the point of view of the traditional antitrust standards, the decisions are not inconsistent. In both the crucial legal question asked was: What were the contracting parties doing or trying to do? not the merely economic one: How will what they are proposing to do affect market performance? It is in connection with the first question only, not the second, that the law would investigate the anticipated effects of, say, a merger on efficiency. The new Sherman Act, like the old, turns primarily on the actions under consideration. And the actions which are forbidden are collusion and exclusion.

Of course, the law has been strengthened, partly under pressure of an active Department of Justice. It impinges upon business activities more than ever before. Well over half of the antitrust proceedings to date have been launched in the last twenty years of the statute's sixty-year life. But there is little to show that the area of per se violation has been substantially extended beyond the area it occupied, conceptually, when Judge Hand wrote the *Corn Products* opinion in 1916 or when the *Reading* case was handed down by the Supreme Court in 1920. *U.S. Steel* (1920) and *United Shoe Machinery* (1918) have to some extent been supplanted. But almost every student admits that these decisions represented the nadir of antitrust legal doctrine. They were probably not good law even when they were handed down.[94]

[94] If Justices McReynolds and Brandeis had been able to sit on both cases, the decisions would certainly have gone the other way.

PART II

An Economic Appraisal of the New Antitrust Policy

CHAPTER 5

Business Integration and Monopoly

LARGE businesses and integration are necessary agencies and inevitable manifestations of a free enterprise system. The firm that competes successfully must be permitted to grow; by the same token, businesses must ordinarily be free to expand if they think they can in this way enhance their ability to serve the customer. Competition requires also that business units be free, ordinarily, to take on new products, new functions, or enter new markets—in short, to integrate.

Under what circumstances may business size and integration constitute a menace to the economy? As far as size alone is concerned, the danger is a familiar and obvious one: the firm may be so large, relative to the total market for the products it sells or buys, that it can exploit its customers or suppliers. The theory underlying the antitrust laws is that except in certain unusual kinds of industries (the public utilities) monopoly will not become a serious problem so long as businessmen are prevented from engaging in collusive or exclusive tactics that suppress or subvert the competitive process. One of the questions we sought to answer in Chapter 3, where we considered antitrust cases involving companies whose size had been "magnified to the point at which it amounts to a monopoly," [1] was whether their growth was no more than the consequence and manifestation of the survival of the competitively fittest or, following the antitrust hy-

[1] *U.S.* v. *Swift & Co.,* 286 U.S. 106, 116 (1932).

pothesis, of monopolization. Our conclusion was that the monopolists convicted during the last ten years have not had their monopolies "thrust upon them" and were not therefore condemned merely because they had been such successful competitors that they stood alone in their fields.

Dangers Inherent in Integration

The only condition necessary for integration to raise the possibility of abuse is the existence of substantial imperfections of competition in some of the fields in which an integrated company operates. The very fact that a company sells in a number of markets, or fulfills a number of functions, in some of which it is subjected to weaker competitive pressures than in others, gives it a leverage and a staying power in its more highly competitive operations that have nothing to do with its relative efficiency there. (It also presumably suffers a handicap in its less competitive operations, compared with nonintegrated firms engaged only in those operations. But its handicaps are the handicaps of "less opulence," rather than the kind of extreme penury to which its less fortunately situated nonintegrated competitors may be subject.) The more favorable access to scarce raw materials that a vertically integrated company may enjoy is merely one variant of the general case, springing from imperfections of competition in the supply of these materials.[2] Similarly, the advantage enjoyed by a company with an accepted brand, when it undertakes the sale of some new product, may be entirely strategic, resting simply on the limited ability of consumers to judge quality without looking at the trade mark. And the elimination of competitors from a market opportunity that inevitably results from the absorption of a customer by a supplier confers a strategic advantage on the integrating firm, entirely apart from any resulting saving in cost, to the extent that market outlets for nonintegrated suppliers are appreciably constricted as a result.

[2] See, e.g., Celler Committee, *The Iron and Steel Industry,* p. 33. In a buyer's market the advantage may, of course, lie with the nonintegrated competitor. See the experience of Republic Steel, *ibid.,* p. 29. But again, the disadvantage to the integrated company at such times takes the form only

If access to the operations conferring such strategic advantages were equally available to all competitors, no unfairness or danger of an extension of monopoly to the more competitive areas would enter. But inequity may be introduced by mere inequality in the ability of integrated and nonintegrated companies to attract capital. This inequality tends to be cumulative; by accentuating the relatively low earning power of the nonintegrated companies, it reinforces the reluctance to invest. It would not follow from the fact that only similarly integrated companies might be able to compete with the dominant firms in aluminum, motion picture production and exhibition, and petroleum refining that integration is the more efficient way of doing business, in the social sense. The nonintegrated aluminum fabricator, motion picture exhibitor, oil marketer, or potential producer of tetraethyl of lead might suffer only the strategic disadvantage of less adequate access to supplies or markets.[3] So integration that links together competitive areas with others in which competition is already seriously defective accomplishes by financial consolidation something very much like what is accomplished by the tie-in prohibited by Section 3 of the Clayton Act: it permits the use of market power in one area to create competitive advantages unrelated to efficiency in others.

The relationship between the American Telephone and Telegraph Company and its wholly owned subsidiary, Western Electric Company, by which the latter enjoys the exclusive right to supply the Bell System with many kinds of equipment, illustrates how integration may pose a threat to competition when one of the markets in which the integrated company sells is insulated from competition. Studies by the Federal Communications Commission showed that there was a distinct tendency for Western Electric to charge its parent prices yielding a much higher profit than it could earn on items sold in open competition with

of lower profits; the disadvantage to the nonintegrated, when supplies are scarce, may drive it out of business.

[3] Cf. Adelman's attempt to reduce the argument that one branch of a vertically integrated firm may subsidize another to a demonstration of nothing more than the "economies of integration." *1951 Symposium*, pp. 141–142; also in 63 *Harv. Law Rev.* 28–30, 34, 52–53 (1949).

other manufacturers of telephone equipment.[4] A Federal District Court found a similar practice consistently followed by the United Shoe Machinery Company:

> United has followed, as between machine types, a discriminatory pricing policy. . . . These sharp and relatively durable differentials are traceable, at least in large part, to United's policy of fixing a higher rate of return where competition is of minor significance, and a lower rate of return where competition is of major significance.[5]

In the case of one machine it reduced its charges progressively when competition was strong and raised them after its major competitor had lost ground in the market.[6] The A & P Company, too, by accepting very low returns or losses for long periods of time in localities where it faced severe competition, while counting on earnings elsewhere to carry the weak retail Units or Divisions, used integration to enhance its competitive position.

Obviously, any company that is integrated horizontally, vertically, or "circularly" will earn divergent rates of return on its various operations. These divergences are the inevitable consequence of varying pressures of competition in different markets. They are not dependent upon company policy. It would be absurd therefore to condemn all such instances of varying profits in which the more profitable operations may be said to subsidize the less profitable.

Nevertheless, the problem of public policy created by these strategic advantages cannot be exorcised merely by demonstrating the absurdity of attacking them whenever and wherever they appear.[7] Integration does put into the hands of its beneficiaries a

[4] *Proposed Report Telephone Investigation,* pp. 326, 382–383. In 1935, for example, Western Electric realized a profit of 42.0 per cent on the cost of panel equipment but lost 37.4 per cent on bare and covered copper wire.

[5] 110 F.Supp. 295, 340–341 (1953).

[6] *Ibid.*, p. 326.

[7] "The trial staff is saying . . . a loss or *even a smaller profit,* in one part of a business implies 'subsidization' from elsewhere in the business. . . .

"To avoid all such subsidization, every phase of a business would have to operate on a cost-plus basis with identical profit margins. . . ." Hansen and Smith, "The Champion Case: What Is Competition?" 29 *Harv. Bus. Rev.*, May 1951, 91.

It is surely just as ridiculous and "anticompetitive" to deny the possibility and danger of "subsidization" (to take an extreme case, Standard Oil

lever which they can use to pry their way into and extend their control over competitive markets. This competitive leverage inherent in integration may appear in a number of possible forms and be exerted in a number of possible ways. (Most of these practices may be employed by any wealthy competitor, integrated or not.) The integrated firm may deliberately "manipulate its margins" so as to exert pressures on nonintegrated rivals more severe than they can cope with, even though their efficiency in the one field they operate in may be superior to that of the integrated unit. Indeed, the latter's margins will inevitably be manipulated as it takes its profits where it can get them and accepts lower returns where competition leaves it no alternative. The more profitable operations thus inevitably subsidize those in the more competitive fields. The subsidy permits a competitive "squeeze," the most dramatic instances of which arise out of vertical integration.

Apart from their denials of the alleged facts, the answers of U.S. Steel executives to allegations before the Celler Committee concerning the unusual profitability of the company's transportation and ore operations failed to meet the merits of the squeeze contentions. They pointed out that independents had access to railroads other than those owned by U.S. Steel—but the rates were identical. They argued that their major competitors were similarly integrated—but the complaints came from the nonintegrated steel makers. They said it was unrealistic to consider the prices and profits in mining and transportation separately from the consolidated profits and end prices of their integrated operations. Nevertheless, to the nonintegrated steel makers, who must operate within the margins fixed by these intermediate prices, the implied profits are anything but fictional.[8]

Similar allegations have been inveterate in the oil industry: that the integrated companies are enabled by their high profits in crude production to carry on subsidized competition in re-

---

of New Jersey subsidized cutthroat competition in certain areas by keeping prices higher elsewhere; so did Alcoa when it applied the squeeze on fabricators) as to attack all "subsidization" per se.

[8] Celler Committee, *The Iron and Steel Industry,* pp. 31–42. For documentation of other price and availability squeezes in steel since World War II, see F.T.C., *Monopolistic Practices and Small Business,* pp. 22–31, 50–54.

fining and marketing; that they are willing to do so in order to control the market and thus to protect the crude oil price.

Prior to 1939, certainly, some of the major oil companies were quite frank to say that marketing and refining were mere appendages of their production investment, and that it was much more important that crude oil revenues be assured than that a profit be earned on other branches of the business. A Gulf Oil vice-president was quoted as saying, "Refineries, you use them to get rid of your crude." A Texas Company prospectus said that the marketing department's "primary function" was to provide "assured outlet for the products of the corporation's subsidiaries. . . ." [9] There seems to be little doubt that marketing investments were not very profitable for a fifteen year period before World War II.

This abuse of integration would not necessarily result in a higher end price for petroleum products than would otherwise prevail; the squeeze on refining and marketing margins (ignoring the probably excessive costs of marketing in this period) means a low price for those functions. However, such a technique, by limiting access of new firms to the level where competition is subsidized and by assuring (or attempting to assure) "orderly marketing" of products at posted prices, minimizes the danger of price rivalry that might otherwise be reflected back into the market for crude. When the purchase of crude oil is confined to a small number of buyers whose heaviest financial stake is in the production of crude itself, the result is likely to be not exploitation of producers but a higher and more stable price than would otherwise prevail. The integrated producer-purchasers of iron ore apparently operate in the same way.[10] Unless the integrated oil companies were making a mistake in integrating and pricing as they did, it would seem to follow that the losses suffered from the lower returns taken to assure a profitable market for crude must have been more than offset by the higher returns on crude assured in this fashion.

In strict logic, one may maintain that the root cause of inequity

[9] T.N.E.C., *Hearings,* Pt. 16 (1939), p. 9153.

[10] L. Gregory Hines, "Price Determination in the Lake Erie Iron Ore Market," 41 *Amer. Econ. Rev.* 650 (1951).

and possible monopoly power issuing from integration is the imperfection of competition in the less workably competitive field that the integrated firm operates in, rather than the integration that ties this operation to others. It is the absence of competition in the supply of telephone service that confers on Western Electric the power both to exploit telephone subscribers and to carry on unfair competition in unsheltered markets. With pure competition in the telephone business, there would be no cause for concern about vertical integration.

However, it obviously does not follow, as J. J. Spengler and others have suggested, that corrective government intervention may therefore properly be directed only against the offending stratum.[11] Where the imperfection is not remediable except at excessive cost (if, for example, it springs from a patent, a natural monopoly, or inexpansibility of supply of some raw material), there may be no practical alternative to attacking instead the financial tie-in which permits one firm to carry the advantages over into other fields. The inelasticity of supply alone confers an advantage on the industrial firm producing its own materials, both in time of inflation and in the long run in an expanding economy facing increasing costs in raw material output. The preferential access that it enjoys, i.e., the vertical integration itself, may be the only imperfection of competition involved. Thus Spengler's prescription (introducing more competition into the imperfectly competitive horizontal stratum rather than condemning vertical integration) represents a counsel of perfection. Were it possible to have an unlimited number of taxi franchises, first-run movie houses, or telephone companies, the exclusive arrangement between a supplier and one of these outlets would be unobjectionable. Were there no scarcity in the supply of Bing Crosby movies, pipelines, iron ore, or desirable sites for generating electric power, the exclusive link of a purchaser with a supplier would not impair competition at the buyer's level. But, given such imperfections, it is the vertical integration which may extend them to otherwise competitive strata.

[11] Spengler, in 58 *J. Pol. Econ.* 347 (1950); Hale, in 49 *Columbia Law Rev.* 940–941, 946–947, 952 (1949).

In addition to arguing that it is unnecessary to destroy vertical integration in order to eliminate its dangers, Spengler has contended that it is undesirable to do so. He has demonstrated that where there are imperfections of horizontal competition imposing monopolistic surcharges in any of the intermediate markets through which materials pass before being sold to the ultimate consumer, vertical integration will make it profitable for the seller in the final market to charge lower prices than before. Thus vertical integration fulfills an important role in restricting the exploitation of the final buyer by suppliers of intermediate materials; and the consumer can only benefit if suppliers with monopoly power are merged with customers downstream. It would seem to follow, conversely, that vertical integration cannot increase total monopoly power. The degree of monopoly depends upon the number of competing sellers within a given horizontal stratum. Each monopolist presumably charges what the traffic will bear in his stratum. The vertical joining of strata cannot lead to more exploitation of the final buyer than before.

However, if a downstream monopolist prices on a cost-plus basis before merging, as most businesses actually do (or if it is restricted to such a pricing formula by a regulatory commission), a supplier who gains control of that customer may thenceforth be in a position to insert a monopoly surcharge *where none existed before,* and see it passed on to the consumer. The supplying firm is particularly likely to do so if the financial interest of its managers in the downstream affiliate is less than in the manufacturing end of the business. The "Spengler effect" occurs only to the extent intermediate goods are passed between affiliates at cost. But this is not the common practice.[12] So one can hardly doubt that the customer ultimately paid in higher fares for the vertical integration at issue in the *Yellow Cab* case,

[12] Most integrated oil companies, thus, transfer crude oil, pipeline services, and refined products from one division to another, not at cost, but at some approximation to the price the downstream division would have to pay if it were not integrated—a price which therefore includes the very "monopolistic surcharges" which, according to Spengler, vertical integration eliminates from the formulation of the ultimate price.

when, after the transfer of financial control, the taxicab-operating companies began to buy the higher-priced cabs of the acquiring manufacturer exclusively.

Similarly, it would hardly suffice to break up Western Electric into three separate and independent production units, as the Department of Justice has proposed, as long as A. T. & T. retained control over these manufacturing subsidiaries. If A. T. & T. were not forced to sever this vertical control, as the Department also requests, what assurance is there that it would deal at arm's length with its three subsidiaries and that as a result their charges would not, like Western Electric's today, be incorporated into the rate structure without any market appraisal of their legitimacy? Telephone subscribers would gain little if any benefit without elimination of the vertical integration as well.

Thus, given pre-existing competitive imperfections, integration may itself permit an extension or magnification of total monopoly power. True, if the separate components of a vertical integration had before joining been exploiting to the maximum any monopoly power they may have enjoyed, the mere combining of seller and buyer might not permit them to do any more. However, even here the merging of interests might permit the further suppression of competition in one of the strata, a more selective exploitation of the less elastic demands for a monopolized raw material, and a mutual reinforcement of monopoly power, such as occurs in the case of package deals, by making more difficult competitive entry at both levels.

When manufacturers of complementary shoe machines, each enjoying a preponderant share of its market, joined in the United Shoe Machinery Company and leased their products in a package, the monopoly power of each undoubtedly reinforced that of the others and made more difficult competitive challenges directed against any one of them. Or to take the case of vertical integration in movies, the link between the producer with exclusive rights to the services of Bing Crosby and the theater strategically situated in Times Square may have increased their combined profitability. The market power of each would perhaps have been more circumscribed, in the absence of integration, by independent producers with better access to Times Square audiences and by independent exhibitors with better access to Bing Crosby films. Thus, it is quite possible for the components of an integration to "subsidize each other," quite apart from the possible efficiency of the combination.

Through the years the oil industry has illustrated how vertical control over the separate strata of an industry, in each or all of which there is imperfect competition, may give rise to greater monopoly power than would otherwise exist. Taking the earliest instance, control of the pipelines by the Rockefeller group in the 1870's and 1880's enabled the Standard Oil Company to cement its monopoly of refining by cutting off supplies of crude oil from its competitors, except at prices that made it very difficult for them to compete. Had the pipelines been owned by a different (even though still monopolistic) group, it is doubtful if they would have favored the Rockefeller combine so consistently. In fact, such an independent monopoly would probably have encouraged competing refineries in order to increase its bargaining power with Standard Oil, which would otherwise have been in a position to dictate its charges. Conversely, Standard's control over refining, achieved by mergers and predatory competitive tactics, gave it preferential access to the lucrative business of pipeline transportation. An independent pipeline company could never count with assurance on the patronage of Standard's refineries. In consequence entry into both transportation and refining was constricted by Standard's integration; the only effective competitors, and they were few, were those who could themselves afford to integrate. (In addition, Standard was enabled by these mutually reinforcing positions in refining and transportation to exploit the independent producers of crude oil, who in turn could escape only by forward integration.)

The Competitive Contribution of Integration

The perplexing problem is that the competitive advantages stemming from gains in efficiency attributable to integration are in practice inseparable from the merely strategic advantages that pose the dangers to society just described. Efficiency gains arise from the fuller utilization of a firm's capacity, whether measured by its physical plant, managerial talents, by-products, technological skills, or the ideas issuing from its research laboratories. The costs of the combined operations are always in some measure joint, and their prices and margins accordingly subject to variation according to competitive conditions in their respective markets. Thus an integrated firm must, if it is to compete vigorously, charge little more than incremental costs in some of its markets, relying on others to make up the larger portion of the joint costs of integrated operations. Yet in so doing it cannot avoid "squeezing" nonintegrated competitors in the more competitive markets, in the sense that it is accepting prices there which it could not long continue to accept but for the returns it obtains elsewhere.[13]

It is practically impossible, therefore, for a large, integrated firm to exploit its socially acceptable advantages, or even to meet competition, without at the same time exploiting those advantages which are purely strategic. Conversely, it may avoid contravening one aspect or phase of the basic proscriptions of the antitrust laws only by a policy of conservatism and inertia, which contravenes another purpose of the law. A policy of eliminating the strategic advantages of integration would seriously undermine the vigor of competition itself, since a prime source of competition in modern capitalism is provided by the ability and incentive of burgeoning giants to press aggressively into new markets by cutting across accepted channels of distribution and trespassing across accepted industrial boundaries, following the diverse logic of their interests and technology.

Integration performs a competitive function even where its advantages are entirely strategic. We have already described Spengler's demonstration that vertical integration may lead to price reduction. The easiest curb on monopoly power, the most

[13] The first (but not the only) reason cited by the Department of Justice in 1920, and accepted by the Supreme Court in 1932, for forbidding the meat packers to sell meat at retail or to handle a long list of other products amounted to nothing more than the efficiency of integration: "through the ownership of refrigerator cars and branch houses as well as other facilities, the defendants were in a position to distribute . . . other . . . commodities with substantially no increase of overhead." *U.S.* v. *Swift & Co.,* 286 U.S. 106, 115 (1932).

effective cure for poor performance, and the one most consistent with free enterprise, is freedom of entry. And this includes, manifestly, the right of an existing business to extend its operations into any area its managers see fit to enter, i.e., to integrate.

By a curious inversion of the concept of competition, Adams suggests that his proposed antitrust commission, set up to root out monopoly power, might require General Motors to confine its attention to automobiles, on the ground that its manufacture of diesel locomotives, refrigerators, and electric appliances "merely represented an *attempt* to aggrandize the firm's size and economic power. . . ." [14] The example is hypothetical but instructive. First, his objective, market structure criterion of monopoly is apparently, after all, to hinge on intent ("an attempt to aggrandize"). Second, the clear implication is that if only big firms would cultivate their own gardens, competition would be keener and monopoly power reduced. Yet the impact of General Motors on railroad locomotives has constituted a competitive revolution.

Having set forth the major economic dangers and benefits of integration and, in summary fashion, of business size, we may now proceed to an examination of the major cases under the new Sherman Act. Have these suits seriously threatened the contributions that size and integration make to competition?

The Alcoa *Decision and the Requirements of Workable Competition*

Did the market performance of the aluminum industry, under the stimulus of such undeniable competitive influences as scrap, imports, and other metals, justify a claim to immunity from antitrust action? It is impossible to assess the complicated record with any pretension to scientific accuracy—as Wallace admitted, after 573 pages of exhaustive inquiry. However, even Wallace's cautious and diffident appraisal concluded that the single seller was responsible for some substantial restriction of output and investment and that an oligopoly would probably have done better.[15]

[14] In 27 *Land Economics* 293 (1951), stress supplied.

[15] *Market Control in the Aluminum Industry,* pp. xxvii, xxix, and Chap. 15.

Alcoa must receive substantial credit for the rapid growth of the American aluminum industry. Its vigorous development of electric power sites and bauxite mines probably resulted in greater expansion of these natural prerequisites of aluminum reduction than would have occurred had the task been left to independent businesses, with no direct stake in aluminum itself, exposed in considerable measure to the risks of dependence on the uncertain requirements of a new industry. The same is probably true of Alcoa's forward integration and the new uses for aluminum which it explored and developed in this fashion. Thus, the company's vertical integration did represent in large measure a socially beneficial exercise of competitive foresight and initiative. Even the price squeeze on rolling mills may be said to have represented a reaction to and a means of probing the opportunities for increasing use of aluminum sheet in competition with other metals, a kind of promotional price discrimination. Alcoa's vertical integration probably contributed also to cost reduction. The record is clear, finally, that aluminum prices and costs have fallen and capacity expanded dramatically over the last half-century.[16]

But it is doubtful that a complete monopoly of United States ingot production was a necessary condition of this development. Economies of scale in neither production nor research appear to require a single producer. Significantly, some of the most important innovations in aluminum must be credited to outsiders, including the United States Bureau of Standards; this suggests that competitive innovation under oligopoly might well have been more fruitful.[17]

And Alcoa's history discloses numerous evidences of monopolistic restrictionism, which the pressure of a few competitors might well have remedied. The lag of investment behind rising demand was particularly flagrant in the boom years 1900–1907 and 1923–1926. Even the expansions of the period 1908–1914, 1926–1929, and 1935–1939 probably fell short of not only the ideal but the attainable. Significantly, E. G. Nourse and H. B. Drury, whose major thesis is that big business can be depended upon to pursue dramatically expansionary pricing policies, cite

[16] *Ibid.*, pp. 10–16, 114, 152, 179–203, 254–257, 390–395.
[17] *Ibid.*, pp. 59, 189–203, 257.

Alcoa's record in the early 1920's as an outstanding example of how business should not behave. They blame its price increases and the aluminum shortages of that period for a substantial retardation in the growth of demand for aluminum, particularly in the automobile industry.[18] In both the 1907 and 1929 depressions, Wallace concludes, "lower prices would have enabled much better utilization of capacity without bringing losses." [19] The successful demand for a 3-cent increase in the protective duty in 1922, and the prompt elevation of the price by the same amount, were surely a further evidence of "unworkable competition." [20] So were Alcoa's high profits, particularly in the monopoly ingot field. Annual returns on stockholders' equity averaging 9.63 per cent during the decade of the 1930's, 16.61 per cent in 1935–1939, and 27 per cent in the latter year (it was considerably higher in ingot production alone) would appear to have justified the "dubious economics" of Judge Hand, when he decided Alcoa enjoyed a monopoly.[21]

Both economics and law appear to agree, then, that the *Alcoa* decision was correct in giving the government the right to lay its hands on the aluminum industry. The next problem was one of economic engineering. Mainly as a result of the disposal of the government's aluminum plants to Reynolds and Kaiser at the end of World War II, but partly also because of distribution of defense contracts after 1950 and the District Court's severance of the link between Alcoa and Aluminium Ltd. (Alted), the monopolized aluminum market has been transformed into an oligopoly.

Is the new market structure likely to produce a better per-

18 *Industrial Price Policies and Economic Progress* (Washington: Brookings, 1938), pp. 203–208.

19 In Elliott, pp. 231, 254–257; see also Wallace, pp. 28, 247–248, and Chap. 14; Stocking and Watkins, *Cartels in Action,* Chap. 6, *passim.*

20 It should be possible for students of American industrial organization to agree on the principle that no industry deserves approval of its economic performance which after thirty-five years of existence demands and obtains a 25 per cent duty on imports. By this standard, competition has been unworkable in other progressive industries, like rayon and chemicals, as well.

21 See Wallace, Chap. 11, and esp. pp. 30–31, 233, 250–252, 258–260, 263; Stocking and Watkins, *Cartels in Action,* p. 231; also p. 60, above.

formance than the old? There are now three large, vertically integrated, domestic producers of aluminum, instead of one. And there is in Canada a huge potential competitor, enjoying unusually low costs. The other United States producers enjoy rights under Alcoa's patents and have been freed of the obligation to license that company under any patents which they may themselves develop in the future.[22]

It seems clear, from Judge Knox's exhaustive assessment, that both Kaiser and Reynolds are inferior to Alcoa in financial strength, in patents and research facilities, and, because of poorer location and dependence on Alcoa for bauxite, in their costs of production. One is left with the fear that the low-cost firm may think twice before competing aggressively with the others, if in so doing it stands a good chance of falling heir again to the monopoly that the final court of appeals condemned "out of Hand." [23] Three domestic sellers of so standardized a product as ingot are in any case hardly likely to engage in vigorous price competition. As for Alted, Congress is likely to exert pressure to keep out its product, in the interest of the new domestic producers; [24] in any event it is unlikely to endanger Alcoa's price

[22] Judge Knox refused to break up Alcoa, because it no longer enjoyed a complete monopoly in virgin aluminum, because of its excellent performance, and because the competitive position of Reynolds and Kaiser appeared reasonably secure. See 91 F.Supp. 333, 401, 416 (1950). Instead he ordered (*a*) dissolution of the "community of interest" between Alcoa and Alted and (*b*) cancellation of the grant-back provisions in the patent licenses which Alcoa had granted to its competitors. Finally, he retained jurisdiction for an additional five years, to permit a later review of the efficacy of the decree.

[23] However, Judge Knox's opinion is reassuring on this score: "I hardly think . . . that normal competitive activity can be used to show an inveterate purpose to dominate an industry. . . . Any such theory, in my judgment, might lead to the vengeful imposition of a penalty upon conduct that is compelled by law." *Ibid.*, p. 415.

[24] See *Business Week*, July 5, 1952, p. 38. Compare the hostility toward relying on Canadian ingot exhibited (at first) by the Celler Committee's *Aluminum* report, by Adams in 41 *Amer. Econ. Rev.* 922 (1951), and by the Joint Committee on Defense Production, *Defense Production Act Progress*, Report No. 20, Aluminum Program, 82d Cong., 2d Sess., Sen. Report 1987 (1952) with the convincing case on the other side made by Anderson, *Aluminum*, pp. 8–9, 30–32, and by Congressman Celler himself,

leadership.[25] On the contrary, the contract, which it signed in 1953, to supply Alcoa with 600,000 tons of ingot over the next six years tended to frustrate the purpose of the 1950 decree to bring it into the American market as a direct competitor. As the Department of Justice complained in its prayer to have the contract set aside, the arrangement gave Alcoa the means for retaining its present dominant share in the American industry as Alted's "principal chosen instrument for exploiting the United States market," a market which Alted was expected to exploit for itself.[26] Finally, the reader need not be reminded that a conservative retardation of investment may occur under oligopoly as well as under monopoly:

Mr. [Congressman] HALLECK. It has been said to me that certain alleged monopolistic positions of some of the larger aluminum-producing companies have intervened to interfere with the increasing production of aluminum. Is that true or not?

Mr. [Charles E.] Wilson [then Director of Defense Mobilization]. It was true; yes.[27]

However, most economists still believe that three or four independent sellers and potential innovators are better than one.

"The Aluminum Program, An Analysis of the Report of the Joint Committee on Defense Production" (privately printed, 1952). See also testimony of representatives of Reynolds and Kaiser before the Celler Committee, *Aluminum,* Hearings, Serial No. 1, Pt. 1 (1951), pp. 111–176, 268.

[25] Nathanial Davis testified that his company would not as a matter of policy undercut American prices, even if its costs were lower, for fear of invoking a rise in the United States tariff. Celler Committee, *Aluminum,* Hearings (1951), p. 440; also pp. 449–450.

[26] *U.S.* v. *Aluminum Co. of America,* Petition in Equity, 1953. Alcoa's answer that there are very few firms in the United States who can use primary aluminum; that such firms are in any case assured adequate supplies of ingot; and that it will be enabled, with Alcan's ingot, to supply to fabricators the semifabricated materials which most of them require (see "Alcoa-Alcan Tie in Court," *Business Week,* Aug. 22, 1953, pp. 88, 90) ignored the contention of the Department of Justice that Alcan should attempt to compete with Alcoa, by offering to American fabricators whatever kinds of aluminum they require, rather than continue to operate here, in effect, through its former affiliate. See the Consent Order, announced April 23, 1954.

[27] Committees on Banking and Currency and Select Committees on Small Business, *Production and Allocations,* Joint Hearing, 82d Cong., 1st Sess. (1951), pp. 17–18.

The immediate need in aluminum ingot is apparently not downward price competition but a price high enough to permit the required expansion of capacity in the face of increasing costs—of transporting bauxite from more distant sources, of generating electric power, of constructing new facilities in an inflationary period. In any event, the introduction of some uncertainty about the division of the market, the likelihood of independent decision making and action with respect not so much to pricing as to research, investment, and product development surely diminishes the prospect of restrictionism in the long run. Judge Knox's decree may not have gone far enough. But the argument of the new critics is that the law goes too far.

Should Alcoa have been subjected to vertical disintegration? Competition in aluminum fabrication is still in some ways burdened by the industry's tight vertical integration. The introduction of two more vertically integrated producers has not greatly increased the availability of ingot to independent fabricators; they continue to be dependent upon their integrated competitors for supplies. The independents' promotion of new uses for aluminum is handicapped by the danger, which became a reality in 1950–1951, of being cut off from supplies. The Department of Justice has therefore been criticized for failing to petition for the separation of Alcoa's fabrication and reduction facilities. The difficulties of the 17,000 independent fabricators during the recent defense program add appeal to this suggestion.[28]

The courts need not hesitate in splitting Alcoa along horizontal lines in 1954 merely because vertical integration has enabled the company in the past to develop new sources of raw material and power and new uses of aluminum. It might be possible to dilute the company's power and increase the competitive opportunities of nonintegrated fabricators, while at the same time preserving the dynamic contributions of vertical integration. For example, part or all of Alcoa's *present* fabrication activities could

[28] "Vertical Integration in Aluminum: A Bar to 'Effective Competition,'" 60 *Yale Law J.* 294, 300 (1951); Senate Select Committee on Small Business, *Material Shortages: Aluminum,* Hearing, 82d Cong., 1st Sess., Pt. 4 (1951).

be split off, while permitting the company to develop whatever new market outlets it chooses.[29] Will a company be likely to innovate through integration if the government may some time later require it to disintegrate? Future divestiture is not the same thing as expropriation. Even the patent monopoly is limited to seventeen years; yet this limited period of exclusive enjoyment of the fruits of innovation is seldom held to vitiate the incentive it offers.

However, to require vertical dissolution whenever an integrated firm both supplies and competes with nonintegrated firms would decree an arbitrary stratification of all industry. If inflation abates, it will be the incompletely integrated ingot producers who will depend on the fabricators, rather than the reverse—particularly since there are now four (including Alted), and it is hoped there will soon be seven, suppliers rather than one. The fact that in 1937 Alcoa's vertical integration compounded the limitation on competition inherent in its ingot monopoly does not mean that vertical dissolution was the best available remedy in 1950, when that monopoly had been sharply curtailed. Vertical integration is a threat to competition only where competition is seriously imperfect in one of the interconnected horizontal strata. To the extent Alcoa's ingot monopoly has been dissipated, the vertical integration, with its possible contributions to efficiency and innovation, may safely be left undisturbed.

Recent actions of the government offer the prospect of considerable relief along these lines. It has been granting contracts for expansion of ingot capacity contingent on the reservation of a minimum portion of the forthcoming ingot for independent fabricators. A long-term purchase contract with Alted would serve the same end. Here is the solution that comes closest to Wallace's proposal of government entry into ingot production itself. Such a contract should improve the market opportunities for independent fabricators and eliminate the one factor which

[29] At one point Adams makes exactly the opposite suggestion: "What the government should have demanded as a minimum . . . was that Alcoa be enjoined from any further *vertical* integration—especially in the fabrication field." 41 *Amer. Econ. Rev.* 919 n. 8 (1951).

makes vertical integration objectionable, while preserving for those firms which can grasp them the social benefits of integration. Even without a government contract, independent fabricators in the United States can undoubtedly look forward to reliable and increasing supplies from Alted, which needs their custom as much as they need its supplies.[30] This will be especially true since the Department of Justice has succeeded in its effort to have substantial changes made in Alted's long term contract to supply Alcoa with 600,000 tons of ingot, a contract that, according to the government, jeopardized not only the prospects of real competition between the two former affiliates, but also the availability of supplies of cheap Canadian ingot to independent domestic fabricators.[31]

Government intervention outside the antitrust laws is probably the only way of assuring fairness in the distribution of scarce materials. Abuse of the power conferred on integrated firms by their control of such materials may justify divestiture upon antitrust prosecution. But the presence of legitimate business considerations may make it impossible to label as simple monopolization such acquisitions by dominant firms, even though nonintegrated fabricators are severely handicapped as a result. In these circumstances, either direct government allocation or, more promisingly, government development (or assistance in development) of additional supplies seems the appropriate remedy.

The history of aluminum also illustrates vividly how government patent and tariff policy can contribute to the construction of impregnable market positions. There were two American producers of aluminum between 1887 and 1893: the Pittsburg Reduction Company (Alcoa's predecessor) and the Cowles Brothers, using the Hall and Bradley patents, respectively. Keen competition between the two was in large measure responsible for reducing the price of aluminum from $5.00 a pound in 1887

[30] See, e.g., *N.Y. Times,* May 22, 1953, p. 36, col. 5.

[31] The Department charged in its petition (pars. 19–23) that nonintegrated fabricators in the United States had had to import metal from Europe at a price greatly in excess of the domestic price because of their inability to secure additional supplies at home or from Alted.

to $0.75 in 1893. At that point the Pittsburg Company launched an infringement suit against the Cowles and won an initial favorable decision. Not until 1903 was the verdict reversed and the validity of the Bradley patent upheld. But then, instead of exchanging licenses, the Cowles sold out to Pittsburg for $1,429,-000 and annual royalties, agreeing in turn to stay out of aluminum refining. The Bradley patent, thus acquired, gave Alcoa an additional three years of legal monoploy at a critical time:

> Had patent protection ended in 1906 it is highly improbable that the Aluminum Company would have attained by that time the degree of size, integration, and power which, after the intervening boom years, faced potential competitors in 1909. . . . Extension of patent protection to twenty years destroyed the opportunity for competitors to enter at a period when conditions were perhaps more favorable than they have ever been since.[32]

High on the list of requirements for effective competition is a more efficient method of adjudicating patent disputes [33] and some limitation on the ability of competitors with patent monopolies to terminate their rivalry completely either with exclusive cross licenses or with one selling out its exclusive rights to the other.

It appears that the tariff on ingot made a substantial contribution to monopoly, not only in the ingot field but also, by helping limit fabricators to Alcoa as their source of supply, in fabrication as well. And it contributed to the monopoly profits which, enhancing the financial power of the company, further discouraged potential rivals. The tariff rate of 8 cents and then 7 cents a pound in the first decade of the century, when Alcoa's annual average price ranged between 22 and 38 cents, doubtless strengthened the company's hand in foreign cartel negotiations and contributed to the extraordinary profits of this decade. The 1913 tariff reduced the rate to only 2 cents a pound, but the postwar recession, marked like the one after 1907 by heavy imports and reduced prices, persuaded Congress to increase the

[32] Wallace, pp. 101 and 5–6; see also Stocking and Watkins, *Cartels in Action*, pp. 221–222.

[33] See Joseph Borkin, "The Patent Infringement Suit—Ordeal by Trial," 17 *U. of Chicago Law Rev.* 634 (1950).

tariff to 5 cents a pound in 1922, at which level it remained until 1930. Alcoa promptly raised its price by the full amount of the 1922 tariff increase, with the result that in 1923 its prices were still some 25 per cent above prewar, while those of copper and tin, the competing metals, remained slightly below.[34] A lower tariff alone—after all, the infant was some thirty-five years old in 1922!—would have made a substantial contribution to more effective competition.

The tariff might have been expected to encourage new domestic producers, or at least expansion of capacity by Alcoa. As for the former, Alcoa effectively precluded the entry of two major interests by buying out the Uihleins, who had secured control of valuable bauxite deposits, and J. B. Duke, who had an excellent power site on the Saguenay River and had made arrangements with George Haskell to go into the aluminum business. As for the latter, despite severe shortages in the intervening years, Alcoa delayed beginning an expansion of capacity until 1925.

Economics of the American Tobacco *Decision*

There is really little possibility of criticizing *American Tobacco* on economic grounds. No economist seems to have anything good to say about either the structure or the performance of the cigarette industry.[35] Where oligopolists are so punctilious in avoiding effective competition as to provide convincing evidence of a general "agreement to agree," if not of actual conspiracy, the economist can scarcely complain that the antitrust laws are condemning "hard" and encouraging "soft" competition.

The only significant economic question about this case is how to frame a decree that will increase competition. There is

[34] Wallace, in Elliott, pp. 252–254; Wallace, pp. 238, 318–320. See also Muller, *Light Metals Monopoly,* p. 236; Stocking and Watkins, *Cartels in Action,* pp. 228–248, *passim.*

[35] See Baum, *Workable Competition;* Nicholls, *Price Policies;* Mason, in 62 *Harv. Law Rev.* 1275 (1949); Kaplan, *Big Enterprise,* Chaps. 5 and 6; Markham, in 41 *Amer. Econ. Rev.* 903–904 (1951); also the more qualified verdict of Tennant in Adams (ed.), *The Structure of American Industry,* pp. 257–265.

little point in merely prohibiting henceforth the "conspiracy" that was probably unnecessary before and is certainly unnecessary from now on to produce an undesirable performance.

The cigarette companies so far have only the implicit injunction not to do those imprecisely identifiable things that caused the jury to find them guilty. Even such a rule may be to some extent salutary. The conviction has apparently helped to engender a more moderate pricing policy.[36] If the Big 3 cannot be forced to compete, at least they can be discouraged from extortionate pricing under a rigid price leadership.

The major impediments to entry and effective competition in cigarettes are not the threat of exclusionary tactics, about which the Big 3 will presumably be more circumspect in the future, but rather the immense cost of advertising, consumer acceptance of the familiar brands, and the regressive federal excise tax. Suppose one manufacturer is willing to get a net price of 4 cents a pack, while another charges 7 cents, or 75 per cent more. Addition of a flat federal excise tax of 7 cents (setting aside the other rigid local taxes and distribution costs) raises the price of the cheaper brand 175 per cent, of the more expensive one only 100 per cent, and reduces the price discrepancy between them sharply. If a manufacturer cuts his price from 7 cents to 4 cents, i.e., by 43 per cent, his final price goes down only 21½ per cent (from 14 to 11 cents). So price rivalry is discouraged. A proportional or progressive excise tax (say 5 cents on the cheaper pack, 10 cents on the more expensive) would assure the firm choosing to compete in price that its full percentage price cut would be passed on to the public.

The antitrust laws cannot eradicate all these influences. But they can do much even here. The Supreme Court has already taken cognizance of the fact that heavy advertising expenditures represent a substantial bulwark of the Big 3's monopoly power.[37] In line with past decrees requiring compulsory licensing in patent cases and condemning otherwise legal practices and relationships when power has been abused, a decree which limited advertising expenditures of each of the Big 3 in the future to a

[36] Tennant, p. 255; Nicholls, pp. 164–166.
[37] See p. 67, above.

certain percentage of gross revenues would seem legally feasible. If economists agree on anything, they probably agree that in cigarettes a limitation of advertising would offer some hope for freer entry and bona fide competition of a socially useful kind.

R. B. Tennant argues that a mere increase in the number of sellers would probably increase the costs of distribution.[38] This argument assumes that competition would continue along present lines exclusively. But, a limitation of advertising and a proportional, if not a progressive excise tax would certainly help preclude such an outcome. And even dissolution alone might help competition take a new tack. The pattern of high advertising expenditures and emphasis on brand seems characteristic of consumer goods industries dominated by a very small number of large sellers, as in cigarettes and soap. In men's suits and shoes, on the other hand, where sellers are more numerous (and there are no technological factors precluding this in cigarettes), there seems to be a good deal more competition on the basis of genuine quality and price.

Economics of the Movie Decisions

Should the movie decisions have turned on an evaluation of the market structure or economic performance of the industry? The severe imperfections of competition in both production and exhibition, resulting from fewness of sellers, extreme product differentiation, and the importance of location of theaters, suggest a particular threat to competition in permitting individual oligopolists to operate at both levels. In these circumstances, vertical integration inevitably reinforced the monopoly elements by increasing the impediments to entry at both levels and made more likely the rigidly channelized, essentially co-operative kind of competition that prevailed between the majors.[39]

Even in these cases, however, it would have been dangerous to condemn the defendants merely because they were few, or few and vertically integrated, or because they enjoyed monopoly power. Their fewness might have mirrored the survival of the

[38] In Adams (ed.), pp. 261–263.

[39] See William Hellmuth, Jr., "The Motion Picture Industry," in Adams (ed.), Chap. 8.

fittest, or the economies of scale, or the limitations of the market. Vertical integration undoubtedly had at least at one time made a dynamic contribution to the development of the industry. The leading producers had the particular incentive, which motivated their huge investments in the construction of new theaters, of obtaining the widest possible audience for their films. Warner Brothers, pioneers in sound movies, claimed that they were compelled to operate their own theaters because of the unwillingness of independent exhibitors to purchase the expensive equipment necessary for "talkies." [40] There may also have been merit in the contention of the major motion picture producers that without the assurance of wide distribution and exhibition which ownership of theaters gave them they would be unable to make the heavy investments required to produce a modern "A" film [41]—although it is doubtful whether heavy investments and guaranteed markets necessarily make for the highest quality product.

It would have been equally undesirable to try to judge the economic performance of the movie industry in rendering an antitrust judgment. Would it be an appropriate task for a court to have to decide, in an antitrust proceeding against movie companies, whether the quality and price of the extraordinarily variegated composite service in question, or the past or prospective contributions to the record of the particular restraints at issue, merit condemnation? Or should it be left to any government agency in appraising the price record of the industry to decide whether the stars or motion picture executives deserve their extraordinary salaries and bonuses? [42]

[40] Hale, in 49 *Columbia Law Rev.* 934 n. 85 (1949).

[41] See Rodney Frank Luther, *The Motion Picture Industry* (unpublished dissertation, Univ. of Minnesota, 1949), 164; Hellmuth, pp. 289–290. Neither writer fully accepts this argument; nor do we.

[42] Adelman criticizes the courts for failing to consider "the adverse effect on the movie-going public" of the monopoly power enjoyed by the Schine chain. Yet his own brief evaluation suggests the futility of such an investigation: "Schine's power . . . enabled it to disregard . . . the demands of the distributors for price maintenance. The public benefits of competition enforced by the big buyer might very plausibly have been called transitory and therefore no offset to the larger drawback of local monopoly. The important thing is that they were never considered." 63

The evils in the movie situation, then, took the form of a noncompetitive pattern of pricing strongly suggesting conspiracy, vertical integration to obtain monopolistic advantage,[43] and market leverage flagrantly exerted to impose unreasonable injury on competitors in both production and exhibition. Most economists would certainly agree that these antitrust offenses of the traditional kind made for less effective competition.

Have the movie suits improved the economic performance of the industry? Or are they likely to do so? So many other violent changes have occurred in the industry since World War II, most notably the new competition of television, that it is very difficult to say. But the burden of proof rests on the critics of antitrust: they must show that the over-all economic outcome is likely to be worse, if they are to censure suits brought to prevent the exercise of market power by dominant firms so as to impose unfair competitive handicaps on other businessmen. It is difficult to see in what way the decisions under consideration could possibly involve any market deterioration. On the contrary, to the extent the decrees are effective in improving the competitive opportunities of independent producers and exhibitors, they can only contribute at both levels to the greater ease of entry which is the prime requisite of workable competition. The divorce of production and exhibition should make it more difficult to enforce an avoidance of price competition down the line, whether collusive or "consciously parallel." Breaking up the big theater chains may diminish their "countervailing power," and so draw down the wrath of Galbraith, but there is no evidence that the chains used this power in any other way than to get monopolistic preferences for themselves.

The movie decrees have by no means stilled the complaints of independent exhibitors. The intensity and volume of these complaints are probably attributable in large measure to the falling off in receipts all over the industry in recent years. But there

---

Harv. Law Rev. 1319 (1949). The courts might have made the gesture of supplying "plausible" economic considerations of the foregoing type, but the results could scarcely have been any more decisive than the results of Adelman's own brief attempt.

[43] Luther, 38, 89; Hellmuth, 273–275.

still appears to be a problem of regulating techniques of distribution like prereleasing (permitting films to be run by selected exhibitors prior to the time when they are generally released) and competitive bidding, in order to prevent unfair treatment of independent exhibitors.[44] However, the continuing difficulties in the industry cannot be traced to disintegration. It seems likely that with declining revenues the independent exhibitors would have been even more seriously discriminated against by the producers if the latter still owned their own houses.

The Proposed Dissolution of A & P

In a civil suit launched after the successful conclusion of criminal proceedings against the A & P Company and its officials, the government's initial proposal was that the company be subjected to vertical and horizontal dissolution, in order to dissipate the power it was held to have abused. The main elements of the program were divestiture of A & P's manufacturing facilities, elimination and dissolution of its centralized buying offices, including its field organization for the purchase of produce, the Atlantic Commission Company (ACCO), and severance of its seven retailing divisions into wholly independent companies. The proposal encountered violent and widespread criticism in contrast to the dissolution orders against the movie companies, even through the rationale was similar. The public was led to believe that dissolution would interfere with A & P's efficiency and that the consumer would consequently pay for it in the end in higher prices.

Little can be said in favor of cutting off A & P's food-processing divisions, and much can be said against it. Large-scale, affiliated production permits real cost savings in the co-ordination of output volume and composition with store needs and shifts in consumer tastes. Some of these savings would be lost if the retail stores severed their intimate relationship with the manufacturing plants that now produce for them evaporated milk, coffee, shortening, bakery products, jams, and jellies. It might be desirable

[44] Senate Select Committee on Small Business, *Problems of Independent Motion Picture Exhibitors,* 83d Cong., 1st Sess., Report No. 835 (1953). See also the *Theater Enterprises* case, 74 Sup.Ct. 257 (1954).

to forgo these savings if A & P had actually "abused" its control of manufacturing in a way that only divestiture could remedy. However, there was really nothing legally or economically objectionable in A & P's manufacturing. The only misuse occurred in the threats to manufacture for itself employed as a means of exacting discriminatory discounts. If the remainder of the dissolution program had been carried out, diminishing the company's massed buying power, control of the Quaker Maid, White House milk, and other processing plants could safely have been left jointly in the hands of the independent successor retail chains. They would have continued to realize the savings that A & P now enjoys as a single monolithic organization.

The consumer would not have suffered seriously with the dissolution of ACCO and A & P's other centralized purchasing offices. Direct carload buying from the shipper or field assembler results in substantial savings compared with produce purchases from terminal markets, but it does not require the maintenance of a field organization such as ACCO now supports. Even individual independent supermarkets buy large-volume produce items by the carload if they have storage space, and small chains like Bohack, Grand Union, Market Basket, and Loblaws do a very large part of their produce business by direct purchase from the shipper. Much of the cost saving of chain produce operation, compared with distribution through terminal market warehouses, is accounted for by the poor location of terminal markets. But there is no reason to suppose that the retail successors to A & P, each with at least $400,000,000 annual sales volume, would not have been able to use A & P's existing strategically located produce warehouses, just as many of their smaller competitors today have their own warehouses and thus avoid depending appreciably on terminal markets or auctions.

Even A & P patronizes terminal markets, inefficient though they are. One of the functions of a terminal market is to supply a cushion; chain produce buyers do not like to buy, in fact cannot always estimate, their full requirements several days ahead of the heavy shopping weekend. Hence a certain amount usually has to come from the markets, to supplement direct purchases. Therefore comparison of A & P's costs of handling produce with those of terminal market wholesalers has no particular bearing on the economic consequences of the dissolution of ACCO.[45] The retailing successors of A & P would presumably have continued to utilize terminal markets for supplementary purchases and to buy most of their needs direct, just as ACCO now does.

Finally, the paramount determinant of profit or loss on produce is the treatment it gets in the retail store, which determines attractiveness to the customer and the rate of spoilage, rather than quality or concessions at the time of purchase. There is no reason to believe that a corporate chain the size of American Stores or First National cannot, like the small, competent independent, ensure that produce receives good treatment.

It is not easy to predict the effect of eliminating A & P's centralized buying offices. It may be that because of its nation-wide coverage the present organization is more effective than a buying office with a more restricted territory in comparing offers and bargaining with suppliers. However, it would be very rash to assert that it operates with significantly greater efficiency than the buying offices of smaller chains. The markets for canned foods, groceries, and meats are quite well organized. Organizations like Biddle and A. C. Nielsen provide price information on a fee basis, and thousands of brokers and salesmen, as well as trade publications, keep chains and wholesalers abreast of market developments.

It seems most unlikely that higher prices would follow a horizontal disintegration of A & P. In the first place, price competition would hardly be diminished if the divisions were made independent of one another. On the contrary, they would then

[45] One commentator implies that it was undesirable to prevent ACCO's receipt of selling brokerage, because this would discourage A & P from performing for itself wholesaling functions, at a cost much lower than average margins for independent terminal market wholesalers. Adelman, in 63 *Q. Jour. Econ.* 249 (1949). Our point is that the latter do a very different job. It seems unrealistic, too, to assume that ACCO is discriminated against if it is not paid selling brokerage. Most of its competitors, if they happened to pay the same price (there is of course no list price for produce) would, in buying direct, assume the costs of hiring buying agents—a cost roughly equivalent to that of the ACCO field organization. See Dirlam and Kahn, in 29 *Ind. Law J.* 10–12 and n. 28 (1953).

be relieved of control from headquarters and would be able to follow a much more dynamic policy than is presently possible. Second, such data as are available on retail and wholesale costs show that it is possible for even smaller organizations than the proposed $400,000,000 chains to operate on gross margins as low and with returns on capital as high or higher than A & P.[46]

Finally, it seems unlikely that dissolution of the giant chain would retard innovation in the grocery field. The most important of all increases in efficiency, the self-service supermarket, was pioneered by independent wholesalers and tiny chains in the early 1930's, and adopted by A & P only after it had incurred substantial and prolonged losses.[47]

The consent judgment finally entered in *A & P* was much less drastic than the government's original proposal. ACCO is to be dissolved, but nothing prevents A & P from immediately setting up another produce-buying subsidiary. However, any successor to ACCO is forbidden to sell to the trade, and hence will not be able to use A & P's massed buying as a means of increasing its brokerage business, as ACCO did prior to 1949. The consent decree will, therefore, prevent the recurrence of what the courts found to be the most objectionable feature of A & P's activities. It is difficult to be enthusiastic about the multiplicity of directives that are laid down with regard to the buying and selling activities of the chain, as a substitute for a politically unfeasible remedy of dissolution. Their effective enforcement would require continuous supervision obviously beyond the bounds of Antitrust Division resources. Indeed, it is hard to understand why A & P itself should have preferred to live henceforth under the shadow of an injunction that extends to the minutest detail of its policy and that must put it at a competitive disadvantage in buying and selling policies. There is a real danger that such a decree will turn the company into a timid competitor. In contrast, the dissolution decrees that have been enforced on Standard Oil, American Tobacco, and Pullman have been advantageous not only to the public, but to the industries and companies themselves, freeing them for more effective and dynamic competition.

[46] *Ibid.*, pp. 22–24.

[47] A & P *Main Brief*, Appeals Case, 173 F.2d 79 (1949), App. A., I, 194–197.

Conclusion

One frequently hears the contention today that the new Sherman Act, or even the old Sherman Act if effectively enforced, would produce market situations noticeably less workable than those which now prevail generally in American industry. Our examination of the integration decisions of the last ten years and the proposals of the government in *A & P* and *Western Electric* have led us to the conclusion that these contentions are not only of very dubious validity but ignore the positive contribution which competition itself, freed of arbitrary private restraints, makes to a strong and progressive economy.

There remains a strong prejudice against dissolution of integrated firms,[48] even when, like United Shoe Machinery Company, they are almost complete monopolies. In *United Shoe,* Judge Wyzanski was unwilling to dissolve the company into three independent manufacturing entities because he could not see how the physical difficulties of independent operation could be overcome. The company's operations are concentrated in one plant (not one building) in Beverly, Massachusetts; it has one set of jigs and tools, one foundry, and one laboratory. However, from the facts stated in the opinion, it would appear that the court in this case was overawed by the difficulties that supposedly attend any change in business organization. The same timidity found expression in the first *U.S. Steel, Hartford-Empire,* and *Timken* decisions. Although private business management in the United States is extraordinarily flexible in meeting emergencies and devising novel methods of operation and organization, the typical judicial attitude in dissolution cases is that reversal or change of present methods of operation would cause incalculable loss. The fact that the United Shoe Machinery Company's operations are centralized in one plant does not inevitably mean that separate and competing companies could not have been set up. Propinquity does not preclude dissolution. Jigs and tools could presumably be divided according to the different types of machinery they were designed for or they could be used co-

[48] See Adams, "Dissolution, Divorcement, Divestiture," 27 *Ind. Law J.* 1 (1951), *passim.*

operatively; the laboratory might be set up on a co-operative basis, at least at the outset; the foundry could be given its independence. Eventually, it could be anticipated, the three successor firms would each tend to develop a full line and hence provide the strong competition that the decree Judge Wyzanski was willing to approve seems inadequate to ensure, since it does nothing (other than requiring sale of shoe machinery) to give competitors a start. The government won, therefore, much less than it did in the *Aluminum* case. It is difficult to see how effective competition requires the preservation of virtually pure monopoly.

Lilienthal has voiced strenuous objections to the proposal of the Department of Justice to dissolve the Western Electric Company into three separate and independent companies and to require the company to sell to A. T. & T. its 50 per cent interest in Bell Laboratories, on the ground that the result will be to destroy a magnificent research organization.[49] There are two reasons why his opinion is not convincing. First, the Hawthorne, Kearny, and Philadelphia plants, which would constitute the nuclei of the independent companies, would be giant organizations, well able to take care of themselves. Second, A. T. & T., with total assets after divestment of roughly $10,000,000,000, should, without jeopardizing the $9.00 dividend, still be able to support Bell Laboratories in the style to which it has become accustomed. The evidence seems to show that, if anything, development in the application of modern electronics to telephones has been hampered by excessive centralization of responsibility for innovation in a monopoly that had, to say the least, conflicting interests in furthering basic research that might render its own equipment obsolescent.[50] The fact stressed by Lilienthal, that Bell Laboratories were able to provide a great deal of help in producing the atomic bomb, does not demonstrate that if we had had Bell Laboratories, Kearny Laboratories, Hawthorne Laboratories, and Philadelphia Laboratories we might not have got the job done even faster. Spurred by competition, the total resources and level of performance of these research organizations could just as

[49] *Big Business,* pp. 102–105.
[50] F.C.C., *Telephone Investigation,* pp. 664–667.

conceivably surpass as fall behind the performance of a single monopolized research group. Where innovation is too expensive for private competitive enterprise, we must look to the government for its effectuation.

Like many other business practices, integration is neither good nor bad. It can be economically beneficent; it is also subject to abuse. If the abuse can be cured without eliminating the integration, well and good. In the case of A & P there was no reason to prohibit ownership of manufacturing facilities by the retailing organizations concerned; the abuses could be cured in other ways more closely related to the company's real transgressions. Judge Wyzanski believed that United Shoe's monopolization of the shoe machinery market could likewise be cured without disintegration. About this we are much more skeptical. With competition introduced into the production of ingot aluminum and government efforts undertaken to assure adequate supplies to nonintegrated fabricators, it would be unwise to forbid Alcoa to integrate vertically, because much more might be lost than gained by thus restricting its activities. On the other hand, A. T. & T.'s control over its manufacturing subsidiaries appears clearly objectionable because the telephone company's monopoly is permanent and has been used to introduce monopoly into unregulated areas that were formerly competitive. Thus, in the *A. T. & T.*, as in the *Paramount, Griffith,* and perhaps the *Yellow Cab* cases, integration has been used to extend the scope of monopoly, and the structure of the market has been such that the abuse could be ended only by ending the integration. It is difficult to see how the economy will be hurt by a correction which cannot help serving the cause of competition.

CHAPTER 6

Exclusive Arrangements

EXCLUSIVE selling and buying arrangements—exclusive dealing agreements, full requirements contracts, or tie-ins—are really a nonproprietary kind of vertical integration. For the seller they provide the same kind, though not usually the same degree, of control over and assurance of market outlets; for the buyer, the same kind of assurance of supply. To both they offer the advantages of a closer co-operation and greater mutual assistance than is ordinarily made available between independent suppliers and customers.

Like integration itself—or marriage!—these arrangements also impose some burdens on the parties thus allied. There are mutual benefits, of course; otherwise the contracts would not be signed or the vows exchanged. But the benefits to one party in the form of control, assurance, or security necessarily entail corresponding obligations on the part of the other, and therefore some loss of freedom of action.

These arrangements (we herewith drop the analogy to the marriage contract, if only because we wish to engender no confusion about the sense in which we have been using the term "double standard" in antitrust) create restraints at three different levels and therefore raise three kinds of problems for agencies concerned with regulating and preserving competition.

First there is the restraint imposed upon the parties themselves, with the possible consequent need to supervise the bargaining relationships between buyers and sellers. In the case of exclusive dealing, for example, the buyer is not the same person as the ultimate customer; rather he is in a position somewhere between that of a truly independent contractor and an employee. The problem arises of maintaining a more or less stable balance of power between the parties, just as in employer-employee relations.[1] Through individual or collective bargaining or (if the public interest seems sufficiently involved) through direct government regulation, a modicum of equity in day-to-day dealing must be achieved. Theoretically, of course, the bargain and the decision to continue or terminate the relationship is a free one, and the question of whether the benefits justify the sacrifices is for each party to decide. But in fact, as is always the case where economic bargaining powers are unequal, one party may be presented with so narrow a choice that he is not so free to accept or reject the arrangement or certain aspects of it as a competitive society would have him be. He may be disadvantaged by some part of the bargain, yet enter upon it because it is the least bad choice available to him.

The second public aspect of these private arrangements is their impact on competitors of either the seller or the buyer (or dealer). The question inevitably arises whether the security that seller or buyer A gains by an exclusive vertical relationship with B is at the expense of insecurity for seller or buyer C. The rivals may of course enter the same kind of arrangements, perhaps only because they find they must do so in order to compete. But if an exclusive contract between A and B imposes undue restraints upon C, the public cannot be indifferent.

Finally, there is the question of the way in which the exclusive arrangement directly affects the consuming public. The consumer interest in effective competition is obviously closely bound up with the sufficiency of access to markets or supplies left to competitors of the contracting parties. However, a contract fair as between the parties and not injurious to competitors may impose an undue restraint directly upon the buying public, for example, by serving as an instrument for price fixing or by forcing ultimate customers to take something they do not want.

[1] See Joseph C. Palamountain, *The Politics of Distribution* (unpublished dissertation, Harvard U., 1951), pp. 147–156, 383–386.

Exclusive arrangements represent a departure from the open, freely competitive market. The departure is only temporary; it lasts, technically, only as long as the exclusive contract runs. It may be only a means of competing even more strenuously and effectively in the final market—of reducing costs and prices, of giving the customer a better product or service. It may not preclude strong competition among buyers or sellers to induce the opposite parties to sign the exclusive arrangement in the first place or to renew it. Yet the "security" and "assurances" that these arrangements provide represent a kind of insulation, however transitory, against the vicissitudes (perhaps socially undesirable as well as privately intolerable) of a completely free market. Sellers and buyers are relieved of the necessity of using price as a method of inducing their opposite numbers to purchase or to supply, if only in the short run. Clearly, this proximate avoidance, limitation, or control of free competitive bargaining is one possible effect that must be considered when the economic consequences of these practices are evaluated.

Exclusive Dealing in Farm Equipment

In the distribution of farm equipment, where the relationship between large manufacturers and their thousands of dealers is always an uneasy mixture of collaboration and conflict, there is continuously thrust forward the issue of equity in the dealings between the parties.

The farm equipment dealer is seldom entirely satisfied with the treatment he receives from his supplier. He resists the manufacturer's pressure to take all the machines in his line; some of them, he knows, are inferior to those of a competitor. He complains that the manufacturer insists periodically on shipping him more machines than he orders. He demands better financial terms, quicker settlement of claims under company guarantees. He asks production engineers why they are so slow to improve machines he knows are defective. He often resists or wishes he could resist the district manager's pressure for "adequate" representation, display, and service facilities, demands backed ultimately by the right of the company to cancel the contract.

The manufacturer defends his distribution policies by urging that they make him better able to compete effectively. International Harvester, for instance, was limited by a 1918 antitrust consent decree to one dealer in each town. Consequently, the company feels that it must insist on the fullest possible support from the lone dealer, and although its officers disclaim full-line forcing, their understandable insistence on "full representation" comes close to it. The practice of shipping machines in excess of orders is another way of ensuring the most intensive possible dealer selling effort; the dealer's hostility to the practice is essentially a recognition that large inventories mean price cutting and may lead distributors in adjoining markets to invade his territory by making distress sales of "bootleg" equipment.[2] In their effort to ensure adequate or full representation, manufacturers also insist that dealers' business establishments be well located, attractive and contain sufficient display and service facilities. Soon after World War II, they urged distributors to build distinctive "prototype" buildings, often making this a condition of receiving or keeping the distributorship. The prescribed buildings were often so distinctive both in appearance and location that dealers feared they would have only a greatly depreciated value for other purposes; the investments therefore exposed them to serious losses if they ever lost the distributorship. These pressures thus generated great resentment; dealers were naturally unwilling to make the heavy investments required, and in some states actually got laws passed prohibiting such practices.[3]

This brief catalogue of the factors engendering friction between manufacturers and dealers indicates that neither side is invariably right or wrong on all issues. Local dealers are certainly not more devoted advocates and practitioners of intensive competition than their suppliers. Many of their grievances are against company policies that force them to compete more intensively. Many of those who lose their distributorships do so

[2] See the analogous problem in the distribution of gasoline, arising from the major companies' "greed for gallonage," pp. 180–187, below. The equities of the situation, the impact on competitors and on the public, will vary depending on whether exclusive dealing is associated with exclusive territorial agency. See p. 198, below.

[3] F.T.C., *Report on Manufacture and Distribution of Farm Implements,* pp. 132–154.

because they do not serve either the manufacturer or the public adequately.

In any event, antagonisms inevitably arise between dealers and the manufacturers, partly because local agents of the supplier in an effort to make a good showing may apply more heat than top management specifically directs or formally permits. The problem cannot be dismissed by saying that the dealer contracts freely with the farm equipment manufacturer and is free to withdraw if he feels unfairly treated. This fiction has been abandoned in the field of labor relations, where it is obvious that inequality of bargaining power makes "freedom of contract" a mockery for the individual worker. Though less of a fiction when applied to the relationship between manufacturer and dealer, particularly before the first contract is signed, the fact remains that the manufacturer can get along without any particular local representative more easily than the dealer can get along without this or that supplier. Once he has taken on a line, invested in distinctive facilities, associated his good will with a particular brand, and built up his local business, he cannot freely shift. Even the move from one supplier to another, if by chance there is available the local franchise of another company, is far from costless; the dealer can never transfer all his clientele to the new brand. Moreover the number of full-line companies is very limited.[4] The right to handle the line of one of them may therefore mean the dealer's entire livelihood and be sufficiently precious to induce him to do things which are not necessarily in his or in the social interest.

In these circumstances, the fact that buyers and sellers find exclusive contractual relationships sufficiently satisfactory to enter into them does not necessarily make them socially acceptable.

[4] The numerous new entrants to the farm equipment field since 1940 are (except for Ford and Ferguson, and the latter is now reported planning to merge with Massey-Harris) highly specialized and cannot offer anything like a full line. *Ibid.*, pp. 66, 102–105. The production of farm implements, considering the entire, highly variegated group as a whole (omitting only tractors), is relatively unconcentrated. But in 1947, 87.6 per cent of the production of tractors, to which the full line is usually attached, was concentrated in eight firms. Information submitted by the Secretary of Commerce to the Celler Committee, *Hearings*, Serial No. 14, Pt. 2-B (1949), p. 1438.

The existence of mutual economic advantages in such an arrangement does not justify a seller's insisting on it. Society may deny either party the right to demand an exclusive tie, merely in the interest of fair dealing between supplier and dealer. But it will be reinforced in this decision by the effect of the arrangements on competitors and on the public. Where one of the parties exerts pressure in such a way as to make entry difficult for others, it should perhaps require convincing positive evidence of the necessity for such arrangements, rather than negative evidence of lack of harmful apparent effects on economic performance—an elusive test, we have argued—to vindicate them. The presumption of antitrust must be against exclusive tactics and in favor of easier entry into oligopolistic markets.

The structure of the farm machinery industry is not greatly different from that of the West Coast petroleum industry: the four leading full-line manufacturers accounted in 1948 for 55.2 per cent and the top eight for 73.6 per cent of total national sales.[5] Since the policies of all the leaders (except Allis Chalmers, which came on the scene late and had to take many nonexclusive dealers) paralleled those of J. I. Case, Judge Nordbye might well have found, as Justice Frankfurter did in *Standard of California*, that exclusive dealing policies have probably helped the equipment firms that dominate the industry maintain their position.

These considerations led the government to institute its cases against the farm equipment companies, the legal aspects of which were summarized in Chapter 4.

The important difference between *Standard of California* and *J. I. Case* is that, in the earlier, exclusive dealing was the clearly established practice and openly avowed policy of all the oil companies and, in the later—where the economic justification for exclusive dealing was probably greater—the practice was far looser. Nonetheless, as we concluded in Chapter 4, a decree which prohibited coercive pressure for exclusive dealing might have been a salutary influence and might have helped to protect dealers (and through them independent competitors) from "unreasonable salesmanship."

[5] 101 F.Supp. 856, 858 (1951). See also, on the petroleum market, p. 183, below.

But formal judicial procedures are ill adapted to dispose of the types of complaints and frictions that inevitably arise in relations between quasi-exclusive dealers and their suppliers. The solution would seem to be (perhaps, but not necessarily, imposed by a decree) the establishment of joint dealer-management committees to hear appeals from contract cancellations, with perhaps ultimate appeal to an impartial arbiter. The procedure might provide for processing less important grievances than cancellations of dealerships.

The point of view of the manufacturers of farm equipment may well be that because there have been only a relatively small number of complaints—let us say that one-half of the 108 instances offered by the government in the *J. I. Case* trial were authentic, though Judge Nordbye thought it was less—the problem is inconsequential, the substantial dangers disproved. But the grievances that reach the government will always be exceeded by those that do not. And where bargaining power is disparate, setting up a formal arrangement for handling complaints is a means not only of reaching mutually satisfactory solutions, but perhaps more important from the point of view of the supplier, of preserving and enhancing the morale of the distributive organization. "Getting close" to the dealers, "leaving the front office door open," discussion of mutual problems at company-run dealer schools—these, like the devices employed in labor relations before the Wagner Act, are not enough to assure the measure of equity or of participation in the "management team" that many dealers now believe is their due.

At the same time, one must be alert to the danger that the course of "fair dealing for dealers" may end up like the "fair trade" movement in injury to the consuming public. Dealers need a Wagner Act much less than labor did in 1935; and the first successes of excessively strong dealer organizations might be in forcing manufacturers to give them exclusive territories and to police "bootleggers" in the industry more effectively than they now do. However, we need have no such qualms about protecting dealers against coercion to handle one manufacturer's products exclusively; the primary purpose here is to protect competitors, hence the consumer as well.

Exclusive Dealing and the Effectiveness of Competition in Gasoline Retailing

Exclusive dealing in petroleum may occur at two levels: the wholesale and the retail. Major oil refiners do not usually have comprehensive exclusive contractual arrangements with their wholesale distributors. The distributors do sign minimum requirements contracts that in effect prevent handling of competitors' products, except in emergency. Besides, the custom of most distributors is to advertise their supplier's brand name as widely as possible (in gasoline more than in home heating oil), and with the supplier's name and colors on their stations it would constitute misrepresentation to shift from one to another, even if the supplier did not object.

Suppliers appear to make much more direct use of their financial strength to produce exclusive dealing on the part of the service station operator. The increasing cost of service stations, which in good locations even in rural areas may run as high as $25,000 to $35,000, puts the major supplier, which can build and lease or endorse the operator's note, in a strategic position to insist on the handling of its products alone. It appears to be true that the operators who lease on short term from the majors —and this includes some 50 per cent of all service stations—are subjected to this kind of pressure in one way or another. There are enough advantages to handling a single full nationally branded line to induce most service stations to be more or less exclusive without further encouragement. However, there is very little question also that the supplier typically exerts a very real influence in making the practice much more rigid than it otherwise would be in the distribution of petroleum products, tires, batteries, and accessories. The relation of financial control over stations to exclusive handling and the nature of the pressures are best conveyed by the following quotations from a survey of the 33 service stations in an eastern town:

> The oil companies want the dealers to push their own line of TBA [tires, batteries, accessories], and frown on their stocking competing products. One dealer said, flatly, he would lose his lease if he carried competing tires and batteries. . . . Others said the sup-

plier "wants" the dealer to go along with its TBA program. The general consensus, clearly, was that a dealer who insists on carrying competing products in considerable quantities is treading dangerous ground. This does not add up to a complete prohibition of competitive TBA enforced by threat of cancellation. Where certain customers express a marked preference for . . . particular brands of accessories, in most cases the dealer will meet their demands. . . . A few dealers keep a very small stock of competing tires . . . on hand. Others, however, go 100 per cent, and refuse to provide customers with any competing brands. . . .

The general attitude expressed toward split-pump, or divided operation, was, roughly; "I wouldn't want it if I could get it, and besides I couldn't get it." . . . Two of the major brand dealers said they would like to have several brands for sale . . . but could not get a contract for any major brand today on a non-exclusive basis. All the other dealers echoed this latter verdict, while also proclaiming a lack of interest in the possibility. . . .

There is a certain special consumer demand for . . . the Pennsylvania grade motor oils. . . . Approximately one-half of the dealers interviewed carried a small stock of these competitive lubricants. . . . *However, the only ones who openly advertise the fact,* exhibiting these motor oils in the show-window, *are the dealers who own their land and buildings,* and have no lease-back arrangement. Although there are no restrictions to this effect written into the contracts, it was quite apparent to the interviewer, and most of the dealers did not hesitate to say so, that the supplier does not want other motor oils carried in stock. . . . Hence, those dealers who are tied to their supplier, yet who are permitted to keep some of these lubricants on hand, keep them in the back room. . . . One reported that his supplier's representative even checks his cellar to make sure he is not carrying too much.[6]

In proceeding against Standard of California the Department of Justice acted to curb a practice that was being used to impose restraints at two of the levels listed at the beginning of this chapter. Certainly it was used to limit access of nonmajors to the service station market. It is likely also that it was or is used with some effectiveness to restrain price cutting. The abovementioned eastern dealer survey has this to say on the subject:

[6] Marshall C. Howard, *Survey of Retail Gasoline Dealers,* reproduced as App. B in his *The Marketing of Petroleum Products.*

Each major supplier "suggests" the proper price to him [the dealer], and dealers accept the "suggestions." There is no reason not to, they say, and any one who has been in the business any length of time does not have to be "educated." [7]

When the economist turns to the question of whether competition in the oil industry under a system of exclusive dealing may nonetheless have been sufficiently workable to vindicate the practice, or more effective than it will henceforth be, he as well as the judge finds himself "set[ting] sail on a sea of doubt." [8] It was for this reason that the Supreme Court majority in the *Standard of California* case prudently refused to apply economic performance tests.

Justice Jackson (joined in dissent by Justices Vinson and Burton) was entirely correct when he said, in a clear statement of the workable competition thesis, that exclusive dealing is "a device for waging competition" as well as for denying competitors access to the market, and that "the retail stations . . . are the instrumentalities through which competition for . . . [the] ultimate market is waged." [9] It is not at all clear that the dominant companies have been able through exclusive dealing progressively to entrench themselves or to eliminate competition among themselves, as the government has claimed in another suit against all the West Coast majors.[10] There are numerous elements of intense competition in the rivalry among majors and independents, for dealers and retail outlets and through dealers, that are genuinely beneficial to both retailers and ultimate consumers.

Lockhart and Sacks, who argue persuasively the need for a more thorough investigation by the courts of the economic consequences of exclusive dealing in Section 3 cases, will apparently be satisfied if courts in the future choose to regard the *Standard* decision as having turned not on the mere "substantiality" of

[7] *Ibid.* See also Bain, *The Economics of the Pacific Coast Petroleum Industry*, I, 203–205, II, 300–301, and III, 101–102.

[8] The phrase is Judge Taft's in *U.S.* v. *Addyston Pipe and Steel Company*, 85 Fed. 271, 284 (1898).

[9] 337 U.S. 293, 323–324 (1949).

[10] *U.S.* v. *Standard Oil of California*, Complaint (1950), pars. 62–64.

the commerce affected by these contracts (6.7 per cent of total gasoline sales) but on the dominant position of Standard (accounting for 23 per cent of all gasoline sales, by all channels) and the fact that the Big 7, all using exclusive dealing, tied up 75 per cent of the stations (and a probably higher percentage of retail sales) in the area.[11]

But even such a finding does not really resolve the economic issue. It does not prove that competition in the industry was unworkable or that exclusive dealing tended significantly to make it so. Consider the very real rivalry among the Big 7, the market impact of the substantial fringe of independents in refining and marketing, the increased efficiency of marketing under methods of controlled distribution, and the industry's impressive record of expansion of capacity and product improvement.

The major oil companies have pioneered in the development of sites for retail gasoline distribution; it seems likely that these sites would not have been so rapidly developed, and such numerous, conveniently situated, and attractive service stations erected on them, had not the refiners been assured that the stations would carry their own products exclusively. Here is an illustration of the familiar Schumpeterian thesis that some degree of monopoly is required for investment and innovation.[12] To protect the good will associated with their brands, they have induced, cajoled, bribed, and forced dealers to maintain clean rest rooms and provide the motorist with many other services. These are intense and in many ways socially beneficial methods of competition. Has their effect been to keep competitors out of the market? Richfield contended that it could not reasonably be accused of foreclosing just because it denied other refiners access to service stations *which it had itself constructed.*[13] The con-

[11] In 65 *Harv. Law Rev.* 940–941 (1952); see 337 U.S. 293, 309 n. 12 (1949).

[12] Another illustration is the possibility that oil companies might (though one could never prove this) have been less willing to invest heavily in exploration and discovery of new sources of crude oil and expansions of refining capacity without controlled market outlets.

[13] 99 F.Supp. 280, 291–294 (1951). Yet much of the acquisition of service stations by majors has involved pre-emption of desirable sites and securing control of already constructed stations by purchase and long-term lease.

tention surely has merit. The history of the oil industry offers many instances of companies which had formerly sold through others deciding to finance the construction of exclusive outlets in order to compete more effectively in the final market with refiners and distributors already entrenched in that market. Exclusive dealing has helped to assure the producer of an unknown brand adequate representation and has thus been a means of affording to a new entrant really satisfactory access to the market.

On the other hand, as we have already pointed out, exclusive dealing by small firms breaking into the market is probably not illegal, nor should it be. We confine our attention therefore to the pursuit of this practice by the dominant firms. As practiced by them, it has undoubtedly had anticompetitive and uneconomic consequences. First of all, the pattern of competition by pre-emption of desirable sites and market outlets has undoubtedly caused waste, contributing to an excessive profusion of service stations, whose construction would not have paid purely as retailing or real estate ventures.[14] In listing the kinds of economic considerations which they feel the courts should take into account in Section 3 cases, Lockhart and Sacks mention the "effect [of exclusive dealing] on bringing additional dealers into the market." [15] However, they recognize this may not be an unmixed economic gain. Do they imply therefore that the Supreme Court should have had to decide whether there were too many gas stations on the West Coast and weigh against this possible waste the economic benefits of competition among the excessively numerous dealers? Or to decide what portion of these offsetting consequences were properly attributable to exclusive dealing, and strike a balance between these, before deciding whether Standard might legally exert its leverage to close a substantial market to competitors? Would such a procedure make the law clearer to businessmen, as the critics of antitrust demand, and diminish the uncertainties of the law as now interpreted?

Second, competition through tied outlets is competition of a channelized and limited kind. Control over these outlets confers on the big refiner a far from universally effective means of

[14] See Bain, II, 239–250.

[15] 65 *Harv. Law Rev.* 926–927 (1952).

limiting price rivalry at both retail and wholesale levels and of limiting access to the market by the smaller, independent refiners and marketers, who are usually the price cutters. (Naturally, then, new entrants have had to resort to the same practice; where existing outlets are exclusive, the new entrant must of course procure his own.) Richfield explained its $20,000,000 investment in retail stations, leased out with a stipulation of exclusive dealing, on the ground that it was "compelled" after World War II to secure an assured market for its expanded refinery capacity. On the other hand, since it would in any case have been compelled by the pressure of capacity to find some outlet for its products, it seems probable that without such a guaranteed market Richfield would have been forced to offer price inducements to get dealers to carry its products, just as Standard of California has apparently been doing in the last few years on the East Coast. The resultant price competition might have taken on a cutthroat character, as it has sporadically in the East Coast region. But the economists and lawyers who have been criticizing the *Standard* decision have not, to our knowledge, been pressing the defense of exclusive dealing that it holds price rivalry in check! Standard has been the price leader on the West Coast and a price cutter in the East largely because in the first it enjoys and in the second it lacks a broad market coverage with controlled outlets.

Moreover, it is difficult to see why many of the mutual benefits and socially beneficent consequences of exclusive dealing require coercion for their achievement. As Justice Frankfurter pointed out, in the *Standard* case, "If in fact it is economically desirable for service stations to confine themselves to the sale of the petroleum products of a single supplier, they will continue to do so though not bound by contract. . . ."[16] If larger and less frequent deliveries are the efficiency by-product of exclusive dealing, there is nothing in the law to prevent refiners granting discounts that measure the cost savings of regularly scheduled, volume purchases. As a matter of fact, some of the major innovations in marketing, notably large-volume operations on low-unit margins, have, like the analogous grocery supermarkets,

[16] 337 U.S. 293, 313–314.

been introduced not by integrated giants and their tied distributors but by independent marketers. These cut-rate operators have often been able to buy their gasoline at favorable prices from major suppliers themselves. There is no reason why suppliers may not continue to give advice, assistance, and free paint to dealers who handle their products as long as these favors are not conditioned on exclusive handling. Nor is there anything in the law to prevent suppliers employing whatever inducements and pressures they wish to get dealers handling their products to keep their rest rooms clean and to provide free air and the like. The only thing they may not legally insist upon is exclusive handling.

In short, the economist can hardly be certain that a law which denies to dominant refiners the right to insist on exclusive dealing will weaken the force of market competition. The probabilities would seem to be to the contrary, and this is after all what the Clayton Act presumed and the *Standard* opinion contends.

What of Justice Douglas' dissent? If Standard is prevented from binding independent retailers, what is to prevent it, he asks, from taking over operation of the stations itself and thus achieving the same objectives even more effectively? This query raises the familiar issue of the double standard in the antitrust laws by which restrictive agreements between separate firms are dealt with more severely than proprietary consolidations.

Lockhart and Sacks would have the courts accept as a conclusive defense of exclusive dealing the prospect that its elimination would be "likely to cause the supplier to obtain the same results through integrating. . . . For, if exclusive dealing is bad, integration, a much tighter connection between supplier and dealer, is worse." [17] The proposal seems both unrealistic and undesirable. The prediction it requires is surely almost impossible. What one can predict with some certainty is that the demand for exclusive representation is, like most demand curves, positively elastic; if courts raise the price, by denying sellers the cheap way of achieving it, less will be demanded. In any event, a firm that wishes to chance its own capital and

[17] 65 *Harv. Law Rev.* 928 (1952).

managerial effort in undertaking a new function must, in a free enterprise system, be permitted to do so, unless the effect is a substantial restraint on competition. It must not be permitted to achieve the anticipated benefits costlessly by coercing businessmen who are supposed to be independent bargaining agents.

It is not necessarily an uneconomic consequence of the *Standard* decision that a major refiner wishing to exercise firmer control over retail outlets than the law now permits must assume the additional risks and responsibilities of acquiring them and running them itself. That full integration may permit greater operating control is balanced by the fact that it is also more expensive. In the face of social security and chain store taxes, it seems in fact unlikely that the oil companies will follow Justice Douglas' invitation, while other, more profitable claims upon their resources remain open for more intensive exploitation, unless the efficiency gains from exclusive handling are greater than on present evidence they appear to be.

F.T.C. Actions against Exclusive Dealing

Our summary in Chapters 3 and 4 made only passing reference to the numerous actions brought by the F.T.C. in recent years against exclusive dealing in the sale of hearing aids, malted milk, spark plugs, cosmetics, shampoo, motor cycles, carbon paper rolls, outboard motors and automobile parts and in candy-vending machines and hardware retailing. Only two of these actions (the cases involving Automatic Canteen Co. and Motion Picture Advertising Service, Inc.) have thus far (April 1954) been tested in the courts since the *Standard of California* decision.

The economic rationale applied by the F.T.C. in these cases is not easy to epitomize. On the one hand, in a case such as *Automatic Canteen,* the Commission appears to have been entirely justified in its condemnation of the company's exclusive dealing contracts with local distributors, although the evidence of market power and competitive impact provided in the findings and opinion was, as usual, skimpy and illogically presented. The finding was that the company had "monopolized" that portion of the market represented by its own tied distributors! Nevertheless, Automatic does occupy a "predominant position" in its business, did use its market power unreasonably, and created a substantial impediment to competitors without a corresponding benefit to the public.[18] Of course, some of the contractual obligations that Automatic Canteen imposed upon its distributors, to which the F.T.C. and Circuit Court objected by implication—the guarantee of a certain sales volume and a certain number of machines in location in proportion to the population of the territory and the agreement to stay out of the business for five years in the event of contract termination—may have been reasonable and unobjectionable. They may have been legitimate conditions for receiving from Automatic exclusive territorial agencies. But since Automatic was at the same time monopolizing the business, the *quid pro quo* was not reasonable from the standpoint of the public interest.

The Trade Commission order against Dictograph Products seems likewise to have been fully justified, for much the same reasons as in *Automatic Canteen.*[19] Thus, in some cases the Commission (or its staff) does seem to have had a clear view of one of the possible evils of exclusive dealing, the unfairness to weak competitors with inadequate marketing outlets.

Yet other decisions by F.T.C. trial examiners seem almost intentionally to disregard the circumstances in which exclusive dealing policies were practiced and to avoid any showing of their competitive consequences. The decisions are content merely to establish the fact that the manufacturer insisted on exclusive dealing (often in exchange for the grant of exclusive territorial distributorships) and to conclude therefrom that "the effect . . . may be to substantially lessen competition . . . and tend to

[18] The Circuit Court of Appeals upheld the F.T.C.'s finding against Automatic under Sec. 3 as well as 2 (f). 194 F.2d 433 (1952). Automatic appealed only the latter finding to the Supreme Court.

[19] Docket No. 5655, Decision, Sept. 24, 1953. Other proceedings where F.T.C. condemnation of exclusive dealing on grounds of injury to competition appears to be justified for similar reasons include *Outboard Marine and Manufacturing Co.,* Docket No. 5882, Initial Decision, Dec. 29, 1952; *Revlon Products Corp.,* Docket No. 5685, Initial Decision, July 15, 1952. In the latter, see pp. 2–3, 8–13.

create a monopoly,"[20] or that the manufacturer had effectively established a "monopoly" in the custom of its tied distributors. Whether these inadequate demonstrations of impact even on competitors represent defects only in the written decisions, not even a study of the record would indicate, since the Commission's legal staff was not interested in developing the facts. The remand of the *Maico* case should remedy this deficiency.

Seizing upon the apparent invitations of *Morton Salt* and *Standard of California* to dilute the rule of reason, the Commission had apparently become so intent on winning cases that it failed to realize the anticipated advantages of flexible and expert regulation of business practices by administrative commissions, rather than by judicial combat. It therefore came perilously close to undermining its very reason for existence. As Justice Frankfurter said in his recent dissent in the *Motion Picture Advertising Service* case:

> The Commission has not related its analysis of this industry to the standards of illegality in § 5 with sufficient clarity to enable this Court to review the order. . . . Apart from uncritical citations in the brief . . . [it] merely states a dogmatic conclusion that the use of these contracts constitutes an "unreasonable restraint. . . ."
>
> If judicial review is to have a basis for functioning, the Commission must do more than to pronounce a conclusion by way of fiat and without explication.[21]

Thus, in these decisions the Commission failed to establish either coercion or unfairness toward dealers, or appreciable exclusion of competitors from a market outlet, or a design to prevent competition among rival channels of distribution.

Tie-ins and Full Requirements Contracts—American Can and National City Lines

There are unquestionably instances in which tie-ins and full requirements contracts could not reasonably be said to impose an unreasonable restraint on purchasers, competitors, or competition. The seller who says, "I'll let you have this if you'll buy

[20] *In the Matter of Beltone Hearing Aid Co.,* Docket No. 5825, Initial Decision, Nov. 10, 1952, p. 2.

[21] 344 U.S. 392, 398, 399, 401 (1953).

that," may be merely competing for customers, the tie-in serving as the same kind of inducement as a price concession. It is difficult in this case to see how anybody is excluded from the tied-in market, in any meaningful sense. Indeed, a tie-in is not necessarily an exclusive arrangement at all: in the *Times-Picayune* case the defendants did not condition their sales of morning advertising space on a refusal of advertisers to patronize their afternoon rival. This is perhaps why the Department of Justice did not proceed against them under Section 3 of the Clayton Act. And there is no evidence that in the first year of the unit rule on general advertising the afternoon independent lost any substantial amount of business, even though the *Times-Picayune's* afternoon affiliate gained tremendously.[22]

Similarly, the seller who offers or agrees to supply whatever quantities the buyer will require in a given period of time may be giving the buyer just what he needs—an assurance of adequate supplies to meet unpredictable requirements.

Did Judge Harris' finding in the *American Can* case, that as there employed tie-ins and full requirements contracts were an instrument of monopolizing, contravene economic common sense? In 1946 American's shares in the national production of cans, sales of cans, and ownership of can-closing machines available for lease were roughly 40, 46, and 54 per cent, respectively.[23] Its share of can sales in the several regional market areas was often higher and sometimes lower, as high transport costs limited the effective range of marketing from particular plants. It seems indisputable that the tying together of two such dominant positions, in cans and machinery, whether by persuasion or rigid company policy, created an additional monopoly power, each position reinforcing the other. So the tie-in or integration itself may have been regarded as economically objectionable. American clearly had substantial market power and extended or cemented it by its tie-in policies. The same conclusion seems

[22] See the figures in 345 U.S. 594, 618, n. 39 (1953). Still, in the second half of the first year the *Item's* lineage ran approximately 6 per cent below the level of the corresponding period in the preceding year, while the combined lineage of its competitors increased substantially. *Ibid.*

[23] 87 F.Supp. 18, 21–23 (1949).

justified with respect to the extremely long-term requirements contracts.

In Judge Harris' evaluation of American's methods of "competitive massage" may be found the attitude one finds in the Robinson-Patman Act and the *A & P* decisions. Large firms are denied the use of various competitive devices to gain or retain customers. Yet the same thing might be said of almost every Section 2 case from *Standard of New Jersey,* in 1911, to *United Shoe,* in 1953. In those cases, as in this, the courts condemned certain business practices which, though not inherently predatory and not unreasonable in other circumstances or if employed by other companies, amounted in the circumstances of these cases to the use of market leverage unfairly to exclude competitors and to maintain a long-established dominant position in the industries concerned.

Tie-ins, like integration, are dangerous only if the contract (or consolidation) embraces one product or operation in which the company enjoys substantial monopoly power. It is this monopoly which provides the lever for extending power into otherwise more competitive areas. Judge Harris' opinion seems to identify the lever in the *American Can* case as the defendant's dominant position (54 per cent) in the provision of can-closing machines for lease. But the major reason for American's dominant position in this field was, apparently, that it rented the machines very cheaply, in order to induce canners to take its cans exclusively. Were there strong patents on the machines, as in *International Salt,* the company's apparent policy of making its money on cans rather than on machines might have reasonably been adduced as additional evidence of an intent to use a legal monopoly in one area to obtain a preferred, profitable position in another. But if American's power in the machinery field, which gave it a leverage to "force" its cans on lessees, issued merely from its willingness to absorb book losses on that phase of the business, it might not seem so clear to an economist as it apparently was to Judge Harris that a monopoly power in one area was used to reduce competition in another, or indeed that the low charge on machines was anything more than an accounting fiction.

In short, American may be regarded as having sold a combined service. It enticed its customers to take the combination by supplying one portion at a low price and by other inducements. Was not the attack on the offer of such a package a blow at integration itself? The dominant can manufacturer had an unusual incentive to develop superior machines for closing cans. It undoubtedly made an important economic contribution in providing for canners a combined service, with accompanying guarantees of performance, efficient repairs, and technical assistance. The only relevant price, the economist might feel, was that of the total package, not of any one part of it. If this combined price were not satisfactory, he might ask, could not the customers have turned elsewhere? And if customers' alternatives were too limited, was it American's tie-in that was responsible or the inability of competitors to offer the services as satisfactorily? Should not the decision have turned, then, on the comparative efficiency or market performance of American and its integrated or nonintegrated competitors?

The answer is no. The law cannot require an appraisal of the relative efficiencies of different firms or of doing business in this way or that. The appropriate question of public policy is not "Is the package bargain the most satisfactory for customer and supplier alike?" but "Are customers given a real opportunity to accept or reject the combination on its merits?" The determination of where one "product" or service ends and another begins, crucial to the identification of tie-ins, is inevitably in some measure arbitrary. When the court ordered American to offer customers cans and machinery separately, it was merely accepting the company's own formal usage; American had itself been offering them separately, so far as formal appearances went, and resorted to various informal pressures and understandings to tie them together. The two did not constitute inseparable parts of a unit; so that it would not have been unreasonable to ask for either one without the other on proportionally the same terms as they were available in combination. The same is true of the supply of cans for any one year, which American tied to the supply for the subsequent four years. It does not follow that American must henceforth fill some canner's order for single cans or for a single day's supply of cans, or that General Motors, denied the right to tie together purchase of its cars and use of its installment credit agency, must henceforth be willing to sell Chevrolets without brake linings or paint.

A decision like *American Can* does not mean that a big company may not compete vigorously. The prohibition of "competitive massage" is, properly, limited to its use in order to tie-in or to secure requirements contracts of unreasonably long duration.

Nor need reasonable "package" bargains be prohibited. Judge Harris recognized that in the canning industry, dependent as it is on variable crops, contracts imposing mutual exclusive and inclusive obligations—exclusive upon the canner, to buy the cans needed solely from one supplier, inclusive on the manufacturer, to supply as many cans as the size of the harvest dictates—are a virtual necessity. So he sanctioned one-year requirements contracts as meeting the needs of both parties, while permitting "competitive influences to operate at the expiration of said period. . . ." And of course nothing in the decision denied American the right to offer canners the opportunity to take its machines and cans together, if they freely chose. The market may now judge the advantages of the combination, as it could not before. In contrast, in the *Times-Picayune* case, six Supreme Court justices were so impressed with the cost savings of integration—thereby doubtless earning an "A" from several economics professors who have been trying to teach them about workable competition—that they forgot to ask whether these savings justified permitting a monopolist to force customers to take advantage of them by promulgating the ineffable unit rule. They might have been justified in their reasoning had the case involved an attack upon a unit *rate,* fairly mirroring these savings, offered to customers without compulsion.[24]

It is too early to judge the economic consequences of the *American Can* decision. The final judgment, entered on June 22,

[24] See 345 U.S. 594, 623–624 (1953). Had the unit rate alone been at issue, the economic question might have arisen whether the unit rate lower than the sum of the two individual rates may not have mirrored a saving in cost, and whether a requirement of separate, full-cost pricing for each service might not have denied customers these advantages.

1950, fell short in essential respects of a substantial alteration in the industry's structure. Because it did not appreciably diminish American's power, amendment of some of its major provisions is still under consideration. Those who advocate horizontal disintegration of the duopoly which dominates the industry, essentially on the ground that such a market structure cannot produce workable competition, should take note of the important ways in which the giant companies have developed the can-making art, and the problematical benefits of dissolution.[25] To the new critics of antitrust, on the other hand, one can only point out that, despite the defendant's predictions to the contrary, in the first sixteen months after the decree, canners had chosen to purchase outright approximately 27 per cent of American's machines.[26] Evidently the package did not suit all the customers. If this greater freedom of choice on the part of canners has any effect at all, it can only contribute to easier entry of competitors into the can industry.

In the *National City Lines* case even the rather mild coercion that characterized the relation of American Can with its customers was absent. Instead the victim arranged, indeed thought up and merchandised, its own exploitation. Particularly in view of the tenuousness of the conspiracy aspect, this decision seems to jeopardize even individual full requirements contracts, reasonably serving the mutual interests of the parties and embracing negligible percentage shares of the relevant markets concerned.

Clearly, *National City Lines* stands at the frontier between competition and freedom of contract, on the one hand, and exclusion, on the other. Competition consists in large measure of offering financial incentives, "free" service, discounts, credit, leases at nominal rentals, assistance in decorating, constructing, or arranging a place of business, in exchange for a contract of

[25] For a judicious review of these considerations, see Charles H. Hession, in Adams (ed.), Chap. 10.

[26] *U.S.* v. *American Can,* Report of the Antitrust Division concerning Pacific American Fisheries (1952, mimeo.), p. 34. By September 1953 American had sold 72 per cent of its machines (Simon Whitney, MS, to be published by Twentieth Century Fund). Whitney reports also that since the decision, canners have shifted their orders from one supplier to another with greatly increased frequency.

sale. Are such inducements to be prohibited if they succeed in getting and holding a customer? Does the *National City Lines* precedent prohibit an engineering firm's granting a ten-year loan to an impecunious steel company, in order to get the latter's order to construct a blast furnace? Does it stand in the way of a can company's building a factory near a large customer, under protection of a commitment by the latter to take all his requirements from that plant, insofar as the latter can supply them? Does it make a mail order corporation subject to penalty for lending money to a dress or tire manufacturer to build a new factory the entire output of which it will take, or an automobile manufacturer for making similar arrangements to secure its supplies of steel? Will such of these financial inducements (and the competition of which they are a manifestation) as are not worth offering except in exchange for long-term full requirements contracts then no longer be forthcoming? And will the result be a poorer market performance?

From the standpoint of the economical utilization of Antitrust Division resources, the *National City Lines* proceeding was almost submarginal. Nevertheless, we doubt that the decision is likely to have harmful economic consequences. The cause of effective competition will not be appreciably advanced in the long run by permitting firms to use their financial resources simply to bind customers to them for long periods of time. This is especially true when the customers are regulated monopolies, like bus lines, taxi, or telephone companies. In an analogous (but, we think, much stronger) case the Department of Justice moved against a company in the business of making loans on real estate for requiring borrowers to take out hazard insurance exclusively through or from it.[27] The Department does not claim that the defendants in this case any more than in *National City Lines* enjoy a monopoly in the lending business, to which they tie their other sales; or that they have achieved or threaten to achieve a monopoly in the tied-in markets—other than, as the complaint puts it, that portion of the business which they obtain for themselves in this fashion. However no evidence is required to show

[27] *U.S.* v. *Investors Diversified Services, Inc.,* 102 F.Supp. 645 (1951), Complaint.

that a company which made over $192,000,000 of mortgage loans in 1949 enjoyed a substantial power to limit the freedom of borrowers in their choice of insurance companies. The defendants clearly were in a position to throw a substantial volume of business in an essentially unrelated field their way and to keep it from competitors; and they did so. The resultant restraint in the tied-in field was surely unreasonable.

The government's definition of monopolizing, without reference to market shares or elasticity of demand, may seem meaningless to an economist. Its use, however, is a sign not necessarily of economic illiteracy but of the irrelevancy of economic evidence except when it helps establish the nature of the act. Monopolizing at law is a coercive and unreasonable course of conduct.

Indeed, it is not clear that suppliers should be encouraged to be investment bankers for their customers at all. Against the possible gain in investment activity resulting from the special interest which may induce a supplier to make long-term loans that no impartial banker would make, the economist must weigh the alternative uses of such funds and the possible distortion of investment when the capital market is circumvented and extraneous criteria guide it.

Where it is necessary for suppliers to offer competitive inducements in the form of services or credit to make sales, it may be presumed they will continue to do so, even if they cannot get an exclusive relationship in exchange. In fact, to the extent that the law strengthens the hand and increases the discretion of purchasers or dealers, sellers may have to compete more vigorously than before for their custom, and perhaps in socially more beneficial ways.[28] Any slackening of competitive efforts that may occur because the law has removed the prize of an exclusive relationship should be more than offset by greater freedom of entry into markets now rendered expensive to penetrate by the necessity of

[28] The big oil companies compete very vigorously for large commercial accounts, usually offering secret discounts from the openly posted prices. The ability of the National City bus lines to bargain for these concessions was seriously restricted by their contractual obligation to buy all requirements from Standard of California and Phillips.

providing capital to customers or of setting up one's own distributive outlets.

Conclusion

Drawing the line between competitive persuasion of dealers and abuse of power requires of course a nice eye and a fine sense of distinction, largely because the problem is one of striking a balance between conflicting legitimate interests. Or, to put it another way, it is extremely difficult, when interests conflict, to carve out from among those interests which seem legitimate to the individual those which conflict excessively with the legitimate interests of others or of society. J. I. Case has a legitimate interest in "adequate representation." But it does not have a legal right to sell only on condition that the buyer be exclusive.

The problem is partly one of defining the limits of socially acceptable representation. From the point of view of single-minded salesmanship, which will admit of no respect in which a competitor's product is equal to one's own, adequate representation and divided loyalties inevitably conflict. But actually, an alert dealer handling two full lines may give better representation than a poor dealer handling only one. Moreover, the dealer has a legitimate interest in a substantial freedom of choice, consistent with doing a good job for the manufacturer. And the consumer's interest may lie in having the dealer sufficiently expert and free to help him choose which particular products meet his particular needs.

The proponents of workable competition have pointed out that, where the market is imperfect in some respects, other imperfections may be required for effective performance. Here perhaps we have the opposite situation. The contention that impure markets, with exclusive dealers (who are not given the opportunity to be anything but exclusive) each vying for the customer's patronage, can provide an effective competitive performance perhaps assumes greater market perfection—insofar as consumer knowledge, discerning powers, and ability to shop around are concerned—than actually prevails. Perhaps, then, inadequate consumer knowledge necessitates an "offsetting perfection": the protection of dealers who are free to shop around and advise their customers. Exclusive dealing is supposed to make for the provision of better service; here is a service it eliminates.

It has been argued that the exclusive arrangement permits an ethical manufacturer to ensure careful fitting and intelligent prescription of hearing aids and thus to avoid the evils of self-service or 5- and 10-cent store distribution in a field where the customer needs expert advice and protection from his own ignorance. The question remains whether exclusive dealing is either a necessary or a sufficient condition for achieving these desirable ends. As for the former, ethical manufacturers might still refuse to sell to 5- and 10-cent stores. As for the latter, see the stipulations as to the facts and agreements to cease and desist from allegedly misleading advertising in the sale of hearing aids.[29]

The question of how much freedom of choice the dealer has a right to demand is complicated by the phenomenon of exclusive territorial agency, which may carry as its logical counterpart, for protection of the supplier, exclusive dealing by the agent. The manufacturer who confers an exclusive distributorship, an arrangement which may have substantial economic advantages, obviously must be permitted at least to hold his dealers to a high level of performance.[30] On the other hand, in the absence of exclusive agency, many of the economic justifications offered by suppliers for insisting on exclusive dealing disappear. The dealer may then reasonably be left to judge when the alleged benefits justify his taking on only one line; and the manufacturer can adequately protect his good will, delivery costs and the like by conditioning his sales and terms of sale on the dealer's achievement in these respects rather than on the socially extraneous criterion of exclusive handling.

These questions of the relative legitimacy of conflicting interests of the parties affected, including the smaller competitor and the consumer, can be resolved only on the basis of the facts

[29] Beltone, Dictograph, Sonotone, and Microtone, F.T.C. Stipulations No. 8277, 8278, 8279, and 8269, June 14, 1952.

[30] On the question of whether a consideration of exclusive agency is or should be relevant in passing upon exclusive dealing arrangements, see Watkins, pp. 209–210, 216, 218–219.

of each case. The courts can decide only whether the actions of the companies concerned, or of their representatives, have overstepped the boundaries between reasonable competitive promotion and exclusion.

Our summary investigations of leading recent cases seem to argue the impracticality of drawing these lines on the basis of purely economic performance. Whether the economist would agree with Judge Nordbye that competition is effective in farm machinery would depend on the economist.[31] The same is true of gasoline retailing. One must concede that an unhampered insistence on exclusive dealing by J. I. Case or Standard of California would be most unlikely in itself substantially to increase their respective market shares. Nor would sweeping antitrust condemnations of exclusive dealing in these industries radically change their performance. Yet it is reasonable to believe, as Justice Frankfurter argued, that a pattern of oligopoly control of markets may be indefinitely extended, and entry continually hampered, by the insistence of all the dominant producers on this marketing practice. It requires overriding proof of the necessity of such practices to justify the use of market leverage to ensconce oligopoly power. The substantiality of the risk that a blanket prohibition of the use of power to exclude competitors from a substantial market "will indiscriminately strike down the good with the bad" [32] has yet to be proved.

Attempts to demonstrate the economically beneficial consequences of exclusive systems of distribution are usually confined to an exposition of their undeniably competitive aspects (the manufacturer imposes exclusive dealing to cut costs or intensify his selling effort), in the same way that opponents of such practices usually confine themselves to a demonstration of their anticompetitive aspects (exclusive dealing excludes competitors). Both arguments are inadequate.

One could hardly discern, from some of the economic discussions of the merits and drawbacks of exclusive dealing, that

[31] Clair Wilcox concluded that competition in this industry was not effective. *Competition and Monopoly in American Industry,* T.N.E.C. Monograph No. 21 (1940), pp. 126–127, 168–170.

[32] Lockhart and Sacks, in 65 *Harv. Law Rev.* 940 (1952).

high on its list of merits from the point of view of the manufacturer is its partial substitution for, as well as limitation of, price competition. This is in large measure what businessmen mean when they say that exclusive dealing is a method of "regularizing distribution." For example, it is difficult to avoid the conclusion that current pressures in the direction of exclusive dealing in electrical appliances are aimed primarily at halting the "chaos" of severe price competition at the retail level.[33] When the Ethyl Corporation confined its licenses to "ethical" jobbers, it was no accidental association that its judgment of their business ethics was based on two criteria—adherence to posted prices and exclusive handling of suppliers' products.[34] A similar association of exclusive handling and resale price maintenance was condemned as an instrument of monopolization in the *Eastman Kodak* decision.[35] American business history presents innumerable instances of collusive price-fixing schemes employing group boycott —i.e., requiring distributors to handle the products of the conspirators exclusively—as the method of excluding and disciplining price-cutting competitors.

How does exclusive dealing discourage price competition? It makes access to the ultimate market more difficult for the smaller manufacturers, who are often perforce price-cutters because their brands do not command widespread acceptance. A tied dealer, who has associated himself exclusively with one well-known brand, is less susceptible to the blandishments of competing suppliers, indeed less free to succumb to them; his patronage can be retained without price concessions. And, concentrating his selling efforts on one brand, he in turn is less likely to use price as a factor in rivalry with other dealers. He is especially unlikely to have to do so where, in exchange for exclusive dealing, he receives his supplier's exclusive territorial distributorship. Exclusive agency simply holds down the number of distributors, each of whom is a potential price-cutter.

Why has the big distributor, exerting what Galbraith has

[33] See "Appliances Head for a Showdown," *Business Week,* July 18, 1953, pp. 66–68.

[34] *Ethyl Gasoline Corp.* v. *U.S.,* 309 U.S. 436, 454 (1940).

[35] *U.S.* v. *Eastman Kodak Co.,* 226 F. 62, 76–78 (1915).

termed "countervailing power," made the least headway in industries like automobiles, petroleum, and agricultural machinery? The reason is that through forward integration, or the quasi-integration of exclusive dealing, the giant manufacturing firms in these industries have developed their own controlled systems of distribution. In this fashion they have prevented big distributors from arising in their fields and have gained substantial immunity against the countervailing power of big distributors to wring price concessions out of them. Price competition breaks out among their tied distributors. But it acts mainly to compress the distributive margins, not to reduce the wholesale price.

It does not follow, because such competition as prevails in a particular industry operates through exclusive arrangements, that the outlawing of such practices will result in a net diminution of competition. The proffering of clean rest rooms and the multiplication of service stations are not the only ways of competing, or necessarily the best available. With dealers freer to buy where they choose and suppliers deriving less advantage from mere ownership or control of service stations, competition in gasoline may focus increasingly on the wholesale (tank-wagon) price to the retailer—heretofore the last to change even in price wars—and the way may be opened for a further application to gasoline retailing of the self-service, large-volume, low-mark-up principle that has so revolutionized the retailing of grocery products. The retailing of hearing aids may lay less stress upon the "custom" service, carpeted floors, and the ultradiscreet salesmen, whose function is to sell the differentiated product and associated services of a particular company, serving the customer as well as possible only within the price and quality (real and illusory) limits set by the "fair representation" requirements of an exclusive dealing arrangement.

CHAPTER 7

Price Discrimination and the Seller

PRICE discrimination has long been suspect among economists. It is an evidence of the existence of imperfect competition and of the exercise of monopoly power. For a seller to be able simultaneously to charge different buyers different prices for the same product (in the absence of differences in the costs of supplying them) there must be some factor preventing the movement of buyers from the dearer to the cheaper market, something blocking the entry of the lower-priced goods or of competitive sellers into the more lucrative market. Price discrimination is the monopolistic seller's method of exploiting the less elastic demand of some of his customers.

In addition, economists have long recognized the possibility of harmful effects of price discrimination on competition—when used by a powerful seller to drive weaker (but not necessarily less efficient) rivals out of business or when extracted by a powerful buyer who thereby obtains unfair advantages over his competitors drawing on the same source of supply. It carries the threat of distorting the process of competition by awarding victory on the basis not of efficiency but of financial strength and bargaining power.

There have been two traditional exceptions to this general condemnation. First, it has been recognized that discrimination by public utilities is justified when it permits fuller utilization of plant and hence lower unit costs on all business done. However, in view of the dangers of monopolistic exploitation or possible unfavorable effects on competition among purchasers, the practice in this area is sanctioned only under government supervision. Second, economists have admitted that discrimination is in some measure both inevitable and inconsequential from the social point of view and that it would therefore be futile to attempt to eliminate it entirely.[1]

Price discrimination has likewise been a traditional object of attack under the antitrust laws. To be sure, the law does not condemn either the practice or the monopoly power which makes it possible, per se. The enforcement agencies are supposed to act only when a substantial public interest is involved—when the practice poses a substantial threat to competition. The Sherman Act has been construed to prohibit the harmful effects of discrimination upon competition at both the seller's and the buyer's level, where the practice represents a means and evidence of monopolizing or unreasonably restraining trade.[2] Section 2 of the Clayton Act (subject always to the qualification, "where the effect may be to substantially lessen competition or tend to create a monopoly") was directed mainly against (or was at any rate effective only against) discriminatory sharpshooting by the seller against its competitors. The Robinson-Patman amendment of 1936 sought to bring the law squarely in opposition to the unfair competitive advantages enjoyed by one buyer over another.

[1] One may find all of the elements of the attitude above described in Alfred Marshall, *Industry and Trade* (London, 1920), pp. 415–418, 439–440, 521, 810–811, and in Harry Gunnison Brown, *Basic Principles of Economics* (rev. ed., Columbia: Lucas Bros., 1947), pp. 24–30, 186, 213. See also Clark, *Studies in the Economics of Overhead Costs,* p. 433 and *passim.*

[2] Price discrimination, with harmful consequences to competition at both levels, was an important element in the convictions of Standard Oil of New Jersey (221 U.S. 1, 1911), American Tobacco (221 U.S. 106, 1911), and A & P. Among the discriminatory practices condemned in these decisions were predatory local price cutting and the use of bogus independents and fighting brands, on the one hand, and the coercion of concessions from suppliers (including railroads), on the other.

The New Criticism and Price Discrimination

Meanwhile, since the formulation of the theory of monopolistic competition, on the one hand, and the passage of the Robinson-Patman Act, on the other, the legal and economic attitudes toward this practice have been re-examined. The theory of workable competition has suggested the following detailed defenses of price discrimination:

1. Oligopolists may be unwilling to chance price reductions unless, possibly under pressure by a big customer, they can make them secretly and selectively; they may similarly be unwilling to attempt promotional pricing except in a selective fashion. To require open, nondiscriminatory pricing may therefore deprive oligopoly markets of their only sources of price flexibility and rivalry.

2. Where producers and markets are geographically dispersed and transport costs important, the ability of some sellers to absorb freight on quotations to distant customers may make it possible for them to compete for such business with, and hence hold down the prices charged by, sellers more favorably situated, who might otherwise enjoy substantial local monopoly power.

3. Where there is excess capacity (for whatever reason, a decline in demand or the relationship between optimum plant size and location and the geographical and temporal configuration of demand), discrimination may permit a fuller utilization of plant.[3]

4. Discrimination in favor of large, perhaps vertically integrated, buyers (particularly in view of the difficulty of measuring precisely the cost saving on large orders, which may dispense with brokerage, save on advertising, and permit a more regular and full utilization of the supplier's plant) may introduce flexibility into the distributive system, helping to compress traditional markups, and prevent or disrupt a rigid stratification of functions.

5. A large buyer which does indeed make possible cost sav-

[3] "The thing that seems . . . in need of explanation is why economists should have thought that other industries were different from railroads. . . ." Clark, *Overhead Costs,* p. 10.

ings on the part of its suppliers may yet, in facing impure markets, have to coerce suppliers into giving it the concessions which its greater efficiency justifies.

In short, price discrimination may increase price flexibility and rivalry at the level of the discriminating seller and among buyers at various subsequent stages; and it may contribute to a more efficient use of resources.

On the basis of such considerations, many economists have concluded that the increasing hostility toward price discrimination manifested in the Robinson-Patman Act itself and, more recently, in the enforcement programs of the Federal Trade Commission and the Department of Justice, has impaired rather than promoted competition and an acceptable performance of industry. They would, in effect, eliminate if not reverse the traditional presumption against the practice.[4]

The Central Legal Issue

The legal issue between the antitrust agencies and their recent critics consists, essentially, of a dispute over the proper interpretation of the "lessening of competition" qualification of the Clayton Act prohibition. As far as effects at the buying level are concerned, the clause clearly exempts discrimination between two buyers who do not compete with each other, either because they perform different functions, like wholesaler and retailer, or because they are located in different areas, or because they are ultimate consumers. On the other hand, most critics of the law would concede the desirability of attacking discriminations which, as practiced by Standard Oil and American Tobacco before 1911, clearly have the effect of substantially impairing the effectiveness of competition as a regulatory force in the market place. The economists among them would probably add, however, that the better policy in such cases would be not to condemn the practice itself, but to proceed under the Sherman Act, as the government did in the afore-mentioned cases, to break up the monopoly power of which the discriminations were but a manifestation and instrument.

[4] Morris A. Copeland, "A Social Appraisal of Differential Pricing," 6 *Jour. of Marketing* 178 (1942).

But there is a broad intermediate area, in which price discrimination could eventually have this undesirable ultimate effect but can be demonstrated in the short run only to have injured or merely taken business away from competitors of the discriminating seller or the favored buyer. There are two separate (though seldom clearly differentiated) rationalizations of the attack on such discriminations. First of all, the antitrust agencies would deny or minimize the distinction between "preserving competition" and "preserving competitors." The way to eliminate competition is to eliminate competitors, and the illegal way to do this is to put them at an unfair disadvantage. To preserve competition, therefore, one must "nip in the bud" practices that may have only a "dangerous tendency" to lead to a substantial lessening of competition; condemnation must not await actual (or even probable) accomplishment of the illegal goal. Thus, the Sherman Act, as we have seen in Chapter 3, prohibits mere attempts to monopolize; illegal monopolizing does not consist in the actual attainment of a preponderant share of the market or even the actual exclusion of competitors, but the use of purely strategic superiorities to put competitors at an unfair disadvantage. Moreover, it was the precise purpose of the Clayton Act to strike directly at unfair trade practices before they actually produced undesirable results.[5]

Second, following the theory that we seek equity in some cases regardless of economic impact, a wrongful injury to an individual competitor is itself an evil to be avoided. It is doubtful that many of the discriminations which have been attacked in the areas of wholesale and retail distribution (in groceries and petroleum marketing, for example) seriously threatened a dangerous reduction in the number of sellers or the intensity of their rivalry. Yet it seems clear the Robinson-Patman Act was passed as a result of the belief that big buyers were obtaining substantial unfair disadvantages over small ones, in no way related to their superior efficiency, and that small buyers were being injured as a result. And the act had the purpose of preventing this injury to individuals.[6] As we have seen in Chapter 4, Justice

[5] *Corn Products Refining Co.* v. *F.T.C.*, 324 U.S. 726, 738 (1945).

[6] In fact, the provision for fixing maximum quantity discount limits

Black's majority opinion in the *Morton Salt* case virtually interpreted it so.

It does not follow, however, that every discount not justified by cost saving or protected by the good faith defense is illegal. The law still requires a demonstration, at least, of reasonable possibility of injury to competition in the market (such as even the dissenters admitted existed in the *Morton Salt* case), and the Commission has not necessarily been exempted by the *Morton* decision from some demonstration of actual or probable substantiality of injury to competitors.[7] But it does mean that it is unnecessary to demonstrate a dangerous tendency toward monopoly or general lessening of competition to establish a violation of the act.

It is here that the issue is joined. As the critics of the antitrust authorities have argued, to prevent price discrimination which merely "injures" or threatens to "injure" competitors (perhaps by no more than a reduction in profits) is to weaken the force of price competition itself. Every time a seller quotes a lower price to get added business, he takes business away from, hence "injures," a competitor in the sense in which the act has been interpreted. Is he as likely to engage in price competition if the only way he can do so is uniformly, on sales to all customers? When Sears Roebuck induced Goodyear to manufacture a private brand tire, on terms that were not available to Goodyear's regular distributors, it surely forced a very violent form of price competition on the industry. Sears achieved no dangerous monopoly power as a result, partly because other large buyers demanded similar concessions, which other rubber tire manufacturers were forced to concede. Yet the discounts to Sears unquestionably took business away from some of its competitors. If the Robinson-Patman Act protects rubber tire companies and

---

sought to protect small businessmen even from those competitive handicaps in buying that fairly mirror cost differences. (See pp. 121, 132–133, above, and pp. 242–245, below).

[7] These issues are by no means settled. Despite the notoriety of some of the leading cases, the F.T.C. has issued only 32 orders under Sec. 2(a) since 1947, according to its Division of Information, and only a fraction of these has been tested in the courts.

regular distributors alike from such price warfare,[8] the consumer may well in the end pay a higher price for his tires.

The Controversy in Perspective

There are two sides to price discrimination—a lower price in the more competitive market, a higher, monopolistic price in the insulated market. The traditional attitude stressed the latter; the new criticism looks mainly at the former. Similarly, one may look at the lower-price side of the coin from two points of view. The traditional distrust springs from its possible predatory character, the low price representing an abuse of power by the big seller or buyer. Economists have more recently been stressing the fact that it represents a necessary concession to obtain business in the area of more elastic demand, and hence is a method of competition. Obviously a consideration of neither aspect of price discrimination alone provides a sufficient basis for economic evaluation or for governmental action.

The distrust of discriminatory price cuts as a method of competition springs in part from the belief that a lower price to one buyer ordinarily means the price to other buyers will be raised correspondingly. Whether or not the elimination of discrimination will mean higher prices on the average thus depends to some extent on whether the discriminating sellers previously practiced "recoupment": Did the tire companies, forced to offer preferential discounts to big buyers, raise the prices charged their smaller customers in order to maintain their average markup over direct costs?

Recoupment is not impossible. Faced by a sharp drop in fuel oil prices in 1949, the oil refiners raised the price of gasoline in order to maintain refinery realizations.[9] There was evidence of the practice in the A & P case, as we shall see. Where sellers are few and powerful, they undoubtedly possess some unused power to raise prices and may be moved to exercise it in order to maintain a customary rate of return. Recoupment is inconceivable

[8] See pp. 242–244, below.

[9] Editorial, "What About Gasoline Prices?" *The Lamp* (Standard Oil Co. of New Jersey), June 1949.

only on the assumption that sellers are already maximizing profits in all markets.[10]

At the same time, recoupment is certainly not necessary or inevitable. There is no reason to believe that sellers who find it necessary to reduce prices to some customers will ordinarily be in a position to make up the loss by raising prices to others. It is doubtful that the tire manufacturers were able to do so, since their various customers were in competition with each other; the low prices to Sears, and Sears's low prices in turn to its customers, probably held down the prices of tires all around.[11] Weak sellers, from whom concessions are most likely to be extracted, are least likely to be able to recoup. Therefore a prohibition of price discrimination may result in higher average prices.

But even if the theory of necessary recoupment is unsound, it does not follow that discrimination necessarily means lower prices on the average. Conceivably, if sellers are denied the right to secure the patronage of valued customers by selective price cuts, they may have to reduce their prices to all in nondiscriminatory fashion instead. The traditional view tends to assume that price competition is possible on a nondiscriminatory basis; the critics tend to assume it is not. Again it is impossible to make a simple choice between these two premises, valid for all times and places.

In this chapter and the one which follows, we shall attempt, insofar as possible (within the limitations of such facts as are available in often frustratingly inadequate legal records), to illuminate the controversy by examining recent leading cases from both perspectives. Since the argument for discrimination is that in the presence of other market imperfections it may produce a better outcome than will be achieved if it is abolished, the task is obviously one of weighing the alleged contributions

[10] See the attempt of Rashi Fein to preserve the theoretical possibilities of recoupment without sacrificing the assumptions of marginalism and Adelman's reply, "Note on Price Discrimination and the A & P Case," 65 *Q. Jour. Econ.* 271 (1951).

[11] See Lloyd G. Reynolds, "Competition in the Rubber-Tire Industry," 28 *Amer. Econ. Rev.* 459 (1938).

of price discrimination to workable competition against its alleged harmful consequences, of comparing the probable consequences of this or that policy in the light of the available alternatives on the basis of the facts in each case.

As we attempted to demonstrate in Chapter 1, public policy toward price discrimination, any more than toward any other phase of antitrust policy, cannot be based exclusively on welfare considerations as defined by the economist. Since conflict between group interests, and between business and consumer interests, appears as nakedly in price discrimination as elsewhere, governmental authorities have to take into account the values placed on security and on equitable resolution of conflicts. Price discrimination is one of the most powerful forces for shifting rewards from one group to another. It frequently determines whether individuals, businesses, and regions will prosper or decay.[12] It is hardly surprising therefore that the Robinson-Patman Act has been so productive of acrimonious controversy, and not merely in academic circles.

The recent controversial cases involving price discrimination (all instituted by the Federal Trade Commission except the Sherman Act case against A & P) may be grouped according to the marketing level and the impact of the discrimination, although some of them fall into more than one category. The classification facilitates consideration of the different economic problems and equities of each kind of situation. The first group of cases are those in which the major alleged threat to competition has been at the level of the discriminating sellers. This type of discrimination, the subject of the present chapter, may be subdivided into two quite different practices: (*a*) the familiar use of local or selective price cutting as a seller's competitive tactic, whether predatory or otherwise, that eliminates or at least injures com-

[12] A large part of the administration of the Interstate Commerce Act has involved the continual compromise between economic principles (often extremely difficult both to formulate and to apply to rate problems) and the rights of established markets, ports, and shippers. A classic study of one of these struggles appears in H. C. Mansfield, *The Lake Cargo Coal Rate Controversy: A Study in Governmental Adjustment of a Sectional Dispute* (New York: Columbia U. Press, 1932).

petitors of the seller, and (*b*) the quite different technique, certainly not the direct concern of the drafters of Section 2 of the Clayton Act, of systematic discrimination (in the form of uniform delivered prices, hence varying mill nets) by a group of sellers serving as the instrument for the elimination of price as a factor in competition among themselves. These two species are illustrated, respectively, by (*a*) the sections of the *A & P* case dealing with the company's retail price policies, *Minneapolis-Honeywell,* and the cases against the manufacturers of spark plugs,[13] and (*b*) the various basing-point cases.

The second broad group of discrimination cases, which are the subject of Chapter 8, involve injury to competition among customers (direct or indirect) of the discriminating sellers. Among these it may be helpful to differentiate, somewhat arbitrarily, (*a*) those directed specifically against the large buyer, like A & P, Automatic Canteen, and the Atlas Supply Company,[14] for having allegedly exercised coercive bargaining power, and (*b*) those directed against sellers discriminating among alternative systems or groups of distributors, as in the above-mentioned *Spark Plug* and *Minneapolis-Honeywell* cases and the actions against Standard Oil of Indiana, the Ruberoid Company,[15] the book clubs,[16] and Sylvania Electric Products.[17]

Discrimination as a Seller's Competitive Tactic

One major facet of the Antitrust Division's complaint against A & P, sustained by the courts, was that the company had misused its massed selling power by operating certain divisions and sell-

[13] *Champion Spark Plug, Electric Auto-Lite,* and *General Motors,* Dockets 3977, 5624, and 5620, Findings, July 10, 1953. See also, among others, *Curtiss Candy,* 44 F.T.C. 237 (1947), and *General Foods,* Docket No. 5675, Complaint, July 7, 1949; Initial Decision dismissing Complaint, Aug. 27, 1952.

[14] Docket No. 5794, Trial Examiner's Initial Decision, June 18, 1951, affirmed by the Commission July 19, 1951, and uncontested.

[15] Docket No. 5017, Findings, Jan. 20, 1950, upheld 343 U.S. 470 (1952).

[16] *Doubleday and Company,* Docket No. 5897, Complaint, June 29, 1951, *Harper and Bros.,* Docket No. 5898, Complaint, June 29, 1951, and companion complaints.

[17] Docket No. 5728, Initial Decision, Dec. 9, 1953.

ing selected products for substantial periods at very low prices with the purpose and effect of driving out local competitors. The leading economist-defender of A & P has confined his observations on selling policy to a defense of the company's promotional pricing (operating individual stores or units at unprofitably low margins in expectation of inducing an expansion of volume and a decline of unit costs sufficient to make the margins profitable) [18] and thus offers no direct defense of the main object of attack, the discriminatory character of the pricing policy. Such a defense may, however, be constructed.

Promotional pricing is a more attractive policy if it can be selective, that is, confined to a particular area or market outlet. To require that it be nondiscriminatory might have effects similar to prohibiting a business from taking losses on its research department without doing the same on all of its operations. Experimental pricing, like research, keeps the market dynamic, competitive. Where there are economies of scale, it may pay off in lower unit costs for the company that has had the imagination (and resources) to risk it. And as long as competition remains effective, despite the disappearance of some less efficient, less imaginative, or merely less wealthy competitors (the government claimed only that A & P had achieved "partial monopoly," whatever that is), resources will in the end be more effectively used, and the gains passed on to consumers.

Moreover, most of A & P's retail price differentiation was, truly, a meeting of competition. Most of the units that ran at a loss for substantial periods did so in an effort to meet the far more aggressive competition of local chains and supermarkets. Many of the instances of local price cutting, such as the running of "specials," sales of meat or produce at or below cost, appear to have been in response to the opening or threatened opening of new stores by competitors. The response to competition, actual or potential, is an important element in workable competition.

However, as we attempted to demonstrate in Chapter 3, what the courts condemned in the *A & P* cases was not promotional pricing or the meeting of local price competition, but an entire

[18] Adelman, in 63 *Q. Jour. Econ.* 239–244 (1949).

course of action by the A & P Company. There is ample evidence in the record that the company consciously used "headquarters profits" and income from profitable retail operations to subsidize competition at the retail level in a highly selective fashion. (A & P officials themselves used the term "subsidy" to describe this practice.[19]) Many of the operations which A & P officials (and, following their usage, the government) described as "in the red" or "at a loss" were not really so: the deficits disappear when to the retail receipts of the unit or division in question were added their proportionate shares in the credits assigned by the company's accounting system to headquarters, e.g., the computed "profits" on manufacturing, ACCO's profits, and quantity discounts on purchases. Some of these retail "squeezes" therefore merely mirrored the efficiency advantages of integrated operations. There were, however, "selected" areas, as the government termed them, where the company suffered losses even after all such credits were allocated.[20] And in many cases the purpose of the local price cutting was clearly predatory—to "turn the heat" on unruly competitors. As A & P divisional headquarters said,

[19] See 67 F.Supp. 626 (1946), Government Brief, pp. 909, 931.

[20] Thus, the Boston unit lost money, after all credits, for five years in succession; the Springfield unit for five successive years. During the years 1932–1940, the Los Angeles Unit lost $1,406,194. 173 F.2d 79 (1949), Government Main Brief, p. 375; A & P Reply Brief Pt. I, p. 485. Moreover, not all the operations that were in the black after allocation of "headquarter's profits" were innocent in the sense that any resultant squeezes mirrored only the acceptable benefits of integration. Entirely apart from the fact that many of the profits were the product of coercive bargaining, it is questionable whether all of them should for analytical purposes be distributed among the retail units before deciding whether any of the latter operated at losses. No company really makes a profit by selling goods to itself, but not all the profits of integrated operations are properly attributable to the division making the final sale either. A & P's capital investments in manufacturing could have earned a return whether or not they were part of the A & P food distribution business. To the extent that the retail stores suffered bookkeeping losses before allocation of that portion of the profits which headquarters investments could have earned even though not integrated with retailing, nonintegrated competitors were being subjected to unfair competitive pressures unrelated either to the relative inefficiency of their retailing or to the superior efficiency of integrated operations.

with reference to the opening of a store in Richmond by an ex-employee, "the hotter we can make our program, the quicker this outfit will realize that they have no place in the supermarket business in Richmond." [21]

A continuing low price policy under the continuous threat of new entrants is indeed an element in workable competition; sporadic destructive price cutting only on the specific occasions and in the specific areas in which the entrants emerge or threaten to emerge is not the same thing. It may not make for workable competition to permit a wealthy company to operate all its stores in a region at a loss for five to eight years. Promotional pricing may make a market more competitive; selective promotional pricing may also be the instrument for making it less so. It does not follow, from the *A & P* case, that the courts will invariably condemn price differentiation which does indeed enhance rather than diminish competition.

Thus one cannot be certain that A & P's illegal price discrimination resulted in lower average prices and margins than would otherwise have prevailed. This was so first because in almost all the instances cited by the court of units selling at a loss, A & P was merely responding to, not initiating, the price cutting. And in the instances of individual zones and stores "turning on the heat," the lower prices were clearly limited in time and space until the threatening competitor could be eliminated or disciplined. This was obviously so where, in order to maintain its accustomed level of earnings, A & P actually raised prices in the

[21] 67 F.Supp. 626, 669 (1946). An Atlantic Division official said, "It might be necessary for us to operate unprofitably for several weeks . . . reducing our line of [*sic*] 10% several weeks prior to the time the competitor plans to open so that people in the community will be impressed with our low prices. . . ." *Ibid.*, p. 668. In an incident leading to reproof from A & P New York headquarters, Mr. King, head of the Pittsburgh unit, "called on two executives of the Streamline Markets in one of their new stores . . . and in a loud voice, publicly, before the employees and customers threatened to commence a campaign to bring about the financial ruin of Streamline Markets." He "zoned all of the Streamline points . . . and the prices in the zone . . . were lower than in any of our regular supermarket zones." *Ibid.*, p. 667. These were not the only illustrations of such practices.

areas in which competition was less keen. An ex-employee testified:

If there was a particular zone where the volume of A & P was low and competition keen, we would reduce certain items in that zone so that it would not effect a price change over the entire system. That works both ways. They could advance prices in certain zones where they felt competition was weak, and they hadn't much competition. . . .[22]

The fact that it was the company (not the Department of Justice) which first spoke of "subsidizing" certain territories shows that it was depending upon its insulation from competition in some areas to meet competition elsewhere, while maintaining the customary dividend rate. In the southern division, an official wrote:

Where stores need special attention because of unusually active competition . . . the stores in those towns should be put into a special zone and given the benefit of lower than average prices. In other towns . . . a little better gross profit rate can be obtained, with the result that the total for the unit will be in line with the program.[23]

The theory of "necessary recoupment" is manifestly unsound, as we have already pointed out. But obviously, also, recoupment may be both possible and profitable, even though according to one kind of economic theory it cannot be; and A & P apparently practiced it.

Nor does the fear seem justified that the decisions will soften the process of competition. The local independents or regional chains who may in the past have been deterred from opening stores near an A & P, for fear of having the "heat" turned on them, may now feel freer to engage in price competition with it. To meet or forestall such rivalry, A & P must maintain a nation-

[22] *Ibid.*, p. 666. See the argument by G. E. Hale that local price discrimination by a geographically integrated firm is the result not of integration but of the varying pressures of competition it faces. This analysis, used by Hale to show the fallacy of "recoupment," also casts doubts on the economic contributions of A & P's discriminatory pricing. "Dispersion: Monopoly and Geographic Integration," 30 *Texas Law Rev.* 444–446 (1952).

[23] *Ibid.*, p. 665.

wide low-price policy and thus exert a more uniform pressure for lower prices and greater efficiency all over the country. (As we argued in Chapter 5, had the civil suit seeking dissolution of the separate geographic retail units been successful, it might have proved a boon to both the public and the company, by permitting each divisional successor to exert whatever competitive pressure it chose without the stigma of being subsidized by others.) The company seems already to have taken this course. There is considerable evidence that during the 1930's, on the other hand, it relied heavily on discriminatory discounts and the ability to meet competition locally rather than on generally low prices or on innovations to improve efficiency.[24] Indeed, the fact that the company was so often on the defensive in protecting its market indicates that it was not, in these cases at least, the dynamic, competitive force it has been depicted. There is a general opinion in the trade that the effect of the Robinson-Patman Act and the *A & P* case has been to turn the competitive energies of the industry toward more efficient methods of merchandising and that A & P is not only a "clean" but also still a keen competitor.

The *Minneapolis-Honeywell* and *Spark Plug* cases involved discriminations allegedly injuring competition both at the selling and buying levels; we confine our attention in this chapter to the former issue. Honeywell, which enjoyed about 60 per cent of the total national sales of automatic temperature controls in 1941, sold its controls to oil-burner manufacturers for resale with their completed units, according to an established schedule of quantity discounts. Accounting studies established a cost justification for the first brackets of the schedule, with the smaller quantities and discounts, but failed to supply such a justification for the larger discounts of the higher brackets, involving some 55 per cent of the total sales. For these discounts, the company offered a good faith defense and a plea that they did not substantially affect competition. A majority of the Federal Trade Commission rejected both contentions. The Commission did not deny that competitors of Honeywell were offering lower prices (even after deduction of the controversial

[24] See p. 169, above.

discounts) to obtain these large accounts, and that Honeywell therefore probably had to grant the concessions (assuming it did not lower its base price) to get the business. But they denied that such an established scale of quantity discounts, unjustified by cost and covering so large a volume of business, satisfied the requirements of a good faith defense, which applies, they pointed out, only to price setting "in particular instances," "to meet the equally low price of a competitor." In short, Honeywell was forbidden to compete for business with a consistently discriminatory price schedule.

The Commission's attack on the pricing of spark plugs was one of a number of proceedings it launched against manufacturers and distributors in the auto parts business. The general purport of the complaints is that the manufacturers have given unwarranted discounts to certain customers, notably to automobile manufacturers in the case of spark plugs and generally to favored wholesale distributors. Because most of these other cases have failed to move even as far as an examiner's decision, because the complaints are singularly uninformative, and finally because of the general lack of recently published information on the automobile parts industry, it is not feasible to attempt to analyze these various cases as a group. We therefore confine our attention to spark plugs.

Champion Spark Plug, Electric Auto-Lite, and AC Spark Plug (a subsidiary of General Motors) account for about 90 per cent of the total national sales of this product. All sell plugs as original equipment to automobile and other manufacturers at 5 to 7 cents each, a price often "below cost." They sell plugs for replacement both to the same manufacturers and to various jobbers and distributors at prices of the order of 22 to 29 cents and higher. (These prices may no longer prevail, but the practice that they illustrate is still followed.) Champion, which at one time had enjoyed 80 per cent of the national market, inaugurated the discrimination between original equipment and replacement plugs long before 1936, when Auto-Lite entered the field. Auto-Lite argued that it adopted the practice in order to break into the original equipment business.

An F.T.C. complaint and the trial examiner's Recommended

Decision attacked this price discrimination as unfairly excluding competing plug manufacturers from the original equipment market and placing them at an unfair disadvantage in competing for replacement business as well, because the replacement business is said to go to the manufacturer of original plugs. The latter exclusion was attributed to two factors: first, the prestige attached to use as original equipment and, second, the fact that automobile manufacturers, persuaded by the favorable price to buy plugs (for replacement as well as original equipment) from one or another of the defendant companies, try to make themselves the sole source of supply for their dealers' replacement plugs, as for other parts. Only if its financial position was very strong, argued the F.T.C. staff, could a plug manufacturer afford to take the losses necessary to obtain the original equipment business until it could reap the gains on the lucrative replacements. Meanwhile the dominant companies, already enjoying the latter trade, are in effect using it to subsidize their competition at the original equipment level. In addition, the discrimination was said to injure competition between the sellers and the automobile companies, who were thereby dissuaded from manufacturing the plugs themselves.[25]

The staff's position in both the *Honeywell* and *Spark Plug* cases seems in many respects unrealistic and excessively doctrinaire.[26] The only injury to competition demonstrated in the first was the fact that Honeywell did obtain and keep the business of most of the favored customers: "To the extent that business is held or diverted to respondent from its competitors by its discriminatory prices and unfair practices, competition has been adversely affected within the meaning of the law." [27] Yet during the years 1937–1941, the period under consideration, Honeywell's sales declined from 73 per cent to 60 per cent of the industry

[25] Actually, since AC is a subsidiary of General Motors and, according to Champion's brief, Auto-Lite has ties with Chrysler, only Ford among the Big 3 would appear to be an unattached user of plugs with the option of buying in the market or manufacturing its requirements.

[26] See Hansen and Smith, in 29 *Harv. Bus. Rev.*, May 1951, 89, some of whose criticisms are summarized here.

[27] 44 F.T.C. 351, 397 (1948).

total. Its competitors' prices were lower and, according to Commissioner Mason's dissent, equally discriminatory.

The proof of injury to competition in spark plugs is confined to statements by independent manufacturers that they could not compete for original equipment business at the 5- to 7-cent price. But the staff never made clear why they cannot do so. For some purposes (in order to demonstrate discrimination between the automobile companies and other buyers for replacement), F.T.C. attorneys argued that the sales to automobile companies for the two separate purposes really constitute one combined transaction, at an average price somewhere between the 6 and 22 cents arbitrarily assigned to each. If this is so, it seems erroneous to predict that independents must assume losses for some undetermined period of time on the below-cost original equipment sales in order to break into the replacement market; insofar as the direct sales to automobile companies are concerned, the connection is immediate. Nor did the Commission make any attempt to measure either the importance of the original equipment prestige as a factor in competition for replacement business (other than to summarize conflicting testimony by stating that in some cases such a preference exists) or the amount of time it would take a new competitor to reap the rewards of an average 6- to 22-cent price to an automobile manufacturer in additional replacement sales at 22 to 29 cents, through other channels. If it is true, as the F.T.C. staff maintained, that the spark plug manufacturers must recoup their losses on original equipment sales through high replacement prices (this would be an interpretation different from the one, mentioned above, to the effect that the original equipment and replacement sales to automobile companies really constitute a single transaction), why would this not offer a rich opportunity to independent plug manufacturers to undercut and take over the replacement markets?

The F.T.C. staff failed, in short, to assess the real competitive disadvantage of independent manufacturers if they are equally efficient and able to offer the same engineering and research services as the three defendant companies. As in the case of heating controls, the industry has become, if anything, more competitive rather than less. Auto-Lite entered the field in 1936, met the Champion pricing pattern, and converted the industry from a duopoly into a triopoly; the three sellers obviously compete vigorously among themselves for additional business. Their assertions remain uncontested that there are no fewer independent manufacturers of spark plugs today than there were in 1936 and that the latter's restricted role is a consequence of their limited scale of operations and technical competence. These considerations undoubtedly moved the Commission itself, in rejecting the trial examiner's decision on this point, to find there was no showing that the discrimination between original equipment and replacement plugs injured competition.[28]

The spark plug companies justified their low prices on original equipment as required to keep the automobile companies from manufacturing the parts themselves. Ford's director of purchases corroborated this. Auto-Lite had the additional justification of having had to meet the pattern already established by its competitors. These facts establish the conformance of the sellers with the spirit of the good faith defense, even though they failed to cite specific equally low prices definitely quoted by competitors in each case (often an impossible requirement). Both Honeywell and the spark plug companies demonstrated that they were able to charge somewhat higher prices than competitors because of the superior quality (or consumer acceptance) of their product; consequently they could not demonstrate that the discriminatorily lower prices they quoted were just as low as those of competitors. Under such a restrictive reading of the good faith defense, Hansen and Smith have pointed out, a company must either match competitors' prices dollar for dollar, thus sacrificing its reputation as a quality producer, or be handicapped in offering the defense.[29]

Apart from the merits of the legal issues, there is no doubt that in both industries the criticized price concessions were necessitated by competitive pressures. On the other hand, the

[28] Findings, *Champion* case, July 10, 1953, p. 6.

[29] 29 *Harv. Bus. Rev.*, May 1951, 99.

same thing can be said generally about all discriminatory concessions; no company grants them, presumably, unless it has to, to get the business. The important economic question, then, is whether a prohibition of discriminatory concessions would have made for more or less effective competition.

There is no doubt that it was easier for the dominant companies in these industries to combat the competition of smaller firms by discriminating than by cutting their general price lists. Auto-Lite did enter the field and meet the other companies on the same level; but it is a large, diversified company. Competitive survival therefore depended in part on factors other than mere efficiency. Thus, the contention that the price discrimination placed independent manufacturers at some unmeasurable disadvantage, for the reasons already summarized, is by no means an unreasonable one. Given such a finding, the F.T.C., while freely conceding that no company offers discounts unless it is forced to do so, might logically refuse to permit the good faith defense to perpetuate a pattern of pricing that is unfair to competitors. And it would place on the defenders of such practices the burden of proof of their harmlessness and of the proposition that no other kind of competition is possible.

Would the economic consequence of establishing a more equitable system of competition have been an inferior or less competitive market performance? It does not follow, from the fact that such competition as has prevailed in the past has been discriminatory, that discrimination is the *sina qua non* of effective competition. Honeywell's prices were consistently above those of its competitors; the company was apparently exploiting the public's acceptance of its brand where possible. Presumably it needed the 55 per cent of the business on which it offered the allegedly illegal discounts. Is there any reason, then, to doubt that, denied the right to discriminate, it would instead have reduced its entire list of prices in order to keep that business? One can only speculate; but such an outcome seems extremely likely, if rivalry in the industry is as keen as Honeywell argued. As Commissioner Ayres pointed out: "The order directs respondent to cease and desist from discriminating in prices, and it may eliminate the discriminations by reducing its high prices as well as by increasing its low prices." [30] If instead Honeywell chose to confine itself to the high-price market, buyers in that market would have been no more exploited than before; the big buyers would still have obtained their favorable prices from competitors; and the dominant firm's share in the industry would have fallen below 60 per cent. It is difficult to characterize any of these alternative results as less workably competitive than the present system.

In spark plugs, similarly, the outcome of a prohibition of discrimination might have been more price competition, for two reasons. First, to the extent smaller companies are placed at a disadvantage by the practice of selling original equipment plugs at cost, their entry into competition would surely have been made easier by its abandonment. Even more important is the possibility that large users would manufacture their own spark plugs, a fact offered in defense of the *status quo*. A discriminatory price concession to the user who threatens to make his own is the cheapest possible way of meeting the competitive threat. Deny to firms the right to meet competition in so selective a fashion and they may have to compete by reducing their general price lists. Auto-Lite and Champion, at least, would certainly have had to consider this policy to keep the trade of the automobile manufacturers. Thus the result which the Trade Commission staff anticipated for the wrong reason (on the theory that if the sellers are forbidden to discriminate in favor of some buyers, they will no longer have to recoup their losses elsewhere, so that the low prices will rise and the high prices fall) would very likely have come to pass.

One possible justification of selective price cuts to big buyers is that, by keeping the latter from going into production themselves, they permit the fullest utilization of the sellers' capacity. But elimination of the discrimination between original equip-

[30] 44 F.T.C. 351, 399 (1948). Hession has pointed out that after passage of the Robinson-Patman Act, American Can Co. reduced its discounts to large buyers but at the same time cut its list price (uniformly) to all buyers. Simon Whitney surmises that the general price cut (replacing the selective discounts) may have been required to keep big customers from manufacturing their own cans (MS, to be published by Twentieth Century Fund).

ment and replacement plugs would not necessarily have caused Ford to make its own, and left the defendants with excess capacity. What the Ford official testified was that his company would do so if it had to pay the 26 cents which was approximately Champion's price to wholesale distributors.[31] This is not the 6 cents which Ford actually paid. Indeed, it is somewhat difficult to reconcile those portions of the spark plug companies' defense in which they cited their superior efficiency as the reason for their dominant position with their fear that nondiscriminatory pricing would immediately cause automobile manufacturers to make their own plugs. The critics of the antitrust agencies seem in this case to have fallen into the error they have elsewhere attributed to those authorities: they assume that when an integrated company performs certain functions for itself it has an advantage because it no longer has to pay someone else a "profit." [32] Ford might "charge" itself 6 cents a plug; but that would admittedly not cover its overhead nor justify the investment. Thus the defense of Champion's discrimination by analogy to a public utility, which has to discriminate to get the added business, fails. Unless Ford might have been more efficient, there is no reason why Champion could not have averaged its prices and still kept the Ford business, thus earning the same revenue and making full use of its capacity, without discriminating.

However, Ford's unexercised option would have kept a downward pressure on the uniform price. It apparently regarded the 26-cent price as richly remunerative. And if it decided that it could produce plugs more cheaply than it could purchase them at nondiscriminatory prices, surely the public interest would in the long run (at the possible expense of excess capacity in the short run) have been served by its doing so.

Hansen and Smith may have scored a debating point in demonstrating that the F.T.C. has at other times objected to the tendency for big business to expand its operations in this fashion.

[31] Brief of Counsel Supporting the Complaint, Docket No. 3977, Aug. 16, 1950, pp. 30–31.

[32] Compare Hansen and Smith, in 29 *Harv. Bus. Rev.*, May 1951, 90–91 and Adelman, in 63 *Harv. Law Rev.* 41–43, 53–57 (1949).

However, they have scarcely supported their own argument in the present context, that the F.T.C. trial examiner here advocated "soft competition," and that his recommended order would have produced a poorer market performance. Nor is their solicitude (rather, their expression of surprise at the examiner's lack of solicitude) for the smaller automobile manufacturers, who lack Ford's alternative and might therefore have been put at a competitive disadvantage if denied the lower original equipment prices, compatible with their own advocacy of hard competition. This is how progress is made under a competitive system. The Ford official testified that if his company decided to make its own plugs it would be compelled to compete for replacement business in order to obtain the necessary scale of production; the 26-cent price would then have been even more vulnerable. In this event, the industry might have faced the problems of excess capacity and cutthroat competition. But the F.T.C. has been attacked in this and related cases as the apostle of soft, not hard competition! Against the danger of excess capacity must be weighed the probability that economic progress is thwarted, on balance, if a supplier can buy off potential competitors with a preferential discount.[33]

The selective price cut on spark plugs sold to Ford, offered to keep it from going into production itself, might have contributed to hard competition if Ford had passed the lower price on as Sears Roebuck did with Goodyear's tires. But, so far as original equipment plugs are concerned, their low price could have been passed on to the new car buyer without in any way endangering the price of replacement plugs; and as for replacement plugs, neither Ford nor Atlas (another favored customer) apparently extended the discounts to their dealers, but they pressed the dealers to buy exclusively from them. Thus at one and the same time the discounts were sealed off and prevented from spreading, and competing spark plug manufacturers and distributors were prevented from breaking into the insulated,

[33] See, for example, the instance in which du Pont dissuaded Standard of New Jersey from embarking on the production of methanol under an I. G. Farben process in this fashion. Stocking and Watkins, *Cartels in Action,* p. 486.

high-price markets. Since automobile companies apparently exert similar pressures on their dealers with respect to all replacement parts for cars and are said to make their greatest profits on the parts business,[34] it appears they use their concerted buying power and threat to manufacture themselves only to line their own pockets.

In all the cases discussed in the present section, it seems clear that the positive evil that antitrust action sought to alleviate, injury to competition at the level of the discriminating seller, was but weakly demonstrated. Even the unfair injury to competitors was inadequately documented. The Commission confined itself to demonstrating the price discrimination and citing the complaints of competing sellers that they could not on individual orders meet the low prices of their large competitors.[35] In no case is it at all clear why the aggrieved competitors could not have quoted equally low, and similarly discriminatory, prices in order to hold their own. If each seller has roughly equal access to both high- and low-price markets, what harm is done by the practice of discrimination? Access was not always equal, but the evidence of substantial inequality of access was in no case entirely convincing.

Yet in each case it was the powerful, larger, better-entrenched seller that discriminated and got the business, without having to disturb the rest of a highly remunerative price structure. It is not an unreasonable attitude to deny to dominant firms the right to hold their markets in this fashion. The evidence we have considered does not suggest that the public need pay a higher price for the establishment of greater equality of competitive opportunity. On the contrary, it suggests that selective, insulated price cuts may have kept competition softer than it would otherwise have been.

[34] F.T.C., *Report on Motor Vehicle Industry,* House Doc. 468, 75th Cong., 3d Sess. (1939), pp. 134–135, 138–139, 1062; F.T.C., *Report on Distribution Methods and Costs,* Pt. 4 (Washington: G.P.O., 1944), p. 92.

[35] For similar evidence in the *Curtiss Candy* case, see Docket No. 4673 consolidated with 4556, Brief of Attorney for the Commission, Nov. 29, 1945, pp. 16–17.

Discrimination as a Method of Suppressing Price Competition

The basing-point cases have generated a tremendous volume of controversy, and the theoretical implications of recent decisions have often been explored far beyond the point of diminishing returns. The frenzy of hostile criticism that beat down on the Federal Trade Commission for its condemnation of the cement industry's basing-point system was generated because hundreds of businessmen who knew that they absorbed freight to meet competition and had no doubt that they were acting competitively were led to believe that they were violating the law. Yet in spite of the outraged and impassioned oratory of attornies for the cement and glucose industries in Congressional hearings, freight absorption has never, except as an integral part of industry-wide, delivered-price systems, figured in Federal Trade Commission complaints or decisions. So, in spite of the fears of Clark, the writers have been unable to read into the basing-point decisions (and in particular into *A. E. Staley*) any rule denying a company the right to absorb freight.[36] None of these cases presented the F.T.C. or the courts with the situation of a single company, acting without reference to an industry-wide pricing practice, absorbing freight either sporadically or systematically in order to compete. Hence we forgo the fascinating exercise of speculating about the effect of the basing-point cases on freight absorption in general or on nation-wide uni-

[36] See pp. 124–126, above. Compare Clark, "The Law and Economics of Basing Points: Appraisals and Proposals," 39 *Amer. Econ. Rev.* 432 (1949), with the *Staley* decision, 324 U.S. 746, 757 (1945). The court's solicitude for the customers located near Staley's Decatur mill, interpreted by Clark as jeopardizing all freight absorption, was merely subsidiary to its effort to decide whether in fact that company's pricing method was protected by the good faith defense. Since in addition to the clear statement in the *Staley* opinion the F.T.C. itself explicitly disavowed, as long ago as 1948, the view that all freight absorption was illegal ("Statement of Federal Trade Commission Policy toward Geographic Pricing Practices for Staff Information and Guidance," mimeo., Oct. 12, 1948), it is hard to share the excitement of an antagonist when he "discovered" the fact in 1953. Austern, "*Tabula in Naufragio*—Administrative Style: Some Observations on the Robinson-Patman Act," *1953 Symposium*, p. 114 n. 26.

form prices for candy bars, chewing gum, and the *Saturday Evening Post*.

In fact, as we pointed out in Chapter 4, only one of the basing-point cases really hinged on the legal consequences of price discrimination. The Corn Products Refining Company, using a single Chicago basing point, discriminated substantially against its nonbase customers, some of whom actually had to move as a result from the nonbase mill area near Kansas City toward Chicago.[37] Obviously Corn Products was unfairly injuring (as well as exploiting) some of its customers by charging them phantom freight. Nor does there seem to have been any economic justification for the practice: it made no apparent contribution to price flexibility or to a fuller use of capacity.

Freight absorption may, of course, make possible fuller use of a seller's plant, but there was no showing that Corn Products' Kansas plant (which alone might absorb freight when selling to customers nearer the Chicago mill) employed the technique for this purpose, or that a single Chicago base was necessary to achieve it. And in any case, freight absorption is legally permissible.

Much of the discussion about the economic consequences of the basing-point decisions has centered on the question of whether it is desirable to impose on the offending industries a system of uniform f.o.b. pricing, which would eliminate all discrimination in mill nets, or to permit nonsystematic, noncollusive, and "non-consciously parallel" freight absorption. Running through these arguments have been differences of opinion about whether any other system than uniform f.o.b. pricing is in fact permissible.

Those who have believed or have chosen to believe that freight absorption is now of questionable legality have predicted the following undesirable economic effects from the abandonment of basing-point systems: price rigidity, because a seller who wants additional business henceforth can get it only by reducing his posted f.o.b. price, thus taking a uniform cut on all his sales; exploitation of local markets by sellers freed from the competitive threat of market penetration through freight absorption

[37] 324 U.S. 726, 728–729, 739 (1945).

by more distant suppliers; and underutilization of capacity of sellers unable to absorb freight to find additional customers. A system of rigid, uniform f.o.b. pricing would involve these dangers, although they may be exaggerated. But because such a system of pricing is not required by law and would on the contrary be politically impossible to enforce in periods of excess capacity or on producers in surplus areas, it seems foolish to linger over these possibilities.

The immediate outcome of the basing-point decisions in steel and cement was the elimination of delivered pricing; each mill posted an f.o.b. price, and buyers paid the actual freight. Prices to distant customers therefore rose. But this termination of freight absorption was also the consequence of the high levels of demand. The higher prices that distant buyers had to pay as a result were in large measure nominal; under the basing-point system, when demand was flush, steel companies refused to serve customers in distant locations, because freight absorption was unprofitable. Thus the basing-point system failed at such times to guarantee the market interpenetration which was supposed to be one of its competitive justifications. Further, the institution of f.o.b. pricing has already had the effect of encouraging the construction of new cement and steel mills in deficit areas, further assuring those areas of supplies in time of future shortages and increasing the ultimate possibility of price competition in those markets. Finally, the elimination of the delivered price computed on the basis of all-rail freight has increased the possibility of price flexibility by encouraging customers to take cheaper forms of delivery. For all these reasons the temporary elimination of theoretically possible freight absorption has been far from a net loss to the buyer.

Moreover, as these industries have again been faced with surplus capacity, freight absorption has returned.[38] Of course even the basing-point system failed to prevent price cutting in steel in periods of slack demand.[39] If the elimination of the basing-

[38] "Real Cost Saving in Steel Due in 1954," *N. Y. Times,* Oct. 4, 1953, Sec. 3, p. 1.

[39] See figures from Lazar and Bean, "Labor Department Examines Consumers' Prices of Steel Products," 157 *Iron Age* 118 (1946), in Kaysen, "Basing Point Pricing and Public Policy," 63 *Q. Jour. Econ.* 297–299 (1949).

point system, with the abandonment of freight books, the introduction of greater uncertainty about whether a price cut will be immediately met by others, and the option of buyers to provide their own transportation, will have any effect at all, it can only increase the likelihood of effective price competition. This may take the form of freight absorption. It may also take the form of variation in f.o.b. mill prices.[40]

One virtue of the basing-point system, as Melvin de Chazeau has suggested, is that it permits competition in service (giving a buyer a choice among a number of suppliers offering a variety of delivery dates, for example).[41] To the extent that this is a real advantage to the buyer, it would appear that the commodity is not entirely standard or uniform; to this extent, then, it is not at all so necessary as proponents of the basing-point system frequently contend to have a pricing system that produces uniform

[40] Compare Kaysen (*ibid.*, p. 296) and Stocking, "The Economics of Basing Point Pricing," 15 *Law and Cont. Prob.* 171–172 (1950) with George Stigler, "A Theory of Delivered Prices," 39 *Amer. Econ. Rev.* 1143 (1949). Though our view is close to that of Kaysen and Stocking, their condemnation of f.o.b. pricing as probably excessively rigid and noncompetitive is not entirely convincing. For instance, the custom of selling cement by submitting bids on job contracts could, under an f.o.b. system, produce substantial price variation and flexibility. More important, where local markets are limited, freight absorption is scarcely less costly than a mill price low enough to assure access to more distant customers. Thus, the basing-point advocates have not made it clear why the Lehigh Valley mills, for instance, could not, even in the absence of freight absorption, be able to sell competitively in New York or Philadelphia. See testimony of Harold B. Robeson, president of Nazareth Cement Company, that the *Cement Institute* decision had forced his price 19 to 28 cents above his Boston, Baltimore, and Philadelphia competitors. Subcommittee, Senate Committee on Interstate and Foreign Commerce, *Study of Pricing Methods,* Hearings, 80th Cong., 2d Sess. (1948), pp. 776–777. He had apparently been absorbing that much freight theretofore; evidently with a soaring demand for cement, it was unnecessary to reduce his base price enough to eliminate the price discrepancies. Had the demand been less strong, the anomaly of which he complained would have disappeared. Meanwhile the f.o.b. system in cement has brought a rather substantial increase in capacity in deficit areas, which in turn may be expected to lead to more price competition. House Select Committee on Small Business, *Final Report,* 81st Cong., 2d Sess. (1951), p. 88.

[41] "Public Policy and Discriminatory Prices of Steel: A Reply to Professor Fetter," 46 *Jour. Pol. Econ.* 562 n. 34 (1938).

delivered quotations by all sellers who want to compete in any given market. This possibility of service competition also undermines to some extent the local monopoly defense of basing-point pricing; the defense is demolished by the continued likelihood of freight absorption in periods of excess capacity and the greater encouragement today to construction of mills in deficit areas. True, such freight absorption is less likely in periods when demand outstrips supply; but neither in such circumstances can a basing-point system induce sellers to absorb freight to challenge local monopolies. If anything, as we have pointed out, the elimination of freight absorption will at such times increase the willingness of manufacturers to supply distant deficit markets.

It is hardly worth while to add to the already overwhelming load of *a priori* commentary on this pricing system. Having dealt briefly with those who cried doom at its condemnation, it may be desirable only to dissociate ourselves also from those who expect great changes now that the system is outlawed. The structure of the industries employing the practice is unchanged. They will hardly turn suddenly to a violent price competition so alien to their habits and interests merely because a useful formula for eliminating it has itself been abolished. It was perhaps naïve for the F.T.C. to have ordered National Lead and its three competitors to stop pricing with the "purpose or effect" of "systematically matching" delivered price quotations, without being able to effect any change in the structure of the industry and without any evidence that the "systematic matching" theretofore had required any collusion beyond what was sanctioned under N.R.A.

It would certainly be even more unrealistic to suppose that, with National accounting for some 60 per cent of the white lead sold in the United States, tying up the pig lead output of American Smelting and Refining (the largest domestic producer of lead) by an agreement that also limited competition between the two companies, and "suggesting" resale prices and submitting bids on contracts identical with those of the other producers, the Commission was unjustified in holding that the industry's zone pricing system was a noncompetitive one! There is room for skepticism about the effects of the F.T.C.'s order. But at least National and its competitors now have to revise their pricing policies; pricing may become more disorderly. Surely no advocate of workable competition could quarrel with an honest effort to undermine one of the manifestations of dominant firm leadership.[42]

[42] The *National Lead* decision raises once again the question of whether a policy of enforcing effective competition can ignore a market structure so monopolistic that it is impossible to formulate an order under Sec. 5 of the F.T.C. Act sufficient to correct its performance. We have rather slighted this strong case for a pure market structure test of monopoly, even in Chap. 2 where we did discuss it directly, because it is obviously not part of the new economic criticism of antitrust that is our primary concern. We return to the question in our concluding chapter.

CHAPTER 8

Price Discrimination and the Buyer

IN CHAPTER 7 we considered the leading recent cases involving price discrimination whose impact was on competition at the level of the discriminating seller. We now turn to those discriminations, or those aspects of the discriminations already discussed, that were supposed to have threatened competition among buyers or their customers. Our division of the cases, placing in one group the actions directed against big buyers coercively exacting discriminatory preferences and in the other actions against sellers granting allegedly injurious functional discounts, is in some measure arbitrary. No seller grants a price concession willingly. Every discount, functional or otherwise, may be regarded as the product of buyer pressure or, what comes to the same thing, the pressure of competing sellers who make it possible for the buyer to demand the lower price of any one of them.

The problem of organization of the cases mirrors a vexing dilemma of public policy. The antitrust agencies have moved in some cases against buyers, in others against sellers. But if every concession is at one and the same time a consequence of buyer pressure and seller competition, can the government be justified in making this distinction? Specifically, should the law ever proceed against coercive bargaining by buyers when such bargaining is simply a manifestation and instrument of competition? Our examination of the cases should help in answering this question.

Discrimination and the Big Buyer

Discriminatory price concessions to large buyers, whether "voluntarily" offered under pressure of seller competition or coerced under threat of withdrawal of custom, may obviously make it more difficult for less favored customers to compete. On the other hand, they may make competition more workable, under certain conditions.

Since this type of price discrimination is not clearly either in the public interest or contrary to it, should there be a presumption against it, as there is against systematic, noncompetitive price matching or predatory local price cutting? Following the logic of pure theory it would seem that the presumption should be favorable rather than the reverse. Only firms with monopoly power can discriminate, and a discriminating monopoly that has been forced by buyer pressure to make downward concessions is preferable to one that is permitted to maintain a uniformly high price. Under perfect competition all producers operate at the point of lowest average total costs, where marginal and average unit costs are equal. When a firm discriminates, at least one of the prices charged must be above marginal cost; this divergence, according to the economist's definition, is the hallmark of monopoly power.

However, the theoretical definition of monopoly power is not a sufficient basis for policy decisions, for reasons already indicated in Chapter 2. Price discrimination is, admittedly, a sign of impure competition. But as the proponents of price discrimination themselves frequently point out, impure competition may none the less be more workable than any feasible alternative. Or, indeed, the purely competitive outcome may in the short run be absolutely impossible: once a crop has been harvested, or a canner's pack completed, marginal costs are almost nil. Therefore the price cannot in the short run possibly equal both marginal and average total costs, even with an infinite number of sellers. In these circumstances, an individual buyer may be able to demand a price somewhere between marginal and average total cost; the sellers may therefore be discriminating, yet may enjoy no monopoly power in any meaningful sense. It follows, therefore, that the ability of big buyers to obtain concessions, a sign of market imperfection only, is by no means an evidence that sellers enjoy excessive monopoly power.

What then are the conditions in which discrimination exacted by a large buyer contributes to workable competition? First, such pressure may represent the only alternative to exploitation of the consumer. Oligopolists may be persuaded to extend secret discriminatory discounts in order to get a large order, when they would be reluctant to reduce their general price list openly. Second, the discriminatory concession must have some means of propagating itself. The typical way is for the favored buyer to pass some of the saving on to his customers; this puts pressure on his competitors, forcing them in turn to demand better terms from their suppliers. Third, the big buyer must not be so powerful that he can exploit his suppliers by denying them normal profits under pain of withdrawal of custom.

The critics of the A & P decisions have either assumed or argued explicitly that the concessions which A & P was able to extract from its suppliers satisfied these conditions. Therefore they contend that A & P's exercise of countervailing power intensified price competition, made for fuller utilization of suppliers' plants, and contributed also to a reduction of wasteful selling expenditures in the industry, partly by shifting the focus of competition from product differentiation to price.[1] But because their argument is almost wholly theoretical, it can never prove more than that a big buyer *may* make competition more effective. They have made very little effort to show that in fact the conditions necessary to produce this on-balance beneficial result were actually present. On the basis of our own examination of the food distribution trade and the characteristics of the markets in which A & P bought, we view with skepticism the assertion that the practices found to be illegal had beneficial effects outweighing the threat to competition and the inequity which they embodied.[2]

[1] See, e.g., Adelman, in 63 *Q. Jour. Econ.* 238 (1949); Galbraith, *American Capitalism,* Chaps. 9 and 10.

[2] The discussion of A & P's buying policies here is a summary of our two articles in 60 *Jour. Pol. Econ.* 118 (1952) and 29 *Indiana Law J.* 1 (1953).

First of all, A & P was not very successful in extracting price concessions from its powerful, profitable oligopolist suppliers, notably soap, cereal, and biscuit companies. There is no evidence it ever tried to bargain for concessions from the highly concentrated producers of evaporated milk. The soap companies simply refused to grant special concessions, even when A & P attempted to apply strong pressure; in fact, A & P believed that they were discriminating against it because they gave only nonpreferential advertising allowances. From Quaker Oats and Ralston, two large cereal manufacturers, A & P received concessions not available to its competitors, but these discounts were on trading items only, that is, products which were not differentiated and which therefore could not be sold monopolistically. Because A & P was unable to get special concessions from the makers of Crisco and Spry, it manufactured its own shortening, dexo. The government had no objection to this manufacture, as such. There was no evidence that A & P secured special concessions from National Biscuit Company or other leading cookie entrepreneurs; it was accused of exerting pressure only on the relatively unimportant Consolidated Biscuit Company.[3] The milk distributors in Buffalo, New York City, St. Louis and Chicago were powerful oligopolists from which A & P was able to extract discriminatory concessions. The discounts were top secret and never, as far as we can learn, passed along to the consumer. Aside from these concessions, however, there is little or nothing to show that during the period covered by the evidence in the trial A & P had received, let alone passed along, concessions from strong sellers. In the words of an authority on the record in the *A &P* case, "It was precisely the highly differentiated products which were most rarely affected by discrimination."[4]

Galbraith singles out for praise the vulnerability of the otherwise impregnable tobacco industry to A & P's countervailing

---

The facts we cite here are more fully documented there. See also our exchange with Adelman, 61 *Jour. Pol. Econ.* 436 (1953).

[3] On these various instances see 173 F.2d 79 (1949), Government Main Brief, pp. 179–180, and A & P Main Brief, pp. 101–102, 244, App. A, II, 354, 360–361, 386, 555–580; also the F.T.C. Decision in *Lever Bros.,* Docket No. 5585, and companion cases, Docket Nos. 5586 and 5587, Dec. 16, 1953.

[4] Adelman, "Comments," 65 *Q. Jour. Econ.* 283 (1951).

power during the period prior to the Robinson-Patman Act. As he points out, the liberal price concessions took the form of advertising allowances. The example is illuminating. A & P's concessions did not prevent the Big 3 from raising their prices in 1931 above the 1929 levels and enjoying unprecedented profits in 1932. When, in 1933, cigarette prices finally broke, a price-cutting orgy ensued in which A & P co-operated. But countervailing power was not responsible for the price cuts. Instead, it was the heavy inroads made by the 10-cent brands that forced the Big 3 to initiate drastic, general, and nondiscriminatory price cuts at the wholesale level in order to meet the competition of the economy brands. A & P's advertising allowances were substantially unchanged from 1932, and it is clear that the chain merely followed the lead of the Big 3 in the 1933 reductions.[5]

On the other hand, A & P did from time to time obtain special discounts from canners and from vegetable and fruit shippers and growers, who are too numerous and unorganized to function like exploitative oligopolists. Their profits are low, as are the profits of even the large meat packers, who are commonly supposed to be in effective control of their market. Price changes are frequent. The products of all but a handful of canners are relatively undifferentiated. Even though the well-known lines of the big canners command a premium over the unknown brands, the profits of these companies have been consistently much below those of the chain stores, indicating that they have little exploitative power beyond the power to recoup their heavy advertising expenditures. Moreover, there is no indication that the concessions which A & P received or its campaign to get generally lower prices than its competitors has had the effect of forcing any reduction of advertising expenditures. On the contrary, since the bargaining pressures of the big buyer have been more effective when applied against producers of unknown brands or against the undifferentiated products of the well-known processors the buying policies of grocery chains have, if anything, probably induced canners to intensify their advertising campaigns in order to strengthen the hold on consumers that alone protects their differentials.

[5] Cf. Galbraith, pp. 127–128, with Nicholls, pp. 119–120, 131 n. 9, and 383.

Certainly a major factor holding in check the exploitative power of food processors are the private brands of the chain stores. But A & P's benefits from the illegal buying concessions were of no consequence in the pricing of the products it manufactured for itself, and relatively unimportant in the case of private label canned goods (which it purchases). These forms of competition, the most important influence which chain stores exert on the prices of nationally branded groceries, remain open to the company.[6]

Thus, the conditions under which price discrimination in favor of a big buyer will promote economic welfare were apparently not satisfied in the *A & P* case. The suppliers from whom the company received concessions were generally those with the least power. There is no way of telling whether, as a general rule, the concessions that it got led to general price reductions. The evidence that has been cited definitely does not support the example, which is becoming part of the mythology of antitrust commentary, of a concession on private brand corn flakes from Ralston-Purina forcing that company to cut the price on its advertised corn flakes as well.[7] It is doubtful also that concessions to A & P made possible fuller utilization of the sellers' resources as a whole, since the chain had to place its orders somewhere, whether or not it received discounts. Only if the concessions dissuaded it from manufacturing for itself would they have permitted fuller utilization; but in this event they were an instrument for keeping competition soft rather than letting it get hard!

The power of A & P compared with that of its suppliers was such that the buyer was much more likely to do the exploiting than the sellers from whom it was able to get favorable prices. Certainly, the special concessions on shipments of fresh vegetables from Florida or Texas seem to point much more to the

[6] On the relative unimportance of discounts as a source of competitive advantage, see data from F.T.C., *Final Report on the Chain Store Investigation,* as analyzed in C. F. Phillips, "The Robinson-Patman Anti-Price Discrimination Law and the Chain Store" 15 *Harv. Bus. Rev.,* Autumn 1936, pp. 62–64.

[7] See Adelman in 63 *Q. Jour. Econ.* 254 (1949) and Galbraith, *American Capitalism,* p. 125.

ability of a buyer accounting for perhaps one-tenth of the total national purchases to get special favors from suppliers with very high sunk costs than it demonstrates appreciable monopoly powers on the selling side of the market. As we have already pointed out, the nature of the canning business and fruit and vegetable growing is such that, when the pack or harvest is completed, marginal costs of production are negligible; rather than lose a sale entirely sellers may take prices far below their long-run marginal costs (those necessary in the long run to keep them in business).

Under Galbraith's optimistic theory of countervailing power such a misdirection of A & P's bargaining is impossible. Having labeled big buyers in general as practitioners of countervailing power and having defined the latter as offsetting "original" power, hence beneficent, he is able to write at length and with conviction about the *A & P* case with only minimal reference to the facts. (In much the same way, he is able to explain the rise of unions in terms of countervailing power, without pointing out that four of the six biggest national unions in the United States today are the Teamsters, Carpenters and Joiners, Machinists, and Mine Workers.) But his theory is faulty. The power of A & P need not be feared, he says, because "concessions are important only when won from positions of original power." Or again, A & P cannot exploit the farmer because "the farmer has no gains to surrender." [8] But on the other hand, he explains the countervailing organization of farmer co-ops as a means of self-protection against big buyers, presumably like A & P. If big buyers, as we are now told, can profit only by exploiting the strong, never the weak, why need the weak ever organize?

The fact is that power is itself dangerous and profitable. Countervailing power is not always or necessarily beneficent, unless one defines it so. The same power may be used to "countervail" or to exploit. It may be used in a way which in the end benefits the ultimate consumer, or it may benefit only its possessor.

We do not mean to imply that A & P got special favors from a very large number of suppliers. Nor do we deny that prior to

[8] *Ibid.*, pp. 147, 125.

the passage of the Robinson-Patman Act the company received sizable concessions from some of the more powerful sellers that now refuse them. What is clear from the case is that the company knew its power, had no hesitation in wielding it, and in numerous instances succeeded in this way in obtaining competitive advantages that had nothing to do with efficiency. What is not clear is that A & P's pursuit of these advantages was so beneficial to the public that it was foolish to forbid the practice.

There remains the possibility that the concessions given to A & P by the canners, grocery manufacturers, and produce shippers might have been no greater than the cost savings on these sales. Since the case was not brought under the Robinson-Patman Act, this possibility was never thoroughly or directly explored by the court; hence a wholly conclusive analysis is hard to provide. However, on the average it was probably true that the countervailing power of the chains was no more than enough to exact from suppliers what they saved them in cost.[9]

The sharpest criticism has been directed against the court's condemnation of A & P's efforts in one form or another to get the equivalent of the brokerage which it claimed it was saving sellers by buying direct. Even apart from its misleading impression that most of the discounts condemned by the *A & P* decisions were justified by the company's performance of brokerage functions,[10] this argument is not wholly convincing, though it is certainly not wholly wrong either. In the first place, produce is more often than not sold through *buying* brokers or agents, especially in California and Texas; the purchaser pays the f.o.b. market price for a car and he, not the grower or assembler, pays the broker's commission. If A & P were refused a discount below the current quotation for such sales, it would in no way be discriminated against; it could not by buying direct be saving the seller any brokerage. If A & P felt that rates charged

[9] See Adelman in 61 *Jour. Pol. Econ.* 438 (1953); Dewey, in 17 *Jour. of Marketing* 281 n. 3 (1953); and note 6, above. Curiously, many persons who complain at the failure of the courts to consider this cost-saving defense in the Sherman Act proceeding against A & P also regard the Robinson-Patman Act, which provides for such a defense, as an economic monstrosity.

[10] On the contrary see pp. 78–79, above.

by buying agents were excessive, it could have—as it did—set up an independent buying organization, but such an organization would save *it,* not the seller, brokerage fees. Moreover, many produce buyers in the northeast, chains and wholesalers alike, establish relationships with shippers whom they trust and buy direct without using any broker whatever.[11] There is no reason for these shippers to quote A & P additional concessions below the market price. The situation is by no means parallel with the marketing of canned goods, for which the seller issues a price list that prevails for weeks or months at a time, and which are usually sold by brokers paid a selling commission by the packer. Prices of produce change daily, even hourly, at the big markets and shipping points, and there is no fixed custom of marketing through brokers paid by the seller. It is hard to avoid the conclusion that the produce shippers who gave ACCO 10 cents off on a case of lettuce were worlds removed from the entrenched oligopolists who, according to critics of the *A & P* decision, collected "phantom brokerage" under the Robinson-Patman Act.

In the purchase of canned goods and other groceries, on the other hand, section 2(c) of the Robinson-Patman Act does impose some unfair discrimination against A & P, as well as against I.G.A. to the extent that they deal direct with manufacturers. But it still is not true that cost savings on sales to A & P necessarily matched the conventional brokerage allowance, or that A & P was typically discriminated against on these purchases when it did not get brokerage or its equivalent. Most canners do not have sales forces; for them brokers fulfill a function that the chains cannot render entirely superfluous. This explains the willingness of canners to keep using brokers, even though they could save the fee by selling only to chains. Payment to A & P of the customary fee would not assure the continuing good will, missionary work, protection against dependence on a single seller, and efforts to obtain the highest price that the broker is supposed to provide the canner. As for those few canners who have their own permanent sales force, it is hard to see why they should permit one

[11] "The trade argues that Acco was more of an encumbrance to A & P in recent years than anything else. . . . Other chains dissolved their own similar operations years ago." *Business Week,* Jan. 23, 1954, p. 32.

buyer to evade its share of the overhead selling expense on the ground it saves them the use of brokers whose services they do not employ!

The tone of some of the correspondence between A & P and its suppliers (Cranberry Canners, for instance, wrote that "any amount of people are taking the same large shipments you do and you are not buying by any different method than the others" [12]), the mutual agreements to keep the discounts confidential, and A & P's refusal to provide records of performance of advertising services, all point to the conclusion that by and large the quantity discounts, cost savings, and advertising allowances were, like brokerage, simply another name for those concessions that big buyers extract or try to extract from small suppliers, by whatever means and under whatever pretext.

None of this is to deny that there may have been genuine cost savings on A & P's big orders or that it may take the exertion of pressure by a big buyer on a supplier to obtain even cost-justified discounts. But Judge Lindley was surely not incorrect in finding no punctilious effort on A & P's part to obtain only what discounts might have been justified in this fashion. And our analysis suggests that the public would not have suffered an appreciable loss had A & P confined its vigorous bargaining to the securing of only those competitive advantages attributable to the superior efficiency of its operations.

The Federal Trade Commission was attacked for its order against Automatic Canteen under section 2(f) on much the same ground as the Department of Justice for proceeding against the A & P Company: "I leave it to you to decide whether this yields tough or soft competition." [13] Automatic probably did over one-half of the business of distributing candy bars and gum through vending machines. It leased its machines to distributors subject to the condition that they not use machines of competitive suppliers and that all confectionery dispensed through the machines be purchased through Automatic. Thus armed with strategic control over access of confectionery manufacturers to this rapidly

[12] 67 F.Supp. 626, 647 (1946).

[13] Austern, "Inconsistencies in the Law," *1951 Symposium*, p. 165. See pp. 130–131, above.

expanding market outlet, the company exacted preferential prices from about 80 of its 115 suppliers. It demanded lower prices than those given to its competitors, submitting its demands to suppliers on a take-it or leave-it basis.

The "toughness" of competition in the vending of confectionery in automatic machines surely left something to be desired from the point of view of the public, although, no doubt, "tough" tactics were employed. Since the candy manufacturing industry hardly conforms to the pattern of a tight oligopoly, and since Automatic Canteen did not pass its concessions on to the ultimate consumer (in contrast with the chain stores, who were enabled by their discounts to sell 5-cent candy bars for 4 cents), the two basic conditions for a monopsonist contributing to more workable competition were absent in this case. In these circumstances there is little conceivable harm the order could have done, and it might, by weakening the extortionate power of a monopoly bottleneck in distribution, have done a great deal of good. The prohibition against exclusive dealing, which was not appealed to the Supreme Court, remains, but the discounts which the company was able to exact were just as important in excluding competitors as the exclusive arrangements, not because they led it to charge lower prices for candy and gum but because they permitted it to offer higher commissions to get its machines in favorable locations.[14]

By admitting more vending machine companies to competition and more candy suppliers to the vending machine market outlet, the order against exclusive dealing has probably diminished the possibilities of exploitation of candy suppliers; the ultimate buyer is unlikely to be affected one way or the other. The order under Section 2(f), it must be admitted, would have placed some legal burdens upon the monopolist who had theretofore been free to exact his toll on the traffic which had to pass his way. This may have been distressing to the company and its attorneys, but it is difficult to see why anyone else should have been concerned.

Ever since 1926, when Goodyear Tire and Rubber signed its

[14] *Automatic Canteen Co.,* Docket No. 4933, Findings, June 6, 1950, par. 11.

first secret contract to supply Sears Roebuck with all its requirements of private brand rubber tires at cost plus 6 per cent, the regular distributors of tires have waged a continuous campaign against the favorable arrangements that have permitted mail order houses to undersell them by a wide margin. In 1936 the Federal Trade Commission, proceeding under the old Section 2 of the Clayton Act, ordered Goodyear to cancel the arrangement, insisting that it get no lower a rate of return over cost on sales to Sears Roebuck than to anyone else.[15] The decision was overruled because the statute at that time permitted discounts justified by differences in quantity. It was in part to close this loophole that the Robinson-Patman Act was passed. The tire manufacturers, however, continued to allow big buyers discounts as much as 30 per cent below the prices charged to the smallest customers. Because they could prove a cost justification for the differentials, it was impossible to attack them except under the quantity limit rule of Section 2(a) of the Robinson-Patman Act. Finally, in 1952, the Commission made use of this authority for the first time to set the limit to quantity discounts on tires at the rate for carload purchases (or 20,000 pounds).[16]

The major issue raised by this order is its obvious conflict with the standard accepted by the antitrust laws themselves, price competition on the basis of efficiency. Under what circumstances does the Robinson-Patman Act permit the F.T.C. to violate this standard? The statute authorizes the promulgation of a quantity limit rule only if it has been shown that "available purchasers in greater quantities are so few as to render differentials unjustly discriminatory or promotive of monopoly." Had the Commission chosen to proceed on the ground that the discounts were merely "unjustly discriminatory," it would perhaps have been able to avoid a serious economic investigation of their impact. But it concluded also that they were "promotive of monopoly." Did it sustain the latter burden of proof?

Briefly summarized, the Commission's argument runs as

[15] 22 F.T.C. 232 (1936); overruled, *F.T.C.* v. *Goodyear Tire and Rubber Co.*, 101 F.2d 620 (1939).

[16] *A Quantity Limit Rule as to Replacement Tires and Tubes,* File No. 203-1, Findings and Order, Dec. 13, 1951, and Jan. 4, 1952.

follows: (1) the number of tire manufacturers has declined from about 100 in 1926 to 21 in 1947, and perhaps as low as 17 in 1951, and the seven largest manufacturers did 86.3 per cent of the business in 1947; (2) in 1926 the independent tire dealers handled about 90 per cent, in 1947 only 52 per cent, of the replacement units; (3) the 63 largest purchasers take 30 per cent of the tires; and (4) the discounts received by these 63 purchasers are so large that they can afford to retail the tires at a price no higher or only slightly higher than their competitors' invoice costs.

An economist can hardly accept these findings as sufficient to warrant outlawing cost-justified discounts that have been so competitive a force in this industry.[17] Sixty-three purchasers doing slightly less than 30 per cent of the replacement tire business are hardly so few as to pose an imminent threat of monopoly. The decline in the percentage share of total sales by independent tire dealers has apparently been attributable in some measure to factors other than the pricing system in the industry (for example, increased sale of tires by service stations). It is in any case difficult to consider it unjust in view of the fact that their share is a smaller percentage of so far greater a volume of total sales that their absolute volume of business has undoubtedly expanded greatly. As for the dramatic demonstration of an increasing concentration among tire manufacturers, the Commission's findings fail completely to convince us that this has been in any way attributable to the quantity discounts to large sellers. Incidentally, the Commission also did not stop to consider (though it did not have to under the terms of the statute) whether the mass distributors of tires, if denied the right to cost-plus contracts, might not buy out tire manufacturers and reap by integration the same benefits they now do by purchase. It is difficult to see how the two biggest distributors, who account for only 10 per cent of total sales, could be accused of violating either the Sherman Act or Section 7 of the Clayton Act if they circumvented the Commission's order in this fashion.

We have already argued that there is, at least in theory, a place

[17] See the convincing Dissent of Commissioner Mason, on which, along with the majority opinion, these observations are based.

for a quantity discount limit provision in an antitrust policy. When competition on the basis of efficiency really threatens monopoly, it will probably be necessary to decide whether it might not be desirable to arrest the tendency by denying to large firms the full benefits of their lower costs. But it is surely not economically sound for the Federal Trade Commission to abandon the basic principle of competition on the basis of such evidence as it offered here that the large discounts, though justified by cost, threaten to erase competition. Moreover, if the rubber tire case is the best one the Commission can find in which to apply this power, it really demonstrates once again the validity of the basic antitrust premise that competition on the basis of efficiency alone will not lead to monopoly!

Functional Pricing and Discrimination

Few pricing practices pose thornier problems than functional discounts. Here the conflicts and cross conflicts of interest among business groups, and corresponding differences of opinion among economists and lawyers, are inevitable because, as the ensuing discussion should show, there is no correct solution except uneasy and continuous compromise.

In an atomistically and purely competitive market the Robinson-Patman Act would pose no obstacle to functional pricing. A wholesaler might obtain a more favorable price than a retailer without objection, because the two would not be in competition. But under pure competition there would be no need for a Robinson-Patman Act. As soon as someone in the distributive process encompasses more than one stage in his operations, it becomes possible and legitimate for him to qualify for a functional discount corresponding to the stage nearer to the ultimate supplier, while competing with nonintegrated sellers at stages nearer the market. Whenever these integrated firms have begun to cut prices, their nonintegated competitors have been quick to complain of "unfair competition," made possible by "price discrimination." And ordinarily the complainants may be correct in contending that their competitive disadvantages do not reflect inefficiencies in the performance of their restricted functions.

If all injured competitors had the opportunity of integrating vertically and readily qualifying for higher-level functional discounts, competition in each stratum could be counted on to keep the respective discounts close to the cost of fulfilling the service. In this event, competitive advantages and disadvantages would mirror only relative efficiency, either within each level of operation or in combining operations. But to the extent there are obstacles to such mobility, there arise possible advantages resulting only from superiority of strategic position. As we pointed out in Chapter 5, if the gross margin (discount) at any one level exceeds the cost of fulfilling the function, part of it may be passed on in such a way as to undercut competitors at another level. Relative size and bargaining power become determinants of business success or failure. In such circumstances, it becomes impossible to supply any irrefutable justification (except in terms of the lesser evil) for leaving the distribution of income to the free play of imperfectly competitive forces in the market.

Standard Oil of Indiana is engaged in "dual operation" in the Detroit area: it sells gasoline both in tank-car lots to jobbers, who store and transport it in smaller quantities to service stations, and directly from its own bulk (storage) plants in tank-wagon quantities to service stations and commercial users. Since 1936, when it adopted the so-called Iowa Plan, it has operated no retail stations; it continues to control over half of its service station outlets in the area by ownership or long-term leases, leasing or subleasing them on shorter contracts to independent operators. Between 1936 and 1940, the period covered by the Federal Trade Commission complaint, it sold its branded gasoline to four jobbers in tank-car quantities at 1½ cents below its tank-wagon price to service stations. All the jobbers sold at retail during this period, Ned's Auto Supply exclusively so. Another jobber, Citrin-Kolb Oil, engaged in some price cutting at both wholesale and retail levels; Ned's price-cut continuously. Openly advertising a price two cents below the prevailing service station price, Ned's apparently increased its gallonage substantially more than the market as a whole. According to the Commission, "this company has been responsible in starting most of the retail price cutting in major-brand gasoline in Detroit over a period of several years." [18] Whatever the cause, price wars abounded in Detroit in this period. Retailers' margins were reduced from 4 and 4.5 cents in 1937 and early 1938 to 3.3 cents in late 1939 and 1940; the lower figure was close to the average cost of operation of the most efficient 25 per cent of the stations, according to a cost survey made in December 1938.[19]

As we saw in Chapter 4, the Commission rejected Standard's patently *ex post* cost justifications and, after the Supreme Court required it to examine the adequacy of the good faith defense, held that the discounts were not made in order to meet competitive offers of gasoline of commensurate quality. In a modified order, it required Standard to discontinue discounts below the tank-wagon price to jobbers on such gasoline as the latter would sell at retail; on such sales, it held, the offending resellers were retailers, not jobbers, and hence entitled only to the tank-wagon price. Second, it forbade Standard to charge a higher tank-wagon price to its retailers than any of its jobbers thereafter would charge their service station customers.[20]

The second part of the 1953 modified order represented a new departure for the Commission. The old order forbade Standard to sell to jobbers at less than tank-wagon prices whenever, as a result, price-cutting independent retailers got their gas more cheaply than Standard's retail dealers. The new requires only that Standard cut its tank-wagon price on branded gas in such circumstances to the level charged by any of its jobbers to their retailer customers. The purpose of both was to make sure that Standard's directly serviced dealers would not have to pay more for their gasoline than any of their retail competitors; but the amendment represents an improvement. As now framed, the order is less likely to result in Standard's refusing to supply any

[18] *Standard Oil Co.,* Docket No. 4389, Findings, Oct. 9, 1945, p. 7. From Sept. 1, 1936, to March 7, 1938, Ned's received regular tank-wagon deliveries but was allowed a half-cent discount under the tank-wagon price; after the latter date, it was accorded jobber status and received tank-car delivery at the 1½-cent discount.

[19] Data from the record cited by Howard, *The Marketing of Petroleum Products,* p. 178.

[20] Modified Order, Jan. 16, 1953, p. 2. On the earlier version of this order, see p. 132, above.

jobbers who undercut the official tank-wagon price. However, Standard might now prefer to eliminate such sales rather than be forced to reduce its tank-wagon price; at the least it would exert considerable informal pressure to prevent undercutting by its jobbers. The pressure is especially likely to be effective if similar orders are obtained by the F.T.C. against the other three majors in the area that sell through jobbers as well as directly to retail outlets.[21]

Even as finally modified by the Commission in 1953, the *Standard of Indiana* decision is extremely vulnerable to criticism. The record convinces the writers, as it did the trial examiner, the Court of Appeals,[22] and two members of the Commission, that Standard was compelled by the competitive offers of other oil companies to give its jobbers a tank-car price. During the years 1936–1940 a large quantity of independent gasoline, Michigan-refined, was pouring into the Detroit market at 3 cents below the prevailing tank-wagon price. At least ten oil companies, in addition to Standard, had marine terminals located in the Detroit area. Shell, Texas, and Gulf were giving discounts below the tank-wagon price equivalent to those Standard allowed its jobbers. Ned's had several offers of discounts below the tank-wagon price from Standard's competitors, including at least one major, Standard of Ohio. After 1938, when it had bulk storage, it is difficult to believe that it could not have obtained a discount of at least 1½ cents off tank-wagon price from any major company. Citrin-Kolb cut its tank-wagon price to a chain of service stations only after the latter had received a competitive offer from Cities Service.[23] Detroit was known as a surplus gasoline area. It is difficult to believe that Standard's discounts to Ned's or Ned's price cutting could alone have been responsible for the city's chronic price wars, as the Commission asserted.

It is precisely in this fashion, by granting concessions on sales to jobbers, able to buy in tank-car lots, that the oil companies com-

[21] The Commission actually has pending parallel suits against Shell, Texas, and Gulf, Docket Nos. 4390–4392.

[22] 173 F.2d 210, 213 (1949).

[23] F.T.C. Docket No. 4389, Transcript of Hearings, p. 1407.

pete with each other for gallonage. Indeed, when it engages in dual operations, each company is actually competing with itself as well. And it is the tank-car market, feeding the independent distributors, which helps hold tank-wagon price and dealer margins to what may well be termed workably competitive levels.[24] By requiring that the major refiners deny to jobbers whatever reward competition requires for fulfilling wholesaling functions (except insofar as they can prove an equivalent saving in cost), the Commission has weakened the incentive to combine wholesale and retail functions and struck a blow for rigid distributive mark-ups, undisturbed by aggressive, vertically integrated competitors.

However, the basic policy question remains: Should Standard be permitted to meet competition by offering discounts from the tank-wagon price? That price is the keystone of the gasoline price structure; the jobber's margin is usually calculated as so many cents per gallon below it; the dealer's margin, above it, is held substantially in check by the relative ease of entry into the field (itself a product of the competition of refiners for market outlets). It is on the tank-wagon price that leadership in the industry focuses. Such price leadership as survives may well be compatible with workable competition. The fact remains, however, that the tank-wagon price is the last to change downward, when market conditions deteriorate. By general convention, the very strong forces of competition in the industry take other channels—notably non-price rivalry, the offer of other inducements to retailers than direct price concessions, and the sale of so-called "surplus" gasoline at tank-car prices to independent distributors. Even if these methods of seeking gallonage combine with some additional competitive influence (independent gasoline in Detroit, or an invading major brand and multi-pump stations, as in the recent New Jersey price wars) to produce a retail price war, the nominal tank-wagon price remains undisturbed often for long periods of time. The suppliers may be forced to offer their dealers in selected areas rebates to keep them in business; but the major brunt of the wars is on the retail mar-

[24] See, in particular, Adelman, in 63 *Harv. Law Rev.* 60–74 (1949).

gin, not on the posted tank-wagon price or the over-all revenues of the major refiners.[25]

During price wars dealers tend to argue, understandably, that the only fair way for majors to compete would be in the tank-wagon price, in a nondiscriminatory fashion, rather than through "surplus" sales to selected jobbers. Even in normal times, they point out, the majors compete for gallonage by competitive construction of service stations and by pressure on dealers to give free services and keep open long hours—all of which bear upon the dealer first and upon the tank-wagon price last. Thus, the solicitude of economist-critics of the F.T.C. for the rights of the major companies to meet competition and for the preservation of competitive pressures on retail margins seems somewhat misplaced, although it is undoubtedly better for the customer to have this kind of competition than none at all. The second part of the modified F.T.C. order, forcing Standard to reduce its own tank-wagon price uniformly to all when its jobbers undercut it, is clearly aimed at eliminating this squeeze on retail margins.

Discriminatory price competition was not necessarily the only kind of price competition possible in the Detroit area in the late 1930's. The large volume of independent gasoline in the Detroit market might have forced the four majors to try to hold their customers by reducing the tank-wagon price had they been denied the right to meet competition only by offering tank-car rates to independent jobbers. Adelman has ridiculed the Trade Commission for citing Sun as a model of fair competition, because that company refused to engage in dual pricing on the ground that it created "a very difficult competitive situation." [26] But it was Sun that was the first of the majors to reduce its tank-wagon price, in 1939, when dealer margins were obviously ruinously low. And Sun has been among the first in the recent New Jersey price wars to offer guaranteed margins to any of its dealers who chose to meet the retail price competition. With the safety

[25] The foregoing represents a brief summary of portions of Dirlam and Kahn, "Leadership and Conflict in the Pricing of Gasoline," 61 *Yale Law J.* 818 (1952).

[26] 63 *Harv. Law Rev.* 70–71 (1949).

valve of price discrimination closed, in short, the majors' protected tank-wagon price structure might have exploded first, instead of last. In the circumstances, it seems an egregious oversimplification to argue that the Commission decision struck a blow for soft competition.[27]

However, there are other possible solutions to the Standard of Indiana dilemmas, perhaps more likely to further the consumer interest than the one chosen by the Commission, yet protecting the retailers from squeezes. The denial to combined wholesaler-retailers of the buying prices to which their performance of wholesaling functions entitles them remains an unquestionably rigid, anticompetitive—indeed discriminatory—solution. It may be that the cost-saving defense represents an adequate compromise between giving them all they can get from major suppliers engaged in dual operation (at the expense of firms in a weaker bargaining position) and giving them nothing at all. However, the probable result of such a compromise concession would be to prevent the major suppliers selling through jobbers at all.[28] And it would involve the Commission, in effect, in continuous price fixing.

The way to assure fairness of functional discounts and to permit them to be granted safely, we have already argued, is to provide for freedom of access to the favored function. Thus, the significant question is whether Detroit dealers had a chance to qualify for the functional discounts that the majors gave to the favored jobbers. It was demonstrated at the hearings that before March 1938, when Ned's had no bulk plant, Standard had denied requests for similar discounts from other dealers buying in similar quantities. In some cases, a group of retailers proposed establishing their own bulk plant facilities and purchasing in tank-car quantities; other dealers already had or offered to obtain bulk storage facilities; all were denied the tank-car price by

[27] See Brief, Amicus Curiae, in the *Standard of Indiana* Supreme Court case, submitted by the Retail Gasoline Dealers Association of Michigan and others; Wallace and Douglas, in 19 *U. of Chicago Law Rev.* 705–710 (1952); Howard, pp. 189–194.

[28] This was the argument of the Empire State Petroleum Association (composed mainly of jobbers and distributors) in its Brief in the Supreme Court case.

Standard.[29] Yet, tied to their supplier by leasing arrangements, the dealers lacked the option of turning to other suppliers in order to force Standard to treat them on a par with Ned's. Here was the real source of inequity.

Divorcement of Standard's owned or leased service stations, control of which gave the company power to hold retail dealers while they were being squeezed, might have achieved the twin goals of competition and equity. It would have allowed the dealers to shop around for gas and thus given them fair access to the wholesaling function. A more practical approach would have been to resurrect the Commission's opinion of thirty years ago holding that, under the Clayton Act, a company may not grant functional discounts to some buyers while denying them to others willing to perform the function.[30] Standard's discounts might thus have been validated on the condition that they be made available to others on equal terms. Thus a major element of unfairness of competition and inequality of bargaining power would have been removed, and with it the justification for a public agency's concern with the equity of functional pricing.[31]

On the basis of the *Spark Plug* (and other similar cases) the Commission has been accused of attacking functional discounts and sabotaging the American system of distribution.[32] The accusation is curious because the Commission has been criticized also for protecting independent wholesalers and retailers against

[29] 41 F.T.C. 263, 277 (1945); F.T.C. Brief, Supreme Court case, p. 8.

[30] See *The Mennen Co.* v. *F.T.C.,* 288 Fed. 774 (1923); also *The National Biscuit Co.* v. *F.T.C.,* 299 Fed. 733 (1924).

[31] Adelman has pointed out correctly that the F.T.C. order in effect required Standard to discriminate against the jobbers. He overlooks the fact that Standard had already discriminated against others willing to perform the function. The Michigan Dealers Association asserted, in its Brief, that its members would have had no objection to Standard's pricing had tank-car prices been available to all who could qualify for them. Under such a rule, the majors might discontinue dual operations and refuse to sell to jobbers at all. However, they would be less likely to do so than under the F.T.C.'s proposed order, which would make it virtually impossible for integrated refiners to meet the competition of nonintegrated suppliers for jobbers' business except by reducing the prices on all their gasoline.

[32] See Brief of Champion Spark Plug Co., Docket No. 3977, Oct. 17, 1950, p. 1.

more efficient competitors in its enforcement of the Robinson-Patman Act. There is probably more merit in the latter criticism than in the former. In the functional discount cases the Commission has, it is true, restricted the granting of price differentials to wholesalers when they happen to be competitors of retailers. It has to some extent, therefore, reduced the incentive for wholesalers to integrate forward. But it has done so only in those cases where nonintegrated competitors would otherwise be at a disadvantage. The beneficiaries of its functional discount policy are thus not only other middlemen, but those small businessmen who have been aroused by the claims of interested parties that the Commission is threatening their existence. Our own criticism is that it is not permitting them to be threatened enough or, alternatively, that it is not protecting their legitimate interests in a way that preserves competition too.

Price Discrimination—Conclusion

Not all of the pricing practices attacked by the F.T.C. in recent years could have been reached under the traditional interpretations of antitrust statutes qualified by the rule of reason, either as traditionally conceived or as modified under the new Sherman Act. This may be the understatement of the year. Yet either because of the unreasonableness of the act or the imminence of serious anticompetitive consequences the rule of reason would certainly not have precluded condemning many of the practices we have considered—notably the predatory aspects of A & P's retailing policies, the collusion or absence of good faith competition inherent in the basing-point and zone price systems, and the coercive pressures for discriminatory concessions exerted by big buyers.

In the other cases, notably *Minneapolis-Honeywell, Spark Plugs, Standard of Indiana,* and rubber tires, the justification would have to be sought in the special purpose of the Robinson-Patman Act, the preservation of equity in competition. Insofar as we have defended some of the latter actions (with the notable exception of the rubber tire case) or the purposes which they sought, on economic grounds, we have been able to do so only because we were not convinced from the evidence that the economic cost of greater fairness of competition would be as serious as other commentators have implied.

The trouble is that the Commission itself provided precious little evidence in the latter cases that it had made even the necessary appraisal of offsetting benefits and costs of its decisions and orders. By failing clearly to show that the acts themselves were unreasonable, that they really posed a serious threat to competition, or even that they really imposed a serious unfair handicap on competitors, by failing finally to consider seriously the economic consequences of its orders or the possibility of achieving the desired results at less economic cost by a different kind of order, in short, by being more legalistic than the courts, the Commission was apparently intent on destroying its own *raison d'être* as an expert, flexible administrative agency.

We have seen how the Commission has found injury to competition in little more than the successful offer or receipt of a discount, so that the qualifying clause of Section 2 ceases to qualify. We have seen how it has interpreted the cost-saving defense in a similarly restrictive fashion and how it has attempted finally to emasculate the good faith defense.

In a way, the weakening of the good faith defense may be regarded as the most serious departure from traditional antitrust doctrine. The assumption of that doctrine was that if firms competed honestly and fairly, i.e. in good faith, they could safely be left alone and might enjoy reasonable assurance to that effect. The recent developments pose many problems for businessmen. For example, sellers face the unenviable choice of meeting precisely the "equally low" price of a competitor, assuming they know it, and thus risking falling afoul of the charge of systematically matching those prices; or not meeting them exactly (cutting sometimes below, as the basing-point decisions suggest might be safer, sometimes not quite so low, as the respondents did in the *Spark Plug* and *Honeywell* cases) and thus surrendering the good faith defense; or, perhaps, letting competitors take away the business and then suing for treble damages!

The consequence is a real threat to the process of competition itself. Price competition takes place by changes in individual offers, over periods of time, under pressure of offers by other sellers. It inevitably operates unevenly between buyers and between one period and another. The Commission now seems to have forced itself into holding that a meeting of competitive offers that results in giving preferences to certain customers, who are enabled as a result to take some business away from *their* competitors, is not a meeting of competition at all but an injury to competition. It ought to supply clearer proof that it has really weighed the offsetting benefits and losses of competition at the levels of both buyers and sellers before interfering so brusquely with price competition. Concerted systems of discriminatory pricing, such as were found in the *Cement,* glucose, *National Lead, Maltsters, Milk Can,* and *Fort Howard Paper Company* cases cannot legitimately take refuge behind the camouflage of the good faith defense. But what was Standard of Indiana to do in the face of an offer by the Red Indian Oil Company to sell Indiana's jobbers Standard of Ohio gasoline at 2 cents below the prevailing tank-wagon price?

But all this is only another way of saying that a discriminatory price cut is always, in the first instance at least, a competitive phenomenon. So we began this chapter by asking whether the law ought ever to proceed against a big buyer, since his pressures represent a competitive force; and we close by asking whether, for the same reason, it ought ever to proceed against a discriminating seller either.

The answer is that our analysis of the key decisions has by no means refuted the underlying purpose of the Robinson-Patman Act and the rationale, implicit if not explicit, of the Commission's policies. On the contrary it has affirmed them. Both are on defensible ground in their presumption against price discrimination, even when the manifestly harmful effects are limited to individual competitors. In almost all cases, the Commission has sought to deny the use or benefits of price differentiation to dominant firms who have used it either as a cheap way of protecting a dominant position without seriously upsetting the market or as a source of competitive advantage unrelated to efficiency. Price discrimination, like coercively imposed exclusive arrangements, plays most often into the hands of the big and wealthy firm, buyer or seller.

PART III

Conclusion

CHAPTER 9

The Proposed Revisions and Appropriate Limits of Antitrust

DAVID LILIENTHAL once wrote an article entitled "Our Anti-trust Laws Are Crippling America." [1] The title was dramatic; it summarized an opinion that is prevalent in America today in legal and business circles. But the article and his later book *Big Business,* despite repeated references to the same idea, provide no evidence that Lilienthal has ever read an antitrust decision from beginning to end.

Assuming he was referring to real and not imaginary antitrust suits, Lilienthal must have meant that if the assets of the American Telephone and Telegraph Company system are reduced from $11 to $10 billion dollars by splitting off Western Electric, if the owners of du Pont are forced to sell the stock in General Motors which they say they do not vote anyhow, if the United Shoe Machinery Company is split up, or if the retailing divisions of A & P had been separated to create seven separate chains each as large as First National or American Stores, or twice the size of Loblaws—then the American economy would be deprived of a prime source of technical progress and military strength. He must have meant that if companies like Standard of California and American Can are forced to offer their dealers or customers the opportunity to take their products on a nonexclusive basis, if Automatic Canteen can no longer coerce its suppliers into

[1] *Collier's,* May 31, 1952, pp. 15–17; see also his *Big Business, A New Era,* Chap. 21.

giving it preferential discounts, or if the steel companies can no longer systematically match each other's prices, the vitality of the American economy will be sapped.

The argument has several parts, as we have seen: (*a*) that there is a new Sherman Act which demonstrates a doctrinaire hostility to business size, integration, efficiency, and competitive tactics heretofore considered harmless; (*b*) that it is these forms of business organization and practice that have been in large measure responsible for the favorable performance of the American economy over the last century and in the last decade; (*c*) that the new Sherman Act must be replaced by a more flexible and sympathetic rule of law based on a realistic appraisal of the economic contributions of the organizations and policies under scrutiny.

Our review of recent developments in antitrust policy has been designed to reveal whether recent policy is as novel as it has seemed to some commentators who wrote directly under the shadow of the decisions, but who apparently read little more than legal headnotes or isolated dicta. We think we have demonstrated that on the whole the cases fall, albeit with some logical extensions of doctrine, into the policy framework within which the acts have been enforced since their inception. The law does just about what Lilienthal, who probably reflects accurately the views of most businessmen, thinks it should do but does not.[2] The traditional presumption against collusive and exclusive tactics and systematic discrimination remains at the core of the law, and this is as it should be.

The amazing thing about the vociferous new criticism of the antitrust laws is the paucity of evidence it has offered to show that antitrust decisions have actually had or even threatened to have the awful economic consequences that they predict so freely. Lilienthal's book is typical in this regard. Our own economic appraisal of the leading recent cases shows why the new critics have been so sparing with their economic facts; there

[2] *Ibid.*, pp. 170–171. For an excellent appraisal of Lilienthal and the broader issues he raises, see Loevinger, in 37 *Minn. Law Rev.* 505, 521–525, 547–548, 551 and *passim* (1953).

simply are very few available to support their fears. Yet on the basis of this sketchy evidence of public necessity, they would, as we shall see, dilute if not eradicate the suspicion with which the law regards the practices of collusion, coercion, and exclusion. We find very little reason to expect harmful economic consequences from the new Sherman Act, and much reason to be enthusiastic about it.

We find, in short, that the legal analysis of many of the new critics has been partisan and their predictions of economic disaster erroneous.

In our appraisal of the leading cases, we asked whether a resurrection of the rule of reason with an economic corpus would have been likely to produce a basically different and economically superior rule of law. Again we found much ground for skepticism.

In this concluding chapter, we consider directly some of the more general arguments for amending the antitrust laws and some of the proposals for converting them into a charter for "effective competition." We must content ourselves in most cases with relatively brief observations.

Mitigating Antitrust Vexations for the Businessman —Uncertainty and Litigation

One of the most popular complaints against the antitrust laws is that they do not provide sufficient certainty for the harassed business executive, who would like to know what he can and cannot do without having to lie awake nights worrying about possible infractions of the law. It is impossible not to be sympathetic with this plea.

A closely related complaint is that the financial burden of an antitrust case is so heavy and its delays so egregious that on grounds of efficiency alone some substitute should be found for cumbrous, anachronistic, adversary legal proceedings. Though even among the cases that go to trial the number of "big cases" is exceeded many times over by those that are disposed of quickly and efficiently, and though there is no simple substitute for the "big case" consistent with the purposes of antitrust, this contention too has merit.[3] For example, the investment bankers and the *Aluminum* trials bear witness to the lawyer's contempt for time. It seems inevitable that conditions in the suspected industries or firms have changed so substantially during the proceedings—in the course of which the attorneys of record are married, become fathers, grandfathers, and pass on to the next world, leaving behind an estate enriched by antitrust practice—as to render any verdict on the basis of the evidence hopelessly out of date. The same complaints have been voiced against utility rate cases, which are even lengthier than antitrust suits and which become even more complicated because changes in costs while old cases are in progress often necessitate new litigation, so that several proceedings may be carried on simultaneously. What seems clear is that a contest of this sort becomes for private unregulated business an ordeal in itself, to be avoided at all costs. By merely threatening suit, it is claimed, the Antitrust Division can extract settlements that perhaps would not be forthcoming if the cases were tried to their conclusion in the courts.

These related complaints, of uncertainty, doubt, delay, and expense, are both substantive and procedural. The first hope of the businessman for a remedy is said to lie in a substantive change in the law—a change that will render the law clear and specific as to what is prohibited.

There are two ways to effect the required substantive change. One might be to list specific practices and declare them illegal per se. This would reduce uncertainty and shorten antitrust suits. If the list were short enough it might satisfy the businessman who is tired of worrying about being a defendant in antitrust suits (though it would in the same measure worry the businessman who is now protected by the antitrust laws); but could one conscientiously propose such a change if one really wished to preserve competition too? If, alternatively, one tried to reach by a list of explicit per se prohibitions all the possible threats to

[3] Victor H. Kramer, "Some Procedural Problems in Protracted Antitrust Trials," Univ. of Michigan Institute, *Federal Antitrust Law,* 1953 (mimeo.), p. 2 and *passim;* also Breck P. McAllister, "The Big Case: Procedural Problems in Antitrust Litigation," 64 *Harv. Law Rev.* 27 (1950).

competition that antitrust now reaches, would any businessman be content with the result? Could such a list omit price discrimination, tie-in sales, exclusive dealing, mergers, price fixing, division of markets, squeezes? Yet who would advocate that all these be made offenses per se? No, they must be prevented only when they are unreasonable, by virtue either of the nature of the actions or their consequences. But we are back, then, at the traditional laws, with all their uncertainties.

The other possible road to certainty by substantive change in the law might be to outlaw certain kinds of market situations—for example, providing for dissolution of any firm in possession of more than 30 per cent of some market, limiting advertising expenditures to a certain percentage of gross revenues, prohibiting the ownership of more than a certain number of patents, and putting an absolute limit to business size. There is something to be said for this road to certainty, but few of the businessmen now critical of the law would favor it. Most economists would probably agree that such proscriptions could be applied only industry by industry, on a discretionary basis. What then becomes of the hope for certainty or for abbreviated antitrust proceedings?

There are some activities that businessmen know today they must not engage in, although if some of the proponents of workable competition as a rule of antitrust have their way even these anchors would be lifted and the law set adrift, as Justice Taft put it, on a sea of uncertainty. They may not agree with each other to set prices or output. They may not make use of a patent to force customers to purchase an unpatented article. They may not collectively use patent privileges to extend control over the prices, production policies, and sales areas of licensees. They may not enter into agreements with competitors to allocate territories. They may not follow a pricing system used by all their competitors that produces completely uniform delivered prices.

Of course difficulties remain. A large firm, especially, must be much more careful than a small before merging with another, before signing a full requirements contract, before bargaining severely with suppliers or distributors, before cutting its prices selectively. But is there any alternative consistent with having an antitrust law? A firm that has power must, in a free society, be held to an unusually high standard of accountability for the way in which it exercises it, consciously or unconsciously. The present law requires above all else that such a firm take unusual precautions to see that its actions are reasonable, honestly competitive, noncoercive, nondiscriminatory. These are onerous restrictions, and they handicap the big firm. But we are told again and again that big companies have internal sources of strength and efficiency, entirely apart from their relations with competitors and completely insulated from all antitrust attack. We are told that they are the most efficient mechanisms thus far devised in the technique of management, so that the government may readily turn over to them in time of emergency vast and novel programs for research, mobilization, or planning.[4] It should surely be possible for them, *before* antitrust complaints are made, to devise managerial procedures and policies that will keep them clear of the law without interfering with their ability to compete. It may be necessary, for complete safety, that they avoid certain competitive practices of dubious legality. But why should an efficient, big, progressive firm have to insist on any form of exclusive arrangement with its dealers or customers, try to get price concessions other than those that are justified by cost, or join with unfree and unenterprising foreigners to exchange exclusive patent licenses and allocate sales territories?

One way to see whether the law is as uncertain as claimed is for the impartial reader to go through the recent cases as we have and ask himself whether, in most of them, a businessman might not have foreseen that he was treading the narrow edge. There is much truth to the observation that it is easy to avoid violating the antitrust laws; what is difficult is to come as close as possible to doing what the law prohibits without violating it.[5] Certainly in view of the language of Section 3 of the Clayton Act, Standard

[4] See Lilienthal; also Kaplan and Kahn in 47 *Fortune,* Feb. 1953, Sec. 2.

[5] See the shrewd observations of Justice Brandeis, quoted by Wallace and Douglas, in 19 *U. of Chicago Law Rev.* 712–713 n. 80 (1952); Edwards, *Maintaining Competition,* pp. 42–49.

of California, Richfield, and American Can must have known they were running some legal risk. A & P was obviously aware (and Automatic Canteen should have been) of the legal hazards of its buying and selling policies, the members of the Cement Institute and the Iron and Steel Institute of their pricing systems, United Shoe of its leases, the Big 5 movie companies of their methods of pricing and distributing films. Even Minneapolis-Honeywell must or should have been worried about the 55 per cent of its sales on which it granted quantity discounts unjustified by cost: it could scarcely have declared with a mind sincere that it was meeting specific competitive offers within the meaning of Robinson-Patman.

One must not exaggerate: Standard of Indiana could hardly have foreseen that it would be forbidden to give its jobbers the customary 1.5 cents off the tank-wagon price; the rubber tire manufacturers, while aware of the danger of the quantity discount rule, probably had no choice about giving the big buyers the discounts they demanded; the distributors of advertising films perhaps had no reason to believe that they were violating the law; even Alcoa must have been genuinely aggrieved (as well as surprised) at being convicted for having expanded capacity so rapidly as to pre-empt all market opportunities! But not even in the Robinson-Patman jungle do all the hazards lurk that one might, from the continuous breast beating by barristers berating the basing-point decisions, be led to fear. A businessman usually knows whether or not he is meeting competition in good faith in making a price cut.[6] He also must know whether he is coercing dealers to drop lines of competitors. As a professor of the Harvard Business School said in discussing the antitrust laws with a group of businessmen who have had numerous encounters with them: "Down deep in one's heart he knows whether he is taking advantage of any one or not and he knows equally well when he is doing the right thing." [7]

[6] See Edwards, "The Bearing of the Robinson-Patman Act upon the Policy of the Sherman Act," an address before the Practicing Law Institute, N.Y., Dec. 6, 1952 (mimeo.).

[7] E. P. Learned, "Integration in American Industry," an address before the American Petroleum Institute, Nov. 9, 1939 (multilithed), p. 19.

To paraphrase the President of the United States, the only ultimate certainty (or security) is in the grave (or prison—and no businessman has yet gone to prison for a genuine antitrust offense). No one knows better than the lawyers crying for more exactness in the antitrust statutes that all legislation makes for uncertainty, especially laws which strive to make exact definitions of offenses. The income and estate tax laws are as uncertain as any others on the books, partly because of the very effort to make them precise. The private motion picture Production Code seeks to achieve "morality" with specific rules and is a nauseating failure.

The second way in which the vexations of antitrust for the businessman, the uncertainty and the threat of endless litigation, could be mitigated would be by a reform of antitrust procedures. There is obviously room for improvement in the administration of the laws. Though the fashioning of such improvements is essentially a legal problem, it may be desirable briefly to consider the kinds of changes that have been suggested.

The Business Advisory Committee of the Department of Commerce has proposed that (*a*) more cases be settled in conference, out of court; (*b*) the Antitrust Division provide authoritative rulings on activities that might be capable of conflicting legal interpretations, and (*c*) the initiation of "major" antitrust proceedings be subject to review by a board consisting of persons of "business, engineering and economic backgrounds." [8]

While at first glance these proposals seem most attractive, we regard them with considerable skepticism. In the first place, it seems reasonable to assume that (unless the purpose is to emasculate the antitrust laws) the conference procedure will not be too dissimilar from the current practice of obtaining consent decrees. Yet the Business Advisory Report deplores the heavy resort to consent settlements in recent years because it feels this results from uncertainty in the law and the willingness of businessmen to accept even undesirable decrees in their desire to avoid litigation. Its proposed "preventive conference procedure" would, in contrast with consent settlements, involve no formal legal proceedings, no filing of complaints in equity, no indict-

[8] *Effective Competition*, p. 20.

ments. This difference is perhaps unimportant; but the Federal Trade Commission's experience seems to show that without the firm backbone provided by legal proceedings trade practice conferences are almost without effect in inducing businessmen to do anything except what they want to do anyhow.[9]

The second proposal has some merit; the Antitrust Division should be willing to say clearly what its view of the law is. But in many cases the problem is not what the law is but what the defendants have actually done, and what have been the consequences. To determine this is no simple task. Indeed, in view of the fact that the Business Advisory Committee, like most of the new critics of antitrust, would abolish *per se* offenses and have antitrust verdicts turn on the "effectiveness of competition" considered in the light of "all the relevant facts," it is difficult to see how the Department of Justice could ever commit itself in advance on the legality of any practice!

The third suggestion of the Business Advisory Council echoes that of the Select Committee on Small Business of the House of Representatives, which has criticized the Antitrust Division for wholly neglecting economic standards in initiating cases. Complaints are still the source of actions, and cases are selected according to whether the Division believes they can be won. Accordingly, the Small Business Committee proposed that the Division set up a comprehensive program to get rid of the concentration of economic power.[10] But the Business Advisory group denies that there is a concentration problem.

Here, from both the right and the left we find impatience with lawyers and politicians and their noneconomic selection of cases. But the wholly dissimilar economic standards that each of these critics would use demonstrate, as we pointed out in Chapter 1, that ultimately the selection of cases must be a political, not an economic affair. Which expert group of economists planned the

[9] "Plans to negotiate more antitrust settlements are running into snags. Chief trustbuster Stanley N. Barnes . . . finds it hard to deal with alleged violators unless formal charges are made in the courts." *Business Week,* Oct. 31, 1953, p. 38.

[10] *Antitrust Enforcement by the Federal Trade Commission and the Antitrust Division, Dept. of Justice—A Preliminary Report,* 81st Cong., 2d Sess., H. Report 3236 (1951), p. 76.

selection of cases for the Antitrust Division would depend on who won the most recent election. It would seem wiser to preserve, in theory at least, an unchanging corpus of legal offenses corresponding roughly to society's unchanging conception of unreasonable actions.

The defects of antitrust procedure, which it is by no means our purpose to minimize, are not confined to the long trials by combat engaged in by the Department of Justice. The Federal Trade Commission too has become notorious for its molasseslike procedure in handling cases and for the inordinately lengthy records that it develops.[11] There is apparently some hope of improving the Commission's bureaucratic performance through change of management, though readers may remember that commentators have been publicly castigating that organization for years with little if any apparent effect.

Proposals to Return to the Rule of Reason, with Workable Competition as Its Guide

S. C. Oppenheim, before his appointment as cochairman of the National Committee to Study the Antitrust Laws, set forth a proposal for rejuvenating the rule of reason in order to permit use of the criterion of workable competition in appraising acts supposed to be violative of the antitrust laws. Because of his official position and because his proposals represent a conscientious effort to reappraise the antitrust laws in the light of the new criticism, it is worth considering their general purport with some care. The main proposal is apparently to have the courts henceforth consider "all the factors and circumstances in any given situation," rather than use the modified per se approach now found in antitrust enforcement. Obviously, some limit has to be put on these factors and circumstances; but the only ones he suggests are "all the relevant facts" a defendant "can muster." If we read him aright, he would leave it to the judge to decide whether the defendant has demonstrated that workable competi-

[11] See *ibid.*, pp. 19, 84–96; the lament of Commissioner Mason, in his *Automatic Canteen* decision, pp. 1–2; and *F.T.C.* v. *Cement Institute*, 333 U.S. 683, 687 (1948).

tion has been enhanced by the practice in question—for example, the discriminatory concession given a big buyer. Since the decision ultimately rests upon economic tests, the judge in turn would refer the matter to a master in chancery, who would be an economist or have an economic assistant.[12]

Oppenheim provides illustrations of his approach: the Supreme Court in the *Standard of California* case should have assumed the responsibility of hearing the evidence on the effect of Standard's contracts on competition in the marketing of gasoline at retail. Similarly, the probable effects of a particular merger should be weighed "by consideration of all relevant economic factors" under the amended Section 7 of the Clayton Act. Even price-fixing agreements would be tested in this manner, giving the defendants their day in court.[13] Applying the new rule of reason to the Robinson-Patman Act, Oppenheim would substitute the phraseology of the qualifying clause of Section 3 for the prohibition of injury to competition with persons now found in Section 2. The cost saving and good faith meeting of competition defenses would both be absolute, together with "other legitimate economic justifications in the distribution system." [14]

For the reader who has managed to survive to this point it should be unnecessary to catalogue our qualms about this proposal for total immersion in the rule of reason. First of all, our fear is that the courts and litigants will drown in the process. The proposal offers not the prospect of greater certainty and shorter litigation (Oppenheim does not pretend that it does) but utter confusion. Economists are no more likely to agree than lawyers; only a disillusioned lawyer or a brash economist could

[12] In 50 *Michigan Law Rev.* 1151, 1159, 1163–1164 (1952).

[13] *Ibid.,* pp. 1181, 1197. Although Oppenheim expresses clearly his hostility to "cartel-like agreements" (*ibid.,* p. 1159), he would treat them differently from other offenses only in that anything involving "joint action among competitors" would throw upon the defendants the burden of proof of showing workable competition was furthered by their cartel (*ibid.,* p. 1165). Where there is no agreement, the burden would presumably be on the government.

[14] *Ibid.,* p. 1202. Oppenheim would also eliminate Sections 2(c), (d), and (e).

believe otherwise. Second, the suggestion is not in line with the doctrine to which Oppenheim wishes the law to return. He says clearly, at the outset:

> Congressional antitrust policy should continue to place major reliance upon negative proscriptions rather than affirmative prescriptions. It should retain the orthodox pattern of a series of "thou shalt nots." These "don'ts" are the hard kernel of governmental intervention that today gives government and businessmen a firm common ground of concurrence in approaches to antitrust.[15]

This has been our contention, precisely. It is difficult to reconcile this view with the one that would subject every antitrust proceeding to a test of economic consequences. It was as a means of characterizing the action, to see whether it fell within the prohibited category, that Chief Justice White made intent the essence of his rule of reason, holding that acts were illegal

> where the surrounding circumstances were such as to justify the conclusion that they had not been entered into or performed with the legitimate purpose of reasonably forwarding personal interest and developing trade, but on the contrary, were of such a character as to give rise to the inference or presumption that they had been entered into or done *with the intent* to do wrong to the general public and to limit the right of individuals. . . .[16]

Most dangerous is Oppenheim's acceptance of a change in the law that would permit any sort of agreement among competitors if judges could be convinced that it enhanced workable competition. He views the *Trenton Potteries* case as one of the first steps in an erring interpretation of the law, in spite of White's explicit recognition that there were certain acts that in themselves were repugnant to the Sherman Act. He would permit businessmen to engage even in price-fixing conspiracies, provided they can at some future date, when and if called upon to do so, demonstrate in any of a great number of ways that the practices produced good economic results. In view of the weak punitive provisions of the antitrust laws, which most of the re-

[15] *Ibid.*, p. 1146.

[16] *Standard Oil Co. of New Jersey* v. *U.S.*, 221 U.S. 1, 58 (1911) (emphasis supplied).

visionists would further dilute by shutting the door to treble damage suits where the violations were not wilful,[17] it is difficult to doubt that the adoption of such a rule of reason would be regarded by the business world as an invitation to "reasonable cartelization" of the economy.

Recognizing the difficulties of enforcing the law as it stands today, we nevertheless feel strongly that to entrust each proceeding to the vagaries of shifts in economic theorizing—which at one moment strongly supports atomistic competition, at another extols the virtues of powerful, foundation-supporting corporations—would not be a desirable change. We would preserve the general principle of the law, that it is the function of government not to assess the ultimate impact of business practices but only to judge whether they are collusive or exclusive in nature.

This investigation does not preclude the application of a certain kind of rule of reason even to restrictive agreements between competitors. Under common law, the concept of restraint of trade originally referred to agreements not to compete arising out of contracts that had some other, more important, purpose. The so-called ancillary restraints might appear in contracts to sell a business or to enter into a joint venture, like Justice Holmes's two stage drivers. Restraints of this character could not be unequivocally condemned without, in many cases, jeopardizing the substantive, and inoffensive, purpose of the contracts: a tailor could not purchase the shop and good will of another without the latter giving some undertaking to refrain from opening up a competing shop next door. Where the restraint, then, was reasonably ancillary to the substantive bargain, limited in time and space to what was required to effect that bargain, and where it carried a *quid pro quo* in exchange for the agreement not to compete, it was enforceable at law.[18]

One can find an echo of this rule of reason even in cases in-

[17] *Effective Competition,* p. 20. Innocent on its face, the proposal needs thorough examination. To adopt it while at the same time increasing the uncertainty of the law by adopting market performance tests of reasonableness would go dangerously far in robbing the laws of their effectiveness.

[18] See Oppenheim, *Cases on Federal Anti-Trust Laws* (St. Paul: West, 1948), Chap. 1.

volving per se offenses. The courts must decide, first of all, what the defendants were doing. In this appraisal they must consider whether the restraint at issue embodied the primary purpose and essense of the agreement or whether it was incidental to some other, socially acceptable purpose. Thus, in one of the first decisions exempting a partial restraint on pricing under the rule of reason, the Supreme Court concluded that the Chicago Board of Trade's primary purpose in forbidding sales outside trading hours, except at the last closing price, was not to effect a substantive alteration of the market price but instead to create an organized competitive market. Thus the Board of Trade rule, which did actually fix prices in a very limited sense, was in effect held ancillary to the primary, legitimate purpose of the agreement.

In several proceedings against international cartel agreements, an important part of the new Sherman Act resurgence of antitrust, the question has arisen explicitly whether the restraints at issue were merely ancillary to the formation of joint foreign ventures (either with domestic or foreign partners) or to exchanges of patent licenses and technical information. In most cases the courts decided, and we think correctly (as we argued earlier in the case of *Timken*), that the restraints were not limited to what was required to effect some other socially acceptable purpose.[19] We cannot here consider each of these cases in detail. But it seems necessary to point out the particular importance of applying to international or foreign contracts the rule of reason implicit in the distinction between ancillary and substantive restraints. First, the special hazards and governmental restrictions on international trade and investment may justify co-operative arrangements that are feasible only with

[19] See the similar judgment of Herbert A. Bergson, "Some Antitrust Problems in Doing Business Abroad" (MS), Univ. of Michigan Institute, *Federal Antitrust Laws,* 1953; also of Sigmund Timberg, "Antitrust and Foreign Trade," 48 *Northwestern U. Law Rev.* 411–426 (1953). It is difficult to find a justification analogous to the one accepted in *Chicago Board of Trade* for the collusive fixing of commission rates by real estate boards. Cf. G. E. and R. D. Hale, "Market Imperfections: Enforcement of the Anti-Trust Laws in a Friction-afflicted Economy," 102 *U. of Penn. Law Rev.* 182–183 (1953).

anticompetitive agreements attached. Thus, joint ventures that would themselves be suspect in domestic trade may be the only feasible way of exploiting foreign markets. If the lawful main purpose cannot be achieved without the attached restraint, the courts should find the latter ancillary, incidental, and hence reasonable. Second, contracts having some restrictive influence on United States exports or imports, direct or indirect, may be legal in the countries where they are put into effect. Since the reach of American laws and the jurisdiction of American courts extends properly only to contracts which directly and substantially affect United States foreign commerce, condemnation should not be extended to all restraints on that commerce, however remote or incidental.[20]

For both these reasons, if it appears that the only way American oil companies could have obtained access to foreign concessions to explore for crude oil was to participate in joint foreign enterprises and in cartel agreements not illegal in the countries whose trade was directly restrained as a result, it would be unreasonable for American courts to find the ventures illegal per se. Similarly, if American companies, even a group accounting for the bulk of domestic output, decide jointly to set up a joint manufacturing subsidiary behind a foreign tariff wall and agree as part of the bargain not to compete with their joint subsidiary, it is hard to see why their agreement should run afoul of a condemnation of price-fixing and market-sharing agreements, even though American exports are incidentally subjected to a collective restraint as a result.[21] If the same technique were used in sharing the California market, the joint venture itself would obviously be suspect, as a direct and substantive restraint of competition in the United States. The same could not be true of a joint venture in England, to which the restraint on American exports is ancillary. It is not the function of American law to preserve competition in the United Kingdom market,

[20] See American Bar Association, Section of International and Comparative Law, *Report of the Comm. on Internat'l Trade Regulation on the Impact of the Antitrust Laws on Foreign Trade,* Aug. 6, 1953.

[21] See the contrary decision in *U.S.* v. *Minnesota Mining and Mfg. Co.,* 92 F.Supp. 947 (1950).

to protect foreign customers from the cartelization that their own laws seldom condemn and sometimes welcome. A rule of reason that exempts agreements representing only ancillary, indirect restraints of American foreign commerce is entirely compatible with the new as well as the old Sherman Act.

A plausible case can be made for extending a similar rule to patents and processes agreements among international (or, indeed, domestic) competitors carrying restrictive covenants, as they almost invariably did prior to the new Sherman Act. Division of markets (by exchange of exclusive rights for stipulated territories), joint ventures in neutral markets, and even price-fixing stipulations may be essential if the main purpose is to be achieved: resolution of patent tangles, freeing the art for further advance, and permitting fruitful collaboration in research. Would companies co-operate so unreservedly, and therefore with such good economic results, if each knew that the fruits of its own research might be used (indeed, would have to be used, under the antitrust laws) by its partner in competition with it?

However, we would be much more skeptical of the desirability of permitting, as reasonably ancillary to patents, trade mark, and processes agreements, such comprehensive cartelizations as have been struck down since 1940.[22] If the law is changed to do so, subject to a workable competition or market performance rule of reason (which is apparently the position of Judge Leahy in the *Cellophane* case), patent owners will be disposed to hold out for such restrictive clauses as a condition for reaching agreement. They will therefore always be able to assert afterward, in an antitrust proceeding, that no agreement could have been reached without meeting the demand. With the law unequivocally opposed, the cartel restraints will probably, as they have so often in the new Sherman Act period, mysteriously cease to be an essential condition of agreement.[23]

[22] See *U.S.* v. *Timken Roller Bearing Co.,* 341 U.S. 593 (1951); *U.S.* v. *Imperial Chemicals Industries, Ltd.,* 100 F.Supp. 504 (1951); *U.S.* v. *General Electric Co.,* 82 F.Supp. 753 (1949); *U.S.* v. *National Lead Co.,* 332 U.S. 319 (1947); *U.S.* v. *General Electric Co.,* 80 F.Supp. 989 (1948).

[23] Standard of New Jersey nominally withdrew from the international

The American market can be assured the benefits of access to foreign-owned American patents without relaxing the prohibition of such direct restraints on competition in the United States as were involved in the agreements between Standard of New Jersey and I. G. Farben, or between du Pont and I. C. I. First, a compulsory working provision for foreign-owned United States patents, providing for compulsory licensing if the patents are not worked with reasonable assiduity, would minimize the bargaining power of the foreign patentee. Second, the richness of the American market would in any case seem to assure the exploitation of commercially feasible patents. The only factor that might lead to nonuse would be the desire of the foreign owner to protect the investments of its American cartel partners who might be injured by its competition; but such a limiting factor would be strengthened by the existence of extensive cartel ties such as resulted in instance after instance of delayed application of foreign chemical processes in the United States between World Wars I and II.[24] Lastly, we place our faith in the competitive ingenuity of American businessmen. Denied access to foreign processes, they may instead seek alternative methods of achieving the same end. Where competing patents block development, pooling agreements may still, of course, be reached. But it requires more convincing proof than has so far been produced to show the necessity for a relaxation of the historic American opposition to substantive, as distinguished from ancillary, conspiracies in restraint of competition. With respect to such agreements, we reject Oppenheim's proposal to restore a rule of reason applying economic tests.

The Clayton Act, however, does call for an assessment of the economic consequences of the practices it lists. Here Oppenheim's suggestions command respect. The former efforts of the

---

petroleum cartel in 1938 and notified its Swedish subsidiary to do so in 1942. F.T.C., *The International Petroleum Cartel* (Washington, 1952), p. 266. Du Pont canceled its Patents and Processes Agreement with I. C. I. on June 30, 1948. *U.S.* v. *I.C.I., Ltd.,* Trial Memorandum No. 1 for Defendants, Feb. 15, 1950, p. 7. In 1945 du Pont canceled its restrictive agreement with Sylvania on cellophane production. *U.S.* v. *E. I. du Pont de Nemours & Co.,* 118 F.Supp. 41 (1953), Finding 581.

[24] Stocking and Watkins, *Cartels in Action,* Chap. 11.

Federal Trade Commission to obliterate the saving clauses of Sections 2 and 3 must be partially reversed. From the economic point of view, there is no reason for requiring a narrower inquiry or a less conclusive demonstration of injury to competition under Section 2(a) than under any other section of the act. And from the legal standpoint as well, the Commission must be required to show greater tolerance toward price concessions made in good faith to meet competition. To the same end, the language of Robinson-Patman ought to be changed to make the good faith clause less restrictive. It should not be necessary for sellers to match exactly the "equally low" price of a competitor and thus run the risk of a charge of conscious parallel action. Restrictive language in the statute can never take the place of administrative discretion in deciding whether a price cut was or was not made in good faith. Here is another instance in which the quest for certainty through statutory formulation has produced results of which few businessmen approve. And where the concession was really in good faith, it should certainly require more substantial showing of injurious competitive impact than apparently suffices under the *Morton Salt* precedent to warrant outlawing it.

But can or should these problems be decided exclusively by economic standards? The Robinson-Patman Act was not passed in order to legislate Chamberlinian-Clarkian workable competition any more than was the Sherman Act. It represents a charter of "fair trade" whose general purpose and provisions probably command even wider acceptance than the resale price maintenance statutes that have usurped the fair trade title. By the standards most of us accept, discounts unjustified by the cost or the performance of function, even though made in good faith, are unfair to the competing buyer who pays the higher price. They are even unfair to the small competitor at the selling level, who must bear their full brunt while his discriminating competitor enjoys the subsidy of higher returns on his other operations.

Nevertheless, as in the case of the fair trade laws themselves, it is obvious that society should not protect free enterprisers against every possible competitive inequity, at the cost of the consumer. So here the considerations of equitable treatment of the individual competitor, which enter Robinson-Patman in the provision outlawing discrimination that impairs competition "with any person" adversely affected thereby, must be balanced against the competitive contributions of price discrimination and the possibly stultifying consequences of its complete prohibition. Our only point is that the considerations of equity cannot be abolished in the name of effective competition.

This is especially so because economists can so seldom predict the alternatives to pricing in a discriminatory fashion or to exclusive dealing. We have found strong reasons for believing that competition might have been more effective in temperature regulators, spark plugs, gasoline, or newspaper publishing were businessmen denied the right to discriminate, tie-in, or sell under exclusive contracts. We have very strong doubts that price competition is fostered when a dominant seller is able selectively to meet every competitive price reduction, wherever and whenever it appears, so as immediately to deny to the chiseler the benefits of his temerity. Yet is not such a firm merely meeting competitors' concessions in good faith? The Robinson-Patman Act, for all the criticisms by lawyers and economists, has certainly not prevented very effective competition in the distributive trades. Tremendous technological changes have followed in its wake. There is even reason to believe that, as far as the big chains are concerned, the act has contributed to those changes by turning their attention from the quest of secret discounts to an improvement of their merchandising activities—improved warehousing techniques, cutting losses in produce by improving refrigeration, prepackaging meat, and so on.

We have no pat solution to suggest for balancing these often imponderable as well as incommensurable ethical and economic considerations. In the *Standard of Indiana* case equity and economics could have been reconciled: the Commission could have ordered the company to make its discrimination equitable, that is, available to all who could qualify on a functional basis. This would have been far preferable to wiping out the differentiation completely. For other cases a workable solution is suggested by Senator Kefauver's proposed amendment to the Robinson-Patman Act, introduced in the Eighty-third Congress.[25] The amend-

[25] S. 1357, 83d Cong., 1st Sess., March 18, 1953.

ment retains the protection of the individual inherent in the wording of Section 2(a) that outlaws discrimination impairing or preventing competition with "any person." However, the bill also makes the good faith defense an absolute one, "unless the effect . . . may be substantially to lessen competition," presumably competition in the market *as a whole*. Unfortunately, owing to *Morton Salt,* this proposed exception to the absolute good faith defense becomes operative upon a demonstration of the mere possibility of anticompetitive impact. The requirement should therefore probably be strengthened to ensure that the good faith defense can be overridden only where the resulting threat to competition is actually substantial.

But no bill can provide a perfect formula for balancing the competitive against the inequitable and monopolistic aspects of discrimination. There is no substitute for a conscientious effort on the part of the F.T.C. to weigh the effects against each other. The new Commission seems prepared to make the effort; our only fear is that it may redress the balance so far in the direction of "economic" standards as to sacrifice the equity which it is also the purpose of antitrust to preserve, without really gaining much in the way of economic performance. A free enterprise system cannot tolerate substantial and continued disparities between its realities and its ideal of a fair field and no favors. Inevitable differences in competitive strength are created by inequalities in the access to capital and the inherent advantages of size, established position, and integration. When these advantages are compounded through coercion, exclusion, and systematic discrimination, it would require more convincing demonstrations than have heretofore been offered that these tactics are necessary for effective competition to warrant our rejecting the economic and social theory underlying the new Clayton Act.

There is another, more fundamental reason for distrusting the positive proposal of the new critics that we take a more reasonable attitude toward these practices. At their very core, the two views, theirs and ours, are in opposition in their attitude toward business power. Traditionally, American society has distrusted concentrated economic power, whether in public or private hands. The antitrust laws are but one expression of that basic hostility. Together with the public attitude of which they are an expression, they have been part of the dynamic equilibrium of forces that has produced the very business system that the proponents of antitrust reform can, not unreasonably, describe as workably competitive. Indeed, the American economy of 1954 is in many ways astoundingly energetic, competitive. But unless one adds also the caveat that the economy is the way it is partly because of public suspicion of business size and power and hostility toward anticompetitive manipulations, one leaves the implication that the business system is so basically competitive that it no longer needs restraints. We do not intend to exaggerate the importance of social and legal constraints or to deny the strong competitive forces inherent in American business. But it would obviously be a logical fallacy of the most elementary sort to conclude that because, today, after twenty years of governmental suspicion and increasing control of private economic power, business acquits itself extremely well, there is no need for the suspicion and the controls may safely be relaxed. With the exception of changes introduced by unfriendly administrations, American business has fundamentally the same institutional characteristics as the system that performed so badly and was so unworkably competitive, so undynamic, so insufficiently innovative, during the years 1929–1939. In our haste to expunge from the record our unfavorable and to some extent unfair verdicts on business size, integration, and competitive tactics, we may be destroying the very forces that have necessitated modification of the earlier verdict.[26]

To illustrate, we may look briefly at the petroleum industry, where, on the basis of crude performance and structure tests, there appears to be very little to criticize.[27] Yet who can doubt the contribution to that present happy situation of the long-standing public hostility to the concentration, collusion, and

[26] *Cf.* Oppenheim's good conduct medal to the trade associations, in 50 *Michigan Law Rev.* 1174 n. 87 (1952). He fails to inquire why trade association activities have been so relatively blameless, or whether they will remain so if his argument convinces Congress to eradicate the per se condemnation of collaborative price fixing.

[27] Dirlam, "The Petroleum Industry," in Adams (ed.), *The Structure of American Industry* (2d ed., New York: Macmillan, 1954).

exclusion in the industry? It was embodied in the 1911 disintegration of the Standard Oil monopoly, the extension of common carrier status to the crude, then product, pipelines—not really effective until thirty-five years after the Hepburn Act was passed—the successful breakup of the Ethyl patent pool with its rigid price fixing and its denial of the essential ingredient of high-test gasoline to independent refiners (who would have failed to survive in today's world of high-compression engines without access to a cheap means of upgrading their gasoline), the attack on the concerted gasoline-buying programs of the major oil companies in the Midwest and on the West Coast, the Federal Trade Commission analysis and the complaints of the Mutual Security Agency against the profiteering and market sharing by the international petroleum cartel, and last, but perhaps most important, the often unreasonably hostile Congressional scrutiny of every major price change initiated by big companies. After all, a concentrated industry does not necessarily produce a good performance autonomously, without external constraints.

Would it not therefore be foolhardy, simply because of a currently good industry performance, to eliminate the certainty that price fixing, exclusive tactics, or mammoth mergers are illegal?

To its proponents an extension of the rule of reason undoubtedly recommends itself as an extension of reasonableness itself. The arguments in its favor are unquestionably plausible and pragmatically appealing. But if the antitrust laws begin to take a less unreasonable view of certain tactics that businessmen have been prone to adopt in the past, our fear is that the delicate balance of forces producing the present performance and seemingly justifying the more reasonable attitude will be upset. If this is permitted to happen, the pendulum may one day swing too far in the opposite direction, toward unreasonable and excessive hostility to the creative, progressive, dynamic tendencies inherent in the American free enterprise system.

Proposals for Strengthening the New Sherman Act

Because our major task in this book has been to examine the contentions of those who, in vigorous support of hard competition, feel that the antitrust laws have been applied too harshly, we have tended to neglect the views of the critics who feel that they are not harsh enough and who would substitute a market structure test for the traditional rule of reason. Although we have serious reservations about this approach, as we indicated in Chapter 2, we must recognize that it has a certain persuasiveness in some situations where the antitrust laws have failed to prevent concentration and where in consequence, without any evidence of collusion or abuse of power by the dominant firm, competition is in some ways at least seriously lacking, for example because of a rigid price leadership. We might of course take refuge in the position that more adequate enforcement of the law in the past would have prevented such concentration and that the theory of the law, therefore, is sound. As a matter of fact, we cannot be sure that this was so. Whatever the historical reason, the solution in such cases would be to break up excessively concentrated market structures.

A typical situation of this sort apparently obtains in the lead pigments industry. There National Lead is the price leader and dominant firm, with about 60 per cent of the business, and a friendly competitor, Eagle-Picher, is the only other producer of consequence. As we pointed out in Chapter 7, the Federal Trade Commission strove to root out the price leadership system prevailing in the industry, but its efforts may prove ineffective because it cannot alter the market structure that produces this behavior.

National Lead had ten widely scattered lead pigment plants; as Commissioner Mason said, it was the Kilroy of the lead pigment industry. If it were broken up, the number of competitors in the industry could be substantially increased. But on what grounds could dissolution be ordered? National has from time to time, in the relatively remote past, engaged in activities apparently violative of the Sherman Act. It was organized in 1891 as a combination of over thirty independent companies; by 1920 it had acquired about twenty more producers.[28] It became the major customer of the largest supplier of pig lead in the United States, American Smelting and Refining, and in return American

[28] *National Lead Company*, Docket No. 5253, Opinion, Jan. 12, 1953, p. 4.

"thereafter refrained from taking any further interest in the manufacture of lead pigments." [29]

What legal action, if any, is indicated? Can National Lead be ordered to disgorge now the acquisitions made more than thirty-eight years ago? One might resolve that, aided by the amended Section 7 of the Clayton Act, the government must prevent similar combinations in the future, but this gives us no present plan of action. The trouble with trying to proceed on economic grounds alone is that it is almost impossible to tell in which direction to move. Commissioner Mason has emphasized the technological competition which the industry (like all monopolies) faces; lead pigments must compete with lithopone, titanium oxide, zinc oxide, and leaded zinc oxide.[30] Other economists would be satisfied to disintegrate the industry, because of the evidence of rigid price leadership. They might point out also in support of their case for the dissolution of giant companies that until recently National Lead tied up the competing product, titanium, too; they might cite as an object lesson the timidity of the Supreme Court which, though sustaining National's Sherman Act conviction in the titanium case, yet refused to dissolve the culprits.[31]

But it is most unlikely that National Lead could now be convicted under our antitrust laws for its control of the lead pigments industry, in the absence of evidence of collusion or exclusion. All we can do is enforce Section 7 of the Clayton Act to prevent further mergers of the type that have brought the company to its present position, attack vigorously such collusive and exclusionary practices as National Lead and du Pont employed in titanium and the F.T.C. found in lead pigments, and leave it to the dynamic processes of technological change to erode National's market power over the long run.

The Federal Trade Commission apparently intends to use Section 7 in the manner suggested. Its first opinion under the amended statute, in the *Pillsbury Mills* case, seems to reject, so far as Section 7 proceedings are concerned, the views of the new

[29] *Ibid.*, Findings, pp. 11–12.

[30] *Ibid.*, Dissenting Opinion, p. 15.

[31] *U.S.* v. *National Lead Co.,* 332 U.S. 319 (1947).

critics who find all degrees of market concentration compatible with workable competition, judged by market performance. It decided that a *prima-facie* case had been made out against Pillsbury's acquisition of its competitors Duff and Ballard, increasing the company's share in sales of baking mixes from 16 to 23 per cent nationally and from 23 to 45 per cent in the Southeast, even though it recognized that a merger of this kind might not necessarily "at present convert the industry . . . from a competitive to a non-competitive pattern. . . ." The decision spells out the Commission's willingness to go along with the Congressional intent to strengthen the antitrust laws in dealing with mergers that pose only an incipient threat to competition:

> We think the present case is the type Congress had in mind—one that presents a set of facts which would be insufficient under the Sherman Act but nonetheless establishes, *prima facie*, a violation of Section 7 of the Clayton Act. . . .
>
> As we understand it, it was this sort of trend that Congress condemned and desired to halt when it adopted the new Clayton Act anti-merger provision.[32]

On the other hand, the Commission equally rejected the views of the advocates of pure market structures, who would prohibit all mergers involving an appreciable amount of commerce. Recognizing that mergers may often intensify competition and reduce market concentration, it refused to apply to them the same diluted tests of substantial impact that have been accepted in Section 2 and 3 decisions. It drew the same distinction that we have ourselves suggested, between exclusive arrangements that limit unreasonably the freedom of choice of independent buyers and exclude competitors from the market, frequently through the use of coercion, and voluntary transfers of property whose probable economic impact, it held, can be judged only by more complicated economic investigations. Whether its insistence on considering "all the relevant factors" goes too far in applying the test of economic results, as Commissioner Mead seemed to fear,[33]

[32] Docket No. 6000, Opinion, Dec. 21, 1953, pp. 13 and 16.

[33] *Ibid.*, pp. 9 and 6–10 *passim;* Concurring Opinion of Commissioner Mead, Jan. 18, 1954. See also Irston R. Barnes, "Economic Issues in the Regulation of Acquisitions and Mergers," 14 *Ohio State Law J.* 279 (1953).

cannot as yet be predicted. It did not preclude at least an initial decision on the side of competition in this case.

The antitrust laws cannot be turned into a statute for the structuring of all markets in the direction of purer competition. Apart from the economic objections to such a program, it would be politically impossible. It is questionable if it is worth devoting the bureaucratic resources necessary to achieve the reordered structure, and it is questionable too whether the resultant discord and confusion might not impair economic performance more than the final restructuring would improve it. Where giant firms have overstepped the bounds of antitrust, there is no sign their efficiency would in most cases be impaired by dissolving them; reduction of power by these means could be accomplished without much loss. But beyond this remedy, we must resign ourselves to the presence of substantial economic power in our community. General Motors, General Electric, A. T. & T., du Pont, Sears Roebuck, Standard Oil of New Jersey—not to mention the United Mine Workers and the Teamsters Union—are all powerful organizations. But their power is held in check by a variety of forces and controls. It would be difficult to make a convincing economic case for their wholesale disintegration.

We reject the proposals for changing the antitrust laws that spring alike from hostility or friendliness to the present American business system. We are unsympathetic to proposals for reorganizing market structures to make them more purely competitive, because we feel that the advocates of the change have failed to demonstrate its necessity. They have not convinced us that so sharp a break with tradition is justified, either because current performance is so poor or because future performance, after reorganization, will be so much better. On the other hand, we cannot welcome the weakening of antitrust proscriptions proposed by the new critics. Not only have they failed to make their economic case for alterations in the law, but our own examination of the cases convinces us that, if anything, the changes would produce a poorer, not a superior economic performance. They would, on the strength of inconclusive economic analysis that does not show what they say it shows, amend a law that does not say what they say it says, in such a way as to jeopardize social, political and economic values that all of us are intent on preserving.

APPENDIX

Excerpts from Antitrust Statutes

Sherman Act, 1890

SEC. 1. Every contract, combination in the form of trust or otherwise, or conspiracy, in restraint of trade or commerce among the several States, or with foreign nations, is hereby declared to be illegal. Every person who shall make any such contract or engage in any such combination or conspiracy, shall be deemed guilty of a misdemeanor, and, on conviction thereof, shall be punished by fine not exceeding five thousand dollars, or by imprisonment not exceeding one year, or by both said punishments, in the discretion of the court.

SEC. 2. Every person who shall monopolize, or attempt to monopolize, or combine or conspire with any other person or persons, to monopolize any part of the trade or commerce among the several States, or with foreign nations, shall be deemed guilty of a misdemeanor, and, on conviction thereof, shall be punished by fine not exceeding five thousand dollars, or by imprisonment not exceeding one year, or by both said punishments, in the discretion of the court.

Clayton Act, 1914

SEC. 2. That it shall be unlawful for any person engaged in commerce, in the course of such commerce, either directly or indirectly, to discriminate in price between different purchasers of commodities, which commodities are sold for use, consumption, or resale within the United States or any Territory thereof or the District of Columbia or any insular possession or other place under the jurisdiction of the United States, where the effect of such discrimination may be to substantially lessen competition or tend to create a monopoly in any line of commerce: *Provided,* That nothing herein contained shall prevent discrimination in price between purchasers of commodities on account of differences in the grade, quality, or quantity of the commodity sold, or that makes only due allowance for differences in the cost of selling or transportation, or discrimination in price in the same or different communities made in good faith to meet competition: *And provided further,* That nothing herein contained shall prevent persons engaged in selling goods, wares, or merchandise in commerce from selecting their own customers in bona fide transactions and not in restraint of trade.

SEC. 3. That it shall be unlawful for any person engaged in commerce, in the course of such commerce, to lease or make a sale or contract for sale of goods, wares, merchandise, machinery, supplies, or other commodities, whether patented or unpatented, for use, consumption, or resale within the United States or any Territory thereof or the District of Columbia or any insular possession or other place under the jurisdiction of the United States, or fix a price charged therefor, or discount from, or rebate upon, such price, on the condition, agreement, or understanding that the lessee or purchaser thereof shall not use or deal in the goods, wares, merchandise, machinery, supplies, or other commodity of a competitor or competitors of the lessor or seller, where the effect of such lease, sale, or contract for sale or such condition, agreement, or understanding may be to substantially lessen competition or tend to create a monopoly in any line of commerce.

Federal Trade Commission Act, 1914

SEC. 5. That unfair methods of competition in commerce are hereby declared unlawful.

Robinson—Patman Act, 1936, Amending Section 2 of the Clayton Act

SEC. 2. (a) That it shall be unlawful for any person engaged in commerce, in the course of such commerce, either directly or indirectly, to discriminate in price between different purchasers of commodities of like grade and quality, where either or any of the purchases involved in such discrimination are in commerce, where such commodities are sold for use, consumption, or resale within the United States or any Territory thereof or the District of Columbia or any insular possession or other place under the jurisdiction of the United States, and where the effect of such discrimination may be substantially to lessen competition or tend to create a monopoly in any line of commerce, or to injure, destroy, or prevent competition with any person who either grants or knowingly receives the benefit of such discrimination, or with customers of either of them: *Provided,* That nothing herein contained shall prevent differentials which make only due allowance for differences in the cost of manufacture, sale, or delivery resulting from the differing methods or quantities in which such commodities are to such purchasers sold or delivered: *Provided, however,* That the Federal Trade Commission may, after due investigation and hearing to all interested parties, fix and establish quantity limits, and revise the same as it finds necessary, as to particular commodities or classes of commodities, where it finds that available purchasers in greater quantities are so few as to render differentials on account thereof unjustly discriminatory or promotive of monopoly in any line of commerce; and the foregoing shall then not be construed to permit differentials based on differences in quantities greater than those so fixed and established: *And provided further,* That nothing herein contained shall prevent persons engaged in selling goods, wares, or merchandise in commerce from selecting their own customers in bona fide transactions and not in restraint of trade: *And provided further,* That nothing herein contained shall prevent price changes from time to time where in response to changing conditions affecting the market for or the marketability of the goods concerned, such as but not limited to actual or imminent deterioration of perishable goods, obsolescence of seasonal goods, distress sales under court process, or sales in good faith in discontinuance of business in the goods concerned.

(b) Upon proof being made, at any hearing on a complaint under this section, that there has been discrimination in price or services or facilities furnished, the burden of rebutting the prima-facie case thus made by showing justification shall be upon the person charged with a violation of this section, and unless justification shall be affirmatively shown, the Commission is authorized to issue an order terminating the discrimination: *Provided, however,* That nothing herein contained shall prevent a seller rebutting the prima-facie case thus made by showing that his lower price or the furnishing of services or facilities to any purchaser or purchasers was made in good faith to meet an equally low price of a competitor, or the services or facilities furnished by a competitor.

(c) That it shall be unlawful for any person engaged in commerce, in the course of such commerce, to pay or grant, or to receive or accept, anything of value as a commission, brokerage, or other compensation, or any allowance or discount in lieu thereof, except for services rendered in connection with the sale or purchase of goods, wares, or merchandise, either to the other party to such transaction or to an agent, representative, or other intermediary therein where such intermediary is acting in fact for or in behalf, or is subject to the direct or indirect control, of any party to such transaction other than the person by whom such compensation is so granted or paid.

(d) That it shall be unlawful for any person engaged in commerce to pay or contract for the payment of anything of value to or for the benefit of a customer of such person in the course of such commerce as compensation or in consideration for any services or facilities furnished by or through such customer in connection with the processing, handling, sale, or offering for sale of any products or commodities manufactured, sold, or offered for sale by such person, unless such payment or consideration is available on proportionally equal terms to all other customers competing in the distribution of such products or commodities.

(e) That it shall be unlawful for any person to discriminate in favor of one purchaser against another purchaser or purchasers of a commodity bought for resale, with or without processing, by contracting to furnish or furnishing, or by contributing to the furnishing of, any services or facilities connected with the processing, handling, sale, or offering for sale of such commodity so purchased upon terms not accorded to all purchasers on proportionally equal terms.

(f) That it shall be unlawful for any person engaged in commerce, in the course of such commerce, knowingly to induce or receive a discrimination in price which is prohibited by this section.

Celler-Kefauver Act, 1950, Amending Section 7 of the Clayton Act

SEC. 7. That no corporation engaged in commerce shall acquire, directly or indirectly, the whole or any part of the stock or other share capital and no corporation subject to the jurisdiction of the Federal Trade Commission shall acquire the whole or any part of the assets of another corporation engaged also in commerce, where in any line of commerce in any section of the country, the effect of such acquisition may be substantially to lessen competition, or to tend to create a monopoly.

Table of Cases [1]

[1] The government cases are alphabetized according to the name of the principal defendant. The listing includes cases before the F.T.C. and also Department of Justice complaints cited in the text.

Besser Manufacturing Co., U.S. *v.*, 96 F.Supp. 304 (1951); 343 U.S. 444 (1952).

B.F. Goodrich Co., F.T.C. Docket No. 5677, Initial Decision, Dec. 10, 1953.

Board of Trade of City of Chicago *v.* U.S., 246 U.S. 231 (1918).

B.S. Pearsall Butter Co. *v.* F.T.C., 292 Fed. 720 (1923).

Bruce's Juices *v.* American Can Co., 87 F.Supp. 985 (1949); 187 F.2d 919 (1951).

Carpel Frosted Foods, F.T.C. Docket No. 5482, Findings, Dec. 13, 1951.

Cement Institute, F.T.C. *v.*, 333 U.S. 683 (1948).

Champion Spark Plug Co., F.T.C. Docket No. 3977, Findings, July 10, 1953.

Champlin Refining Co., U.S. *v.*, 341 U.S. 290 (1951).

Clayton Mark & Co. *v.* F.T.C., 336 U.S. 956 (1949).

Columbia Steel Co., U.S. *v.*, 334 U.S. 495 (1948).

Corn Products Refining Co. *v.* F.T.C., 324 U.S. 726 (1945).

Corn Products Refining Co., F.T.C. Docket No. 5502, Proposed Findings, June 6, 1950; Order 47 F.T.C. 587 (1950).

Curtiss Candy Co., 44 F.T.C. 237 (1947).

Dictograph Products, Inc., F.T.C. Docket No. 5655, Decision, Sept. 24, 1953.

Dictograph Products, Inc., F.T.C. Stipulation 8278, June 14, 1952.

Distillers Corporation-Seagrams, Ltd, F.T.C. Docket No. 6047, Complaint, Sept. 24, 1952; Consent Settlement, March 8, 1954.

Du Pont, *see* E. I. du Pont de Nemours.

Doubleday and Company, F.T.C. Docket No. 5897, Complaint, June 29, 1951; Remand, Sept. 1953.

E. C. Knight Co., U.S. *v.*, 156 U.S. 1 (1895).

E. I du Pont de Nemours & Co., U.S. *v.*, 118 F.Supp. 41 (1953).

Electric Auto-Lite Co., F.T.C. Docket No. 5624, Findings, July 10, 1953.

Excelsior Motor Mfg. & Supply Co. *v.* Sound Equipment, Inc., 73 F.2d 725 (1934).

Fashion Originators' Guild of America, Inc., *v.* F.T.C., 312 U.S. 457 (1941).

General Electric Co., U.S. *v.*, 80 F.Supp. 989 (1948).
General Electric Co., U.S. *v.*, 82 F.Supp. 753 (1949).
General Foods, F.T.C. Docket No. 5675, Complaint, July 7, 1949; Initial Decision Dismissing Complaint, Aug. 27, 1952.
General Motors Corp., U.S. *v.*, 121 F.2d 376 (1941).
General Motors Corp. and AC Spark Plug Co., F.T.C. Docket No. 5620, Findings, July 10, 1953.
Goodyear Tire and Rubber Co., 22 F.T.C. 232 (1936); 101 F.2d 620 (1939).
Griffith, U.S. *v.*, 334 U.S. 100 (1948).

Harper and Brothers, F.T.C. Docket No. 5898, Complaint, June 29, 1951.

Imperial Chemical Industries, Ltd., U.S. *v.*, 100 F.Supp. 504 (1951).
Independent Grocers Alliance Distributing Co., F.T.C. Docket No. 5433, Order, March 17, 1952; 203 F.2d 941 (1953).
International Salt Co., Inc., *v.* U.S., 332 U.S. 392 (1947).
Investors Diversified Services, Inc., U.S. *v.*, 102 F.Supp. 645 (1951).

J. I. Case Co., U.S. *v.*, 101 F.Supp. 856 (1951).

Kiefer-Stewart Co. *v.* Joseph E. Seagram & Sons, Inc., 340 U.S. 211 (1951).

Lever Bros. Co., F.T.C. Docket No. 5585, Decision, Dec. 16, 1953.

Maico Co., Inc., F.T.C. Remand 5822, Dec. 15, 1953.
Mennen Co. *v.* F.T.C., 288 Fed. 774 (1923).
Microtone Co., F.T.C. Stipulation 8269, June 14, 1952.
Minneapolis-Honeywell Co., F.T.C. Docket No. 4920, 44 F.T.C. 351 (1948); 191 F.2d 786 (1951); 344 U.S. 206 (1952).
Minnesota Mining & Mfg. Co., U.S. *v.* 92 F.Supp. 947 (1950).
Morton Salt Co., F.T.C. *v.*, 334 U.S. 37 (1948).
Motion Picture Advertising Service Co., F.T.C. *v.*, 344 U.S. 392 (1953).
Motion Picture Patents Co. *v.* Universal Film Mfg. Co., 243 U.S. 502 (1917).

Nash *v.* U.S., 229 U.S. 373 (1913).
National Biscuit Co. *v.* F.T.C., 299 Fed. 733 (1924).

National City Lines, Inc., U.S. *v.*, 186 F.2d 562 (1951).
National Lead Co., U.S. *v.*, 63 F.Supp. 513 (1945); 332 U.S. 319 (1947).
National Lead Co., F.T.C. Docket No. 5253, Findings, Jan. 12, 1953.
New York Great Atlantic and Pacific Tea Co., Inc., U.S. *v.*, 67 F.Supp. 626 (1946); 173 F.2d 79 (1949); Civil Action 52–139, S.D. N.Y., Sept. 15, 1949; Consent Decree, Jan. 19, 1954.
Northern Securities Co. *v.* U.S., 193 U.S. 197 (1904).

Outboard Marine and Mfg. Co., F.T.C. Docket No. 5882, Initial Decision, Dec. 29, 1952.

Paramount Pictures, Inc., U.S. *v.*, 334 U.S. 131 (1948).
Pick Mfg. Co. *v.* General Motors Corp., 80 F.2d 641 (1935); 299 U.S. 3 (1936).
Pillsbury Mills, Inc., F.T.C. Docket No. 6000, Order and Remand, Dec. 21, 1953.
Pullman Co., U.S. *v.*, 50 F.Supp. 123 (1943).

Quantity Limit Rule as to Replacement Tires and Tubes, F.T.C. File No. 203–1, Findings and Order, Dec. 13, 1951, and Jan. 4, 1952.

Reading Co., U.S. *v.*, 226 U.S. 324 (1912).
Reading Co., U.S. *v.*, 253 U.S. 26 (1920).
Revlon Products Corp., F.T.C. Docket No. 5685, Initial Decision, July 15, 1952.
Richfield Oil Corp., U.S. *v.*, 99 F.Supp. 280 (1951); 343 U.S. 922 (1952).
Rigid Conduit, *see* Triangle Conduit and Cable Co., Inc.
Rubber Tires, *see* Quantity Limit Rule as to Replacement Tires and Tubes.
Ruberoid Co., F.T.C. Docket No. 5017, Findings, Jan. 20, 1950; 343 U.S. 470 (1952).
Russelville Canning Co. *v.* American Can Co., 87 F.Supp. 484 (1949); 191 F.2d 38 (1951).

Schenley Industries, Inc., F.T.C. Docket No. 6048, Complaint, Sept. 24, 1952; Consent Settlement, March 8, 1954.
Schine Chain Theaters, Inc. *v.* U.S., 334 U.S. 110 (1948).
Signode Steel Strapping Co. *v.* F.T.C., 132 F.2d 48 (1942).
Sinclair Refining Co., F.T.C. *v.*, 261 U.S. 463 (1923).
Socony-Vacuum Oil Co., Inc., U.S. *v.*, 310 U.S. 150 (1940).

Sonotone Corp., F.T.C. Stipulation 8279, June 14, 1952.
Spark Plug, *see* Champion, Electric Auto-Lite, *and* General Motors Corp.
Staley Co., *see* A. E. Staley Mfg. Co.
Standard Oil Co. *v.* F.T.C., 41 F.T.C. 263 (1945); 43 F.T.C. 56 (1946); 340 U.S. 231 (1951); Docket No. 4389, Modified Order, Jan. 16, 1953.
Standard Oil Co. of Cal. *v.* U.S., 337 U.S. 293 (1949).
Standard Oil Co. of Cal., U.S., *v.*, Civil Action 11584-C, S.D. Cal., Complaint, May 12, 1950.
Standard Oil Co. of N.J. *v.* U.S., 221 U.S. 1 (1911).
Swift & Co. *v.* U.S., 196 U.S. 375 (1905).
Swift & Co., U.S. *v.*, 286 U.S. 106 (1932).
Sylvania Electric Products Inc., F.T.C. Docket No. 5728, Initial Decision, Dec. 9, 1953.

Theater Enterprises, Inc. *v.* Paramount Film Distributing Corp., 74 Sup. Ct. 257 (1954).
Times-Picayune Pub. Co. *v.* U.S., 345 U.S. 594 (1953).
Timken Roller Bearing Co. *v.* U.S., 83 F.Supp. 284 (1949); 341 U.S. 593 (1951).
Trans-Missouri Freight Assn., U.S. *v.*, 166 U.S. 290 (1897).
Trenton Potteries Co., U.S. *v.*, 273 U.S. 392 (1927).
Triangle Conduit & Cable Co., Inc., *v.* F.T.C., 168 F.2d 175 (1948).

United Shoe Machinery Corp., U.S. *v.*, 110 F.Supp. 295 (1953).
United States Steel Corp., U.S. *v.*, 251 U.S. 417 (1920).

Western Electric Co., U.S. *v.*, Civil Action 17–49, D.N.J., Complaint, Jan. 14, 1949.

Yellow Cab Co., U.S. *v.*, 332 U.S. 218 (1947); 80 F.Supp. 936 (1948); 338 U.S. 338 (1949).

Bibliography

Adams, Walter. "The Aluminum Case: Legal Victory—Economic Defeat," 41 *Amer. Econ. Rev.* 915 (1951).

——. "Dissolution, Divorcement, Divestiture: The Pyrrhic Victories of Antitrust," 27 *Indiana Law J.* 1 (1951).

——. "Is Bigness a Crime?" 27 *Land Economics* 287 (1951).

——. *The Structure of American Industry*. New York: Macmillan, 1950.

Adelman, Morris A. "The A & P Case: A Study in Applied Economic Theory," 63 *Q. Jour. Econ.* 238 (1949).

——. "Business Size and Public Policy," 24 *Jour. of Business* 269 (1951).

——. "Dirlam and Kahn on the A & P Case," 61 *Jour. Pol. Econ.* 436 (1953).

——. "Effective Competition and the Antitrust Laws," 61 *Harv. Law Rev.* 1289 (1948).

——. "Integration and Antitrust Policy," 63 *Harv. Law Rev.* 27 (1949).

American Economic Association. *Readings in the Social Control of Industry*. Philadelphia: Blakiston, 1943.

Anderson, Dewey. *Aluminum for Defense and Prosperity*. Washington: Public Affairs Inst., 1951.

A New Look at Antitrust Enforcement Trends, Antitrust Law Symposium. New York: Commerce Clearing House, 1950.

Antitrust Law Symposium, 1952, 1953. New York: Commerce Clearing House, 1952, 1953. These are annual symposia on the antitrust laws, representing the proceedings of the Section on Antitrust Law, N.Y. State Bar Assn. Titles for earlier years vary.

Bain, Joe S. *The Economics of the Pacific Coast Petroleum Industry.* 3 vols. Berkeley: U. of Calif. Press, 1944, 1945, 1947.

Baum, Warren C. *Workable Competition in the Tobacco Industry.* Unpublished dissertation, Harvard Univ., 1949.

Bowman, Ward S. "Toward Less Monopoly," 101 *U. of Penn. Law Rev.* 577 (1953).

Burns, Arthur R. *The Decline of Competition.* New York: McGraw-Hill, 1936.

Business Advisory Council, U.S. Department of Commerce. *Effective Competition.* Washington: G.P.O., 1952.

Business Practices under Federal Antitrust Laws, 1951 Symposium. New York: Commerce Clearing House, 1951.

Celler Committee. *See* U.S. Congress.

Chamberlin, Edward H. "Product Heterogeneity and Public Policy," 40 *Amer. Econ. Rev., Papers and Proceedings* 85 (1950).

Clark, John Maurice. "The Law and Economics of Basing Points: Appraisals and Proposals," 39 *Amer. Econ. Rev.* 430 (1949).

——. "The Orientation of Antitrust Policy," 40 *Amer. Econ. Rev., Papers and Proceedings* 93 (1950).

——. *Social Control of Business.* 2d ed. New York: McGraw-Hill, 1939.

——. *Studies in the Economics of Overhead Costs.* Chicago: U. of Chicago Press, 1923.

Conference on Business Concentration and Price Policies. *See* National Bureau of Economic Research.

Copeland, Morris A. "A Social Appraisal of Differential Pricing," 6 *Jour. of Marketing* 177 (1942).

Dewey, Donald. "Anti-Trust Policy and the Big Buyer: Further Misgivings about the A & P Case," 17 *Jour. of Marketing* 280 (1953).

Dirlam, Joel B., and Kahn, Alfred E. "Antitrust Law and the Big Buyer: Another Look at the A & P Case," 60 *Jour. Pol. Econ.* 118 (1952).

——. "The Integration and Dissolution of the A & P Company," 29 *Indiana Law J.* 1 (1953).

——. "Leadership and Conflict in the Pricing of Gasoline," 61 *Yale Law J.* 818 (1952).

——. "A Reply," 61 *Jour. Pol. Econ.* 441 (1953).

Edwards, Corwin D. *Maintaining Competition.* New York: McGraw-Hill, 1949.

——. "Public Policy and Business Size," 24 *Jour. of Business* 280 (1951).

Elliott, W. Y., *et al. International Control in the Non-Ferrous Metals.* New York: Macmillan, 1937.

Ellis, Howard S., ed. *A Survey of Contemporary Economics.* Philadelphia: Blakiston, 1948.

Federal Communications Commission. *Proposed Report Telephone Investigation.* Washington: G.P.O., 1938.

Federal Trade Commission. *Monopolistic Practices and Small Business.* Staff Report for Subcomm. on Monopoly, U.S. Senate Select Comm. on Small Business. Washington: G.P.O., 1952.

——. *Report on Manufacture and Distribution of Farm Implements.* Washington: G.P.O., 1948.

Fulda, Carl H. *Food Distribution in the United States: The Struggle between Independents and Chains.* Assoc. of American Law Schools, Comm. on Auxiliary Business and Social Materials, 1951 (mimeo.).

Galbraith, John Kenneth. *American Capitalism, The Concept of Countervailing Power.* Boston: Houghton Mifflin, 1952.

Griffin, Clare E. *An Economic Approach to Antitrust Problems.* New York: American Enterprise Assn., 1951.

Hale, G.E., "Vertical Integration: Impact of the Antitrust Laws upon Combinations of Successive Stages of Production and Distribution," 49 *Columbia Law Rev.* 921 (1949).

——. "Size and Shape: The Individual Enterprise as a Monopoly," 1950 *U. of Ill. Law Forum* 515.

Handler, Milton. "Anti-Trust—New Frontiers and New Perplexities," 6 *The Record of the Ass'n of the Bar of the City of New York* 59 (1951).

——. *A Study of the Construction and Enforcement of the Federal Antitrust Laws.* Temporary National Economic Comm. Monograph No. 38. Washington: G.P.O., 1941.

Hansen, Harry L., and Smith, Marcell N. "The Champion Case: What Is Competition?" 29 *Harv. Bus. Rev.*, May 1951, 89.

Heflebower, Richard B. "Economics of Size," 24 *Jour. of Business* 253 (1951).

Howard, Marshall C. *The Marketing of Petroleum Products.* Unpublished dissertation, Cornell Univ., 1951.

Kaplan, A. D. H. *Big Enterprise in Our Competitive System.* Unpublished MS, Brookings Inst., 1952.

—— and Kahn, Alfred E. "Big Business in a Competitive Society," 47 *Fortune,* Feb. 1953, Sec. 2.

Kaysen, Carl. "Basing Point Pricing and Public Policy," 63 *Q. Jour. Econ.* 289 (1949).

Keezer, Dexter M., ed. "The Antitrust Laws: A Symposium," 39 *Amer. Econ. Rev.* 689 (1949).

Levitt, Theodore. "The Dilemma of Antitrust Aims: Comment," 42 *Amer. Econ. Rev.* 893 (1952).

Lilienthal, David E. *Big Business, A New Era.* New York: Harper, 1953.

——. "Our Anti-Trust Laws Are Crippling America," *Collier's,* May 31, 1952, pp. 15–17.

Lockhart, William B., and Sacks, Howard R. "The Relevance of Economic Factors in Determining Whether Exclusive Arrangements Violate Section 3 of the Clayton Act," 65 *Harv. Law Rev.* 913 (1952).

Loevinger, Lee. "Antitrust and the New Economics," 37 *Minn. Law Rev.* 505 (1953).

McLaren, Richard W. "Related Problems of 'Requirements' Contracts and Acquisitions in Vertical Integration under the Anti-Trust Laws," 45 *Ill. Law Rev.* 141 (1950).

MacLaurin, W. Rupert. *Invention and Innovation in the Radio Industry.* New York: Macmillan, 1949.

Markham, Jesse W. "An Alternative Approach to the Concept of Workable Competition," 40 *Amer. Econ. Rev.* 349 (1950).

——. *Competition in the Rayon Industry.* Cambridge: Harvard U. Press, 1952.

——. "The Nature and Significance of Price Leadership," 41 *Amer. Econ. Rev.* 891 (1951).

Mason, Edward S. "The Current Status of the Monopoly Problem in the United States," 62 *Harv. Law Rev.* 1265 (1949).

Miller, John P. *Unfair Competition.* Cambridge: Harvard U. Press, 1941.

Muller, Charlotte F. *Light Metals Monopoly*. New York: Columbia U. Press, 1946.

Mund, Vernon. *Government and Business*. New York: Harper, 1950.

National Bureau of Economic Research. "Conference on Business Concentration and Price Policy." Unpublished papers, 1952.

Nicholls, William H. *Price Policies in the Cigarette Industry*. Nashville: Vanderbilt U. Press, 1951.

Nutter, G. Warren. *The Extent of Enterprise Monopoly in the U.S., 1899–1939; A Quantitative Study of Some Aspects of Monopoly*. Chicago: U. of Chicago Press, 1951.

Oppenheim, S. Chesterfield. "Federal Antitrust Legislation: Guideposts to a Revised National Antitrust Policy," 50 *Mich. Law Rev.* 1139 (1952).

Rahl, James A. "Conspiracy and the Anti-Trust Laws," 44 *Ill. Law Rev.* 743 (1950).

Rostow, Eugene V. "Monopoly under the Sherman Act—Power or Purpose," 43 *Ill. Law Rev.* 745 (1949).

——. "The New Sherman Act: A Positive Instrument of Progress," 14 *U. of Chicago Law Rev.* 567 (1947).

Schumpeter, Joseph A. *Capitalism, Socialism and Democracy*. 2d ed., New York: Harper, 1947.

Schwartz, Louis. "Potential Impairment of Competition—The Impact of Standard Oil of California *v.* United States on the Standard of Legality under the Clayton Act," 98 *U. of Penn. Law Rev.* 10 (1949).

Seager, Henry R., and Gulick, Charles A., Jr. *Trust and Corporation Problems*. New York: Harper, 1929.

Spengler, J. J. "Vertical Integration and Antitrust Policy," 58 *Jour. Pol. Econ.* 347 (1950).

Stevens, W. H. S. *Unfair Competition*. Chicago: U. of Chicago Press, 1915.

Stocking, George W. "The Economics of Basing Point Pricing," 15 *Law and Contemp. Prob.* 159 (1950).

——. "The Law on Basing Point Pricing: Confusion or Competition," 2 *Jour. Public Law* 1 (1953).

—— and Watkins, Myron W. *Cartels in Action*. New York: Twentieth Century Fund, 1946.

——. *Monopoly and Free Enterprise.* New York: Twentieth Century Fund, 1951.

Sunderland, Thomas E. "Changing Legal Concepts," 24 *Jour. of Business* 235 (1951).

Timberg, Sigmund. "Antitrust and Foreign Trade," 48 *Northwestern U. Law Rev.* 411 (1953).

U.S. Congress, Committee on the Judiciary, Subcommittee on Monopoly Power, U.S. House of Representatives (Celler Committee), 81st and 82d Cong., *Study of Monopoly Power. Hearings.* Washington: G.P.O., 1949–1952.

U.S. Congress, Committee on the Judiciary, Subcommittee on Monopoly Power, U.S. House of Representatives (Celler Committee). *Aluminum.* 82d Cong., 2d Sess., H. Report No. 255. Washington: G.P.O., 1951.

U.S. Congress, Committee on the Judiciary, Subcommittee on Monopoly Power, U.S. House of Representatives (Celler Committee). *The Iron and Steel Industry.* Committee Print. Washington, G.P.O., 1950.

U.S. Congress, Temporary National Economic Committee. *Investigation of the Concentration of Economic Power. Hearings, Monographs and Reports.* 76th and 77th Cong. Washington: G.P.O., 1938–1941.

"Vertical Forestalling under the Antitrust Laws," 19 *U. of Chicago Law Rev.* 583 (1952).

Wallace, Donald H. *Market Control in the Aluminum Industry.* Cambridge: Harvard U. Press, 1937.

Wallace, Robert A., and Douglas, Paul H. "Antitrust Policies and the New Attack on the Federal Trade Commission," 19 *U. of Chicago Law Rev.* 684 (1952).

Watkins, Myron W. *Public Regulation of Competitive Practices in Business Enterprise.* 3d ed. New York: National Industrial Conference Board, 1939.

Weston, J. Fred. *The Role of Mergers in the Growth of Large Firms.* Berkeley: U. of Calif. Press, 1953.

Index